ORIGINALISM AS FAITH

Originalism as Faith presents a comprehensive history of
the originalism debates. It shows how the doctrine is rarely
used by the Supreme Court, but is employed by academics, pundits, and judges to maintain the mistaken faith that
the Court decides cases under the law instead of the justices'
personal values. Tracing the development of the doctrine
from the founding to present day, Eric Segall shows how
originalism is used by judges as a pretext for reaching
politically desirable results. The book also presents an
accurate description and evaluation of the late Justice Scalia's jurisprudence and shows how he failed to practice the
originalism method that he preached. This illuminating
work will be of interest to lawyers, law students, under-
graduates studying the Court, law professors and anyone
else interested in an honest discussion and evaluation of
Originalism as a theory of constitutional interpretation, a
political weapon, and an article of faith.

ERIC J. SEGALL is the Kathy and Lawrence Ashe Professor
of Law at Georgia State University College of Law. He is
the author of *Supreme Myths: Why the Supreme Court Is
Not a Court and Its Justices Are Not Judges.*

Originalism as Faith

Eric J. Segall

Georgia State University College of Law

CAMBRIDGE
UNIVERSITY PRESS

University Printing House, Cambridge CB2 8BS, United Kingdom

One Liberty Plaza, 20th Floor, New York, NY 10006, USA

477 Williamstown Road, Port Melbourne, VIC 3207, Australia

314–321, 3rd Floor, Plot 3, Splendor Forum, Jasola District Centre, New Delhi – 110025, India

79 Anson Road, #06–04/06, Singapore 079906

Cambridge University Press is part of the University of Cambridge.

It furthers the University's mission by disseminating knowledge in the pursuit of
education, learning, and research at the highest international levels of excellence.

www.cambridge.org
Information on this title: www.cambridge.org/9781107188556
DOI: 10.1017/9781108105316

First published 2018
Reprinted 2018

Printed and bound in Great Britain by Clays Ltd, Elcograf S.p.A.

A catalogue record for this publication is available from the British Library.

Library of Congress Cataloging-in-Publication Data
Names: Segall, Eric J., author.
Title: Originalism as faith / Eric J. Segall.
Description: Cambridge [UK] ; New York, NY : Cambridge University Press, 2018. |
 Includes bibliographical references and index.
Identifiers: LCCN 2018017258 | ISBN 9781107188556 (hardback) |
 ISBN 9781316640463 (paperback)
Subjects: LCSH: United States. Supreme Court. | Constitutional law–United States–Philosophy. |
 Constitutional law–United States–Interpretation and construction. | Judicial review–United
 States. | Origin (Philosophy) | BISAC: LAW / Constitutional.
Classification: LCC KF4552 .S44 2018 | DDC 342.73001–dc23
 LC record available at https://lccn.loc.gov/2018017258

ISBN 978-1-107-18855-6 Hardback
ISBN 978-1-316-64046-3 Paperback

To Lynne, Jessica, Sara, and Katie, the women and girls in my life. You light my dark, warm my cold, and fill my heart with love and pride every single day.

CONTENTS

CONTENTS

ACKNOWLEDGMENTS

This book would never have been possible without the help, support, and friendship of so many people. For reading earlier drafts, I owe great debts to Bill Hausdorff, Jack Balkin, Geof Stone, Mike Ramsey, Mitch Berman, Richard Posner, Erwin Chemerinsky, Bill Edmundson, Richard Kay, Patrick Wiseman, Steve Griffin, Michael Rappaport, Mark Pulliam, Chris Green, and Rick Hasen. My two research assistants, Chadwick Preston Roland and Derek Schwahn, provided enormous help and assistance. My deans, Steve Kaminshine and Wendy Hensel, gave me all the support and encouragement anyone could ask for.

Although it may be hard to believe, social media helped me evaluate more clearly many of the issues discussed in this book. My many Twitter conversations with Evan Bernick, Chris Green, and Jonathan Adler were more than valuable. I owe special thanks to Mike Dorf, my Blogger-in-Chief at Dorf on Law, for allowing me to publish countless tirades about New Originalism and Justices Scalia, Thomas, and Gorsuch. Those posts generated many of the ideas in this book.

I want to thank everyone at Cambridge University Press for their work on this book, especially Matt Gallaway, who believed in this project from the start.

Thank you to the *Cornell Law Review*, the *University of Pennsylvania Journal of Constitutional Law*, the *Washington University Law Review*, *Constitutional Commentary*, the *Fordham Law Review*, the *University of Richmond Law Review*, and the *Wake Forest Law Review* for granting me permission to use substantial parts of my essays in those journals for this book.

My close and smart friend Carolyn Wood allowed me to ruminate about originalism and judges during our many long walks, and she always made my ideas better and more focused. Dick Posner and I spent hours and hours hashing out many of the ideas expressed in this book. His work in general has inspired my thinking for a long time.

Most of all, my dear wife Lynne's constant and incredible support, patience, wisdom, and judgment kept me going when my energy was low, my will was ebbing, and I struggled with doubt. As always, she kept me moving on.

AUTHOR'S NOTE

"As this book went to print, the Court handed down *Janus v. AFSCME*, the background of which is discussed in detail in Chapter 8. In this decision, five conservative Justices invalidated (on free speech grounds) the laws of twenty-three states requiring public employees to pay partial union dues whether or not they joined the union. The Justices engaged in this aggressive act of judicial review by overturning a unanimous 1977 Supreme Court decision that held exactly the opposite and without any support in the original meaning of the First Amendment. Justices Thomas and Gorsuch, the two self-avowed Originalists on the Court, joined the opinion in full without comment. This brand new case perfectly reflects this book's thesis: Originalism is a method of constitutional interpretation that is nothing more than a misleading label for conservative results for some (the Justices) and an article of faith for others including many legal scholars and the public at large."

PROLOGUE

Erwin Chemerinsky

One of the consequences of the November 8, 2016, presidential election is that originalism lives on as an important approach to constitutional interpretation. If Hillary Clinton had won the presidency, she would have renominated Merrick Garland or perhaps someone younger and more liberal to replace Justice Antonin Scalia. There would have been a majority of justices appointed by Democratic presidents for the first time since 1971. Originalism would have been relegated to dissents, especially by Justice Clarence Thomas. Conservative law professors would have continued to champion originalism and would have used it to criticize liberal decisions. But as a method of constitutional interpretation invoked by the Court, it would likely have faded into obscurity.

Everything, though, is different because Donald Trump won the presidency. Neil Gorsuch, a self-avowed originalist, and not Merrick Garland, replaced Antonin Scalia. It will be President Trump who fills any other vacancies in the next three years, and his list is filled with conservatives with strong Federalist Society ties. If Trump gets one other Supreme Court vacancy to fill, it will create the most conservative Supreme Court since at least the mid-1930s. And if that occurs, there will be a conservative Court for a long time to come. As I write this in November 2017, John Roberts is 62 years old, Samuel Alito is 67, and Clarence Thomas is 69. Neil Gorsuch is 50. It is easy to imagine them being together on the Court for another 15 years or longer.

All of this means that originalism is likely to be more important for constitutional law than ever before. This is what makes Eric Segall's magnificent book so significant. Professor Segall does a masterful job showing the different types of originalism, demonstrating their fatal flaws, and revealing that even those who purport to be originalists – like Scalia and Thomas – often abandon originalism when it does not serve their ideological agendas. Professor Segall's book is particularly important in tracing the history of constitutional interpretation in the Supreme Court and in the scholarly literature.

Ultimately, Professor Segall's detailed examination of originalism points to the central and inescapable problem with the theory: Originalism can be defined in a way that provides significant constraint on justices, but only at the price of unacceptable results. The only way to rescue originalism from this problem is by defining it in a way that eschews constraints, but then it becomes indistinguishable from non-originalism. There is no middle ground: Either originalism constrains at the price of unacceptable outcomes, or it offers no constraints and is not really originalism (despite some scholars and judges wanting to call it that).

As Professor Segall shows, the primary defense of originalism has been the desire to constrain judges and to try to keep constitutional decisions from being based on the values of the men and women on the Court. For example, as described by Professor Segall, this was how Robert Bork initially defended originalism in 1971, and it is how Larry Solum did so in 2017 in urging the Senate Judiciary Committee to confirm Neil Gorsuch.

But the only way that originalism can achieve this constraint is for the justices to truly be tied to the original meaning, even when it produces unacceptable consequences for our contemporary society. Under this approach, as Professor Segall explains, *Brown v. Board of Education* was likely wrong; the same Congress that voted to ratify the Fourteenth Amendment also voted to segregate the District of Columbia public schools. As Judge Bork and Justice Scalia explained, there would be no heightened protection against sex discrimination under equal protection; that never was part of the original meaning of the Fourteenth Amendment. In fact, the requirement for equal protection would not apply to the federal government at all. There would be no protection of privacy rights – whether to purchase and use contraceptives or to engage in private consensual homosexual activity.

As Professor Segall explains, Robert Bork was overwhelmingly denied confirmation by the Senate in 1987 precisely because this cramped view of the Constitution was deemed so unacceptable to a majority of senators and a majority of Americans. If the Constitution is truly "dead, dead, dead, dead," as Justice Scalia said, and if the Court must adhere to the original meaning, it would vastly change constitutional law – and in a way that few would support.

Moreover, the desire for value-neutral judging in constitutional cases is an impossible quest. No constitutional right is absolute, and there inevitably is a balancing of the government's interest against the claim of a right. In the language of constitutional law, this balancing is called "strict scrutiny" or "intermediate scrutiny" or "rational basis review," depending on the right or type of discrimination involved. But what is a "compelling" or an "important" or a "legitimate" government interest inevitably requires a value choice.

To take a single example, laws prohibiting same-sex marriage at the very least must meet rational basis review under equal protection. Gays and lesbians cannot marry, while opposite-sex couples can. Even if heightened scrutiny is not used for sexual orientation discrimination, this discrimination still requires that the government interest be rationally related to a legitimate government purpose. Every justice on the Court therefore had to face the question of whether there is any legitimate reason to keep gays and lesbians from marrying. Originalism cannot provide that answer.

But originalists have an alternative: They can forego constraint and develop a theory that allows the justices discretion to avoid unacceptable results. Professor Segall points to how some who call themselves originalists like Professors Will Baude, Randy Barnett, and Jack Balkin embrace this form of originalism. Baude, for example, defends the Supreme Court's decision in *Obergefell v. Hodges*, which struck down state laws prohibiting same-sex marriage, under his theory of originalism. But then as Professor Segall powerfully shows, originalism and non-originalism become indistinguishable. More generally, if the meaning of a constitutional provision is stated at any abstract enough level, almost any result can be justified. Scholars can call it originalism if they want, but the constraint on judging that inspired originalism is gone.

Of course, as Professor Segall also suggests, there might be other approaches to constitutional interpretation that put significant constraints on the justices without embracing originalism. Constitutional judicial review – the power of the courts to strike down laws and executive actions – could be eliminated. Alternatively, Professor Segall favors allowing courts to give great deference to political choices and striking laws down only when the evidence of unconstitutionality is compelling.

But this raises the most important question: Are we better off as a society allowing unelected justices to give meaning to our Constitution and striking down government actions, or would we be better off greatly constraining, if not eliminating, the power of the Court to strike down laws or executive actions? Do the benefits of decisions like *Brown v. Board of Education, Griswold v. Connecticut,* and *Roe v. Wade* outweigh the costs of rulings like *Lochner v. New York, Hammer v. Dagenhart,* and *Shelby County v. Holder?*

I do not know how to answer that question. In Chapter 10, Professor Segall speaks of originalism as a matter of faith. So is all judicial review. I have that faith and believe that society is better off with an unelected judiciary able to enforce the Constitution, including by applying its open-ended language to contemporary problems.

But I confess that faith is a lot harder in the face of what the Supreme Court is likely to be for a long time to come. This is the context for Professor Segall's wonderful book, and it is the context for constitutional law after the 2016 presidential election.

1   ORIGINALISM AND JUDICIAL REVIEW

We are all Originalists.

Justice Elena Kagan[1]

Faith: A firm belief in something for which there is no proof.

Merriam-Webster Dictionary[2]

How should judges interpret and apply the US Constitution, which in many important aspects is over 200 years old? America's founding fathers owned slaves, denied women most basic rights, and inhabited a world devoid of the modern technologies that shape our everyday life. Even the important Thirteenth, Fourteenth, and Fifteenth Amendments to the Constitution, ending slavery and extending the promise of equality to all Americans regardless of race, were ratified by the people a half-century before women could vote. Should today's judges try to discover what the constitutional text meant at the time of its enactment so very long ago, what it means today, or both? If the answer is both, how much weight should judges give to the text's original meaning when it is inconsistent with our modern values and priorities? These questions frame the originalism debate.

Originalism today is a theory of law and politics. Therefore, this book summarizes and analyzes the academic debates over originalism, how elected officials and the popular media discuss the subject, how judicial nominees and legal experts have talked about originalism in judicial confirmation hearings, and how judges use or don't use originalist sources in their written opinions.[3]

The 1787 Constitution and its Amendments place limits on our elected leaders, but we rely primarily on unelected, life-tenured federal judges to enforce those restrictions. Judicial decisions interpreting the Constitution sometimes define who we are as a people and a country.

Speaking at the dedication of a new Supreme Court building almost one hundred years ago, Chief Justice Charles Evan Hughes emotionally said, referring to the Supreme Court, the "republic endures, and this is the symbol of its faith."[4] This book asks how our highest Court should resolve hard cases implicating this country's most fundamental values and commitments.

Some of those constitutional commitments are precise, such as that the president must be thirty-five, and each state is entitled to two senators, regardless of population. Other provisions, the ones that most often lead to lawsuits, are phrased more broadly. For example, the government may not abridge "freedom of speech," or impose "cruel and unusual punishments."[5] No state shall deny to any person the "equal protection of the laws" or "due process of law."[6] Judges have a difficult time interpreting and applying these kinds of limitations because the language itself cannot resolve most litigated cases, and scholars often disagree about the history surrounding the ratification of these provisions.

Lawyers, judges, legal scholars, and Supreme Court commentators frequently debate the importance of the Constitution's original meaning to present-day cases.[7] Some believe that originalist sources, such as the ratification debates and early Court decisions, should play a decisive or primary role, whereas others think that originalism is just one of many considerations that judges should consider when deciding cases. Other important factors may include tradition, political practices, modern cases, pragmatic concerns relating to the authority of the judiciary, and the real-world consequences of each case.

In addition to disagreeing over the relevant sources of constitutional interpretation, the legal community hasn't reached consensus over how deferential judges should be to other political decision makers such as legislatures (state and federal) and chief executives (presidents and governors). For example, Chapter 2 argues that the founding fathers thought judges should overturn state and federal laws only when such enactments clearly violated the Constitution. Only a small minority of constitutional scholars or judges embrace that position today, and outside a few specific areas of constitutional law, the Supreme Court has not acted with that degree of deference on a consistent basis for well over a century.

Court observers also disagree over how appropriate it is for judges to decide cases based on their own values, politics, and unique experiences. Some scholars and commentators think judges should try their best to keep personal values in check when deciding legal disputes, while others argue that the vague text and contested history in dispute in most constitutional cases means that the subjective value preferences of the judges ultimately influence their decisions. Where that is true, the argument goes, judges should carefully examine and explain the personal values that form at least part of the rationale for their written opinions.

As a descriptive matter, Supreme Court justices sometimes employ the Constitution's original meaning to justify their legal decisions. The justices are excellent lawyers who know how to present evidence to support their arguments and distinguish counterarguments that stand in the way of their preferred results. When original meaning is helpful, the justices use it, and often with great rhetorical flourish.

The justices' use of original meaning to explain and justify their decisions has many positive benefits. We define our national identity in part by our Constitution, which serves as a constant reminder to the American people of intergenerational agreements that we do not need to renegotiate. When the justices connect us to our past by supporting their decisions with persuasive evidence of prior agreements, they cultivate and maintain a distinctively American approach to hard public policy questions. In addition, judicial appeals to original meaning might suggest that the justices are following the decisions of the founders not imposing their own personal values.[8] The justices want the American people to have faith that their decisions are grounded in prior law, not personal predilection, and references to originalist sources make that goal easier.

That Supreme Court justices sometimes use ratification-era evidence to support their decisions, however, reveals only a small part of a much more complicated story. In many divisive cases, the Constitution's original meaning played at most a marginal role in the justices' analysis compared to prior decisions and their personal evaluations of consequences. Some notable examples include decisions perceived at the time by many scholars as progressive such as *Brown v. Board of Education* (separate but equal schools can never be equal),[9] *Roe v. Wade* (right to abortion is constitutionally protected),[10] and *Obergefell v. Hodges* (same-sex marriage is constitutionally required),[11] as well as cases perceived by scholars at the time to be conservative such as *Citizens United v. FEC* (corporations and unions have the same free speech rights as individuals),[12] *Seminole Tribe v. Florida* (states have sovereign immunity under the Constitution even when sued by their own citizens),[13] and *Shelby County v. Holder* (states have equal state sovereignty that Congress must recognize absent a strong interest).[14]

One famous originalism critic observed that in most well-developed areas of constitutional law, "originalist sources ... played a very small role compared to the elaboration of the Court's own precedents. It is rather like having a remote ancestor who came over on the Mayflower."[15] Another scholar, writing shortly after Justice Scalia's death, argued that "before and after Scalia, justices will use history when they believe it supports their ... conclusions and ignore it when they believe it doesn't."[16]

There is abundant political science literature suggesting that the justices' values writ large, including but not limited to partisan politics, much more than legal interpretations of text and history, drive the Court's decisions.[17] If these scholars are correct, and the Constitution's original meaning matters to the justices only when that meaning supports their policy preferences, then it is at best unclear how important originalism is to the Court's decisions.

Scholars who belong to the school of thought known as Legal Realism also believe that the justices use the original meaning of the Constitution, and all other formal legal doctrines, strategically to support their preferred policy results.[18] These academics argue that there are just too many decisions at odds with or not supported by text, original meaning, or prior cases to reach any other conclusion.[19] Legal realists argue that judges should take account of pragmatic concerns and consequences much more than formulaic legal rules.

This book argues that political scientists and legal realists are correct that the justices' decisions are driven primarily by their personal values. Therefore, the justices should be transparent about the minimal role original meaning plays in constitutional litigation. This lack of originalist focus could possibly change, but until it does, the justices should honestly and accurately describe the basis for the decisions they make.

Some judges, law professors, and lawyers object to legal realism on the basis that it fails to take seriously how judges themselves see their roles. No justice, for example, would admit that it is her personal value preferences, not the law, that drives her decisions. No nominee to the bench would ever make such a statement during her confirmation hearing. The legal realist account, therefore, neglects this internal perspective and is inaccurate.

There are three major responses to that argument. First, the American people often assume and take for granted that politicians will bend the truth, to say the least, from time to time. That same realistic stance should apply equally to judges, and most of all to Supreme Court justices, who have almost complete discretion because their decisions are not reviewed by any higher court.

Second, none of us truly understand the complex motivations that drive many of our important decisions. I may think I choose a certain course of action for one set of reasons, but much more may be impacting that choice than I know. Some degree of objectivity outside the internal perspective can bring light to many decisions people make, including judges. As Judge Posner has remarked, "the internal perspective has proved inadequate" to explain how judges actually behave.[20]

Third, and most important, as Chapters 7–9 of this book show, the justices' decisions bear a remarkable, though certainly not perfect, correlation to what we would expect to be their policy preferences. At the end of the day, it really doesn't matter how the justices perceive themselves if their collective decisions bear an uncanny resemblance to what we would expect their policy preferences to be. As Professor Frank Cross has observed, "It is difficult to find a professed originalist, in the judiciary ... who believes that the original meaning of the Constitution is significantly different from his or her personal policy preferences."[21] I would extend that quote to non-originalist Justices as well.

For the purposes of this book, my legal realist claim is narrow. It is limited to Supreme Court cases (unlike other judges, the justices are not bound by prior decisions), and it is not true that the justices can reach any possible conclusion in every case. The justices can, however, usually rule for either party within the boundaries of what most people would agree is reasonable judicial decision making. The issue this book addresses is what role, if any, originalism plays and should play in that decision making.

A. ORIGINALISM THEN AND NOW

Over the last fifty years, the originalism debate has changed dramatically. The first wave of strong originalists, responding to the liberal decisions of the Warren and early Burger Courts, argued that the Court should not strike down state and federal statutes absent a strong showing by the plaintiff that those laws clearly violated the framers' original intent.[22] This kind of deferential approach to judicial review could form the basis of a coherent and defensible method of constitutional interpretation. This brand of originalism, however, has largely died away, and only a handful of academics or judges today support it.[23]

Many modern originalists believe that it is the original meaning of the text, not the intentions of the framers, that matter, and they do not adopt a strong presumption of legislative validity. Indeed, some self-styled originalists today argue that ratification-era evidence "runs out" in constitutional cases, and when that occurs, judges must "construct" legal doctrines to decide those disputes.[24] According to some of these "New Originalists," these judicial "constructions" should not contradict the original meaning of the text, but also cannot be derived from that text. When judges enter what these scholars call the "construction zone," originalist sources are of little use to the ultimate resolution of the controversy.[25] An interesting question is why so many scholars self-identify as originalists even though they admit that original meaning analysis does not help resolve many litigated constitutional cases.

Some of the scholars who believe in the "construction zone" use the label "originalist" as a rhetorical or political device to indicate a generally conservative or libertarian approach to constitutional adjudication,[26] while others suggest that their preferred method of interpretation is more legitimate than theories put forward by legal scholars who reject the originalist label.[27] These New Originalists criticize "living constitutionalism," which they argue allows judges too much discretion to impose their personal values in the guise of constitutional law. For example,

Professor Larry Solum, in testimony in front of the US Congress during the Neil Gorsuch confirmation hearing, said that "originalist judges do not believe that they have the power to impose their own values on the nation by invoking the idea of a 'living constitution.'"[28] This critique of those who believe in the "living constitution" rings somewhat hollow, however, given the admission by many New Originalists that text and original meaning are of little use when the Court enters the so-called construction zone.

The overwhelming need for many judges and scholars to emphasize originalism as the dominant mode of constitutional interpretation may also stem from a desire to have faith that the Supreme Court decides cases under the law, not according to the justices' personal values. This faith, however, gets in the way of a fruitful discussion of how the highest Court in the land engages in its most critical function – the resolution of constitutional cases often implicating our most fundamental values. If one of the primary goals of originalism is to limit the effects of the justices' personal politics and preferences on constitutional decision making, a better approach would be for judges to adopt a deferential, clear error rule for constitutional cases. However, many New Originalists contend that they are more concerned with judges interpreting the Constitution correctly than constraining judicial discretion. This disagreement among originalists about its most important purposes suggests we must define originalism carefully.

B. WHAT IS ORIGINALISM?

What does it mean to say that someone is an originalist? At her confirmation hearing in 2010, liberal Justice Elena Kagan said, "We are all Originalists."[29] In 2017, Justice Gorsuch, a conservative, approved Kagan's comment at his confirmation hearing.[30] Yet, there are substantial differences between Justices Kagan and Gorsuch, as well as other judges and legal scholars, over how best to interpret the US Constitution and how substantial a role original meaning should play in that interpretation. Even among self-proclaimed originalists, their theories are "rapidly evolving . . . constantly reshaping themselves in profound ways in response to . . . critiques, and not infrequently splintering further into multiple, mutually exclusive iterations."[31] There is no single definition of originalism just as there is no overarching agreement among non-originalists as to the best way for judges to interpret the Constitution. However, some broad and important generalizations can lead to a workable starting point to discuss the originalism debate.

Few constitutional scholars or judges argue that original meaning is irrelevant to constitutional interpretation.[32] In the words of Professor Mitch Berman, "not a single self-identifying non-originalist of whom I'm aware argues that original meaning has no bearing on proper judicial constitutional interpretation. To the contrary, even those scholars most closely identified with non-originalism... explicitly assign original meaning or intentions a significant role in the interpretive enterprise."[33] Another eminent scholar has said that most non-originalists "accord the text and original history presumptive weight, but [simply] do not treat them as authoritative or binding. The presumption is defeasible over time in the light of changing experiences and presumptions."[34]

I am also not aware of any scholar or judge who believes that applying the original meaning of the Constitution to modern problems should be the exclusive method of constitutional interpretation in every case. Although a few early originalist scholars, such as Raoul Berger and Lino Graglia, came close to holding this belief, neither said that original meaning must always trump non-originalist case law. Moreover, both men linked their advocacy of originalism to a strong presumption in favor of the validity of state and federal legislation. These scholars advocated for judicial deference just as strongly as they did for originalism.

The real difference between originalists and non-originalists, therefore, is not whether founding-era evidence should play any role in how judges interpret the Constitution, but how strong a role. For the purposes of this book, an originalist judge or scholar is someone who believes the following three propositions: (1) the meaning of the constitutional text is fixed at the time of ratification; (2) judges should give that meaning a primary role in constitutional interpretation; and (3) pragmatic modern concerns and consequences are not allowed to trump discoverable original meaning (although adhering to precedent might).[35] A non-originalist is someone who believes that postratification facts and consequences may trump original meaning, or are just as important as original meaning, to judges faced with difficult constitutional questions.[36]

There are long-standing debates among originalists over whose intentions matter (the drafters or the ratifiers) and the appropriate sources judges should consult when they attempt to ascertain original meaning. For example, James Madison did not allow the release of his constitutional convention notes until after his death many years later, at least partly because he felt that those notes should be irrelevant to judges trying to interpret the Constitution.[37] Should those notes be relevant today? Although this book touches on these kinds of questions, its primary focus is on what Justice Antonin Scalia famously called "the great divide" in constitutional law.[38] This "divide" is the difference between originalists and non-originalists over how much weight to give evidence of the original meaning of constitutional text, not internal debates between and among originalists over what kind of ratification-era evidence is fair game for judges and scholars.[39]

There is a difference between judges reviewing history and past political practices to help decide cases and their use of originalist-era sources. For example, in a recent separation of powers case involving the president's power to make recess appointments when the Congress is out of session, the justices reviewed the long history of these appointments from the founding to the present.[40] This focus on the importance of historical evidence occurring well past (sometimes hundreds of years past) the founding would not be considered by most scholars and judges an originalist method of interpretation. Originalism may possibly be consistent with the relevance of historical events far removed from ratification, but not if those events can trump original meaning, which is quite often the case.

Chapter 2 examines what the founding fathers thought about constitutional interpretation and how the justices engaged in judicial review prior to the Civil War. This summary shows that, although judicial review was contemplated by the men who wrote the Constitution and the voters who ratified it, they expected judges to employ this powerful tool only when the alleged constitutional violation was clear (unless the challenged law dealt directly with judicial power or procedure).

Chapter 3 discusses in broad strokes how the Supreme Court used originalist-era evidence from the late nineteenth century to the end of the Warren and Burger Courts. This period may seem unduly lengthy for just one chapter, but the reality is that our modern conversation about the proper use of originalism is largely, though certainly not exclusively, the product of the last fifty years. As one judge noted, the "modern form of originalist theory actually appeared in the 1980s as the American public, government officials, and academics felt the effects of the Warren Court's decidedly non-originalist jurisprudence."[41]

Around the time the Warren Court ended, a few legal scholars, who I will label the "Original Originalists," began critiquing the liberal judicial decisions of the 1960s and early 1970s on the basis that the justices failed to rest their judgments on the Constitution's text or the framers' original intent. These scholars argued that unelected, life-tenured judges should not strike down state and federal laws absent clear evidence that those laws violate the Constitution. In the words of Thomas Colby, "[o]riginalism was born of a desire to constrain judges. Judicial constraint was its heart and soul . . . ."[42]

Around the same time, conservative politicians began embracing this originalism critique as an argument against *Roe v. Wade*'s legitimacy and a few of the Warren Court's criminal procedure decisions. By the time Ronald Reagan won the presidency in 1980, the legal and political groundswell for an originalist movement was in place.[43] Chapter 4 details the work of these Original Originalists and the social, legal, and political forces that brought their work to light.

Liberal critics including both legal scholars and Supreme Court justices challenged these originalist assumptions and arguments. Chapter 4 also summarizes and evaluates this side of the debate and its implications for both the Supreme Court and our societal conversation about the meaning of the Constitution.

In response to these liberal critics of originalism, a second wave of conservative academics, with the able assistance of Justice Antonin Scalia, tried to change the doctrine to make it more acceptable to scholars and judges. These second-generation New Originalists developed a more visible political posture converting the originalism debate from a largely inside the legal academy and "inside the Beltway" conversation to a broader and more accessible societal argument about the proper role of the Supreme Court in our system of government.

After Presidents Ronald Reagan and George H. W. Bush appointed five Supreme Court justices, and large numbers of conservative lower court judges, the judicial restraint urged by many of the Original Originalists gave way to a much more aggressive form of originalism that is the most common brand today. Some New Originalists advocate that judges give substantial protection to economic liberty, states' rights, and gun rights, and some even suggest that judges use the Ninth Amendment and/or the Fourteenth Amendment's Privileges or Immunities Clause to enforce judicially enforceable rights not mentioned in the Constitution. Chapter 5 analyzes the work of these New Originalists, the impact of their project on constitutional interpretation, and the critical responses by both liberal and conservative scholars.

Chapter 6 discusses the work of a third generation of academic originalists, who modified the doctrine yet again to respond to New Originalism's critics. Some of these academics argue that originalism has always been "our law," while others suggest that judges should adopt a strong originalist approach to constitutional interpretation because the best lawmaking occurs during the time the people vote for and approve constitutions.[44] This chapter argues that the first approach is largely inaccurate under any meaningful definition of originalism, while the second proposal to justify originalism, while presenting an interesting and bold thesis, does not adequately support its conclusion that judges should prioritize original meaning over other modes of constitutional interpretation.

No book could comprehensively review and evaluate all the various originalism theories and paradigms advocated by law professors, judges, and legal scholars; such an effort would require multiple volumes. This book tries to cover as many as possible. Most of that discussion is normative. However, an essential descriptive point this book makes is that no modern Supreme Court justice has consistently voted in an originalist manner. The two justices most associated with originalism are Antonin Scalia and Clarence Thomas. Chapter 7 argues that neither justice was/is an "originalist" in any reasonable sense of that term.[45] These descriptive points suggest that we cannot have a reasonable debate over the proper role of originalism in real cases (as opposed to a theoretical discussion) without recognizing the difficulties even allegedly pro-originalist justices have had applying the doctrine.

Chapters 8 and 9 demonstrate that ideology, not text, original meaning, or any other prior legal rule or intellectual precommitment, has driven Supreme Court opinions for most of our history. These chapters also argue that, absent strong deference to other political decision makers, personal ideology will inevitably trump prior legal doctrine or rules as the most important factor motivating Supreme Court justices.

The final chapter argues that many originalists and judges advocate for the doctrine to maintain faith that Supreme Court decision making is largely a law-like enterprise as opposed to the aggregation of judicial value preferences. This faith allows the justices to maintain their prestige and authority for many Americans who believe strongly in the sanctity of text. As Professor Jamal Greene has keenly observed, "Constitutionalism is often called our civic religion and the originalism movement ... is conspicuously commingled with an evangelical movement ... The United States is the world's most religiously developed democracy, and a substantial number of Americans are at best ambivalent toward the use of reason and creativity in exegesis of sacred texts..."[46] Many Americans want to have faith that modern judges are simply applying our fundamental text despite the reality that constitutional doctrine often follows the politics and the values of the justices, who have the final say about what that text means.

The American people pay a large price for this mistaken faith that the original meaning of the text drives Supreme Court decisions. The loss of transparency obscures how our highest Court operates. The Supreme Court, and the experts who follow and write about the Court, should accurately describe constitutional interpretation. Pretending that the original meaning of the text has ever played, does play, or likely will play a large role in generating judicial decisions in hard cases misleads the American people about the true nature of one of the three branches of the federal government.

Some important judges and scholars, however, have offered a more realistic account of how the Supreme Court decides cases. Almost a century ago, Justice Cardozo observed that the "great generalities of the constitution have a content and significance that vary from age to age."[47] One of the most important constitutional law scholars of this generation, Laurence Tribe, has said that it is imperative that judges "avoid all pretense that [constitutional interpretation] can be reduced to a passive process of discovering rather than constructing an interpretation."[48] Erwin Chemerinsky has argued that efforts to reduce judicial discretion are largely hopeless and that "constitutional law is now, will be, and always has been largely a product of the views [and values] of the Justices."[49]

These legal realist views of the Supreme Court are not intended to and should not undermine the Court's essential role in shaping and maintaining America's commitments to the separation of powers, federalism, and limited government. The text and history of the Constitution are natural starting points for constitutional interpretation and, where decisive, should govern. However, most litigated constitutional cases involve vague principles not concrete expectations.[50] In these cases, which are often the most important and implicate conflicting contemporary values, originalist reasoning may at times be important as a symbolic reminder of our past, but it is unlikely to replace the justices' preferences as the engine of constitutional interpretation.

There are two coherent responses to the limited role text and original meaning actually play in constitutional litigation. We could demand that judges defer significantly to more accountable governmental officials and strike down laws only when the evidence of unconstitutionality is compelling. Unless the plaintiff produces evidence that a challenged law or practice clearly violates constitutional text or virtual universal agreement among scholars and historians concerning the reasons for that text, the plaintiff would not meet her burden of proof. This clear error rule, if adopted by judges, would leave much more power in the hands of elected officials and would require that major social change occur through Article V's amendment process, not Supreme Court decisions. This approach would also decrease the role that the justices' personal values play in their decision making. Although I prefer this model of constitutional interpretation, it is unlikely that the Supreme Court will ever embrace it.

The only other rational choice is to encourage the Supreme Court to accept and admit that prior legal rules, whether based on text, original meaning, or prior cases, although at times relevant, do not generate results in hard cases. Whether the justices are wrestling with abortion, affirmative action, campaign finance reform, gun control, or other contemporary problems, the justices' experiences, personal values, and evaluations of consequences inevitably play the major role in the resolution of those disputes. Despite that recognition, however, the American people can still have faith in the Court by understanding the essential structural role the justices play in resolving difficult and controversial constitutional questions. There is great benefit in having a third branch of government be a place where we can peacefully resolve many of our most contentious societal disagreements. But the Court can play that role without pretending that its decisions are based on the values of people living centuries ago in a world very different than our own. It is not in vague text or disputed historical accounts of the origins of that text, but in the justices' characters, judgments, and values, that the American people must ultimately place their faith.

2 JUDICIAL REVIEW AT THE BEGINNING

It is Emphatically the Province and Duty of the Judicial Department to say What the Law is.
> Chief Justice John Marshall in *Marbury v. Madison*[1]

Since our country's beginning, legal scholars have debated how judges should interpret the US Constitution. This chapter discusses how the founding generation viewed judicial review, details a few early and mid-nineteenth century decisions in which judges struggled to come to terms with their new authority, and evaluates an important law review article written by Arthur Machen at the turn of the twentieth century focusing on constitutional change. Machen's treatment of the subject, the first one of its kind, helps frame the issues raised by the rest of this book.

A. THE FOUNDERS AND CONSTITUTIONAL INTERPRETATION

Prior to the Constitution's ratification in 1787, no country had ever authorized judges to veto laws enacted by a sovereign. The founding fathers, many of them lawyers, believed in the rule of law and the supremacy of a written Constitution. Although the Constitution's text does not expressly grant the power of judicial review to the federal judiciary, there is little doubt that the Constitution's drafters and the voters who ratified it expected judges to strike down laws that clearly or obviously exceeded constitutional limitations.

Alexander Hamilton wrote the most important pre-Constitution defense of judicial review. He justified the practice in *The Federalist Papers*, which were a group of essays written by Hamilton, James

Madison and John Jay to persuade the people of New York to adopt
the new Constitution. In "Federalist No. 78," Hamilton explained why
judicial review was a necessary component of the new constitutional
structure and why the power to veto laws did not make the judicial
branch too powerful.

Hamilton explained judicial review by observing that the Constitution was our country's supreme law. Therefore, "no legislative
act ... contrary to the Constitution, can be valid. To deny this, would
be to affirm, that the deputy is greater than his principal; that the
servant is above his master; that the representatives of the people are
superior to the people themselves; that men acting by virtue of powers,
may do not only what their powers do not authorize, but what they
forbid."[2]

After arguing that legislators cannot be the judges of their own
powers in a system of limited government, Hamilton wrote the
following important paragraph about the judicial responsibility to
enforce the Constitution:

> The courts were designed to be an intermediate body between the
> people and the legislature, in order, among other things, to keep the
> latter within the limits assigned to their authority. The interpret-
> ation of the laws is the proper and peculiar province of the courts.
> A constitution is, in fact, and must be regarded by the judges, as a
> fundamental law. It therefore belongs to them to ascertain its
> meaning, as well as the meaning of any particular act proceeding
> from the legislative body. *If there should happen to be an irreconcilable
> variance between the two,* that which has the superior obligation and
> validity ought, of course, to be preferred; or, in other words, the
> Constitution ought to be preferred to the statute, the intention of
> the people to the intention of their agents.[3]

This paragraph explains the founding fathers' rationale for allowing
judges to set aside laws that are inconsistent with the Constitution. The
Constitution is supreme law, the judges' job is to interpret the law, and
if there is an "irreconcilable variance" between a law and the Constitution, judges must enforce the Constitution, not the law.

This description of judicial review made some people fearful that a
governmental body that could veto laws would be the most powerful
organ of government. Hamilton responded that this worry was

misplaced because judges would have "no influence over either the sword or the purse; no direction either of the strength or of the wealth of the society; and can take no active resolution whatever. It may truly be said to have neither FORCE nor WILL, but merely judgment; and must ultimately depend upon the aid of the executive arm even for the efficacy of its judgments."[4] In other words, the judicial branch has no control of the military or the budget, and therefore must rely on the people's confidence to maintain its power.

Chief Justice John Marshall echoed Hamilton's justifications for judicial review in the 1803 landmark case *Marbury v. Madison.*[5] In that opinion, the Chief Justice formally announced the doctrine of judicial review. He justified it by noting that it "is a proposition too plain to be contested that the Constitution controls any legislative act repugnant to it ... Certainly all those who have framed written Constitutions contemplate them as forming the fundamental and paramount law of the nation, and consequently the theory of every such government must be that an act of the Legislature repugnant to the Constitution is void."[6] Marshall said it is the job of judges to make that determination, in a case properly before them because "it is emphatically the province and duty of the judicial department to say what the law is."[7] Marshall concluded that judges faced with a statute that conflicts with the Constitution have a legal duty to support the Constitution and declare the law void.

Although the people who wrote and ratified the Constitution expected judges to exercise judicial review, they did not agree on two important questions regarding this new judicial authority. What sources of law did they think judges should use to interpret the Constitution, and what level of deference did judges owe to state and federal laws?

As to the first question, the people at the time did not have prior experience with a supreme federal Constitution judicially enforceable through the Courts, but they did have ample exposure to the interpretation of other legal documents such as statutes, contracts, and wills. They viewed constitutional interpretation as "an exercise in the traditional legal activity of construing a written instrument" and thought that the usual "methods of statutory construction" would be used by judges in constitutional cases.[8]

The founding fathers generally believed that judges should look to the law's intent, but they did not necessarily mean the subjective understandings of the drafters. Instead, they thought judges should discern the legal meaning of the text in the context of the entire statute. The focus was primarily on the law's language and its context, not legislative history or other extrinsic aids.[9] The search for meaning was generally not a "historical inquiry into what the parties actually wished to accomplish" but a focus on the objective legal meaning of the terms.[10] To the extent they thought that the intent of the people at the time of ratification was germane to determining the meaning of unclear constitutional language, the relevant intent belonged to the people at the state ratifying conventions, not the drafters of the new Constitution.[11] Of course, this is not to say that evidence of the ratifiers' intent was deemed by judges completely irrelevant to the interpretative task, but such evidence was used only in service of determining the legal meaning of the text.

The founders discussed how to interpret vague legal language, and there are comprehensive historical accounts of those debates.[12] Moreover, most originalists today do accept that original meaning, not original intent, is the appropriate question for originalist judges.[13]

A more difficult question is what level of deference the founding fathers thought judges should give to state and federal laws alleged by plaintiffs to be unconstitutional. The founders' original expectations about this question are important for several reasons. Many of today's originalists, such as Professors Richard Kay, Michael Paulsen, John McGinnis, and Mike Rappaport, argue that judges should exercise judicial review consistent with how the founders viewed that authority.[14] If the founding fathers believed in much more limited judicial review than exercised by today's judges, then these scholars' calls for more deferential review is at least consistent with the original meaning of the Constitution.

However, many other scholars who self-identify as originalists, such as Professors Randy Barnett and Ilya Somin, advocate for a strong system of judicial review where the government has the burden of proof to justify most laws infringing personal liberty.[15] If aggressive judicial review is inconsistent with the founders' original ideas about judicial review, as this book argues, then historical

sources do not justify many of the theories of constitutional interpretation advocated by modern originalists.

Both Alexander Hamilton and Chief Justice John Marshall seemed
to assume that the judicial task of deciding whether a law is inconsistent
with the Constitution was mostly mechanical. To Hamilton, as he wrote
in "No. 78," judges should only make such a ruling when there was an
"irreconcilable variance" between the two. In *Marbury*, Chief Justice
Marshall used as an example of such a case a hypothetical law passed by
Congress allowing guilt for treason to be established by one witness
even though the Constitution explicitly requires two witnesses.[16]

Numerous scholars have reviewed pre-*Marbury v. Madison* state
and federal cases to try to ascertain the views of the people at the time
on the appropriate deference judges should give to legislative acts. The
majority view is that people at the time thought judges should exercise
judicial review rarely and only when judges were sure there is a clear
inconsistency between a law and the Constitution. For example, Larry
Kramer, the former dean of Stanford Law School, canvassed the
relevant cases and concluded that judicial review was infrequently exercised and only when the law obviously violated the Constitution.[17]
Similarly, Professor Sylvia Snowiss reviewed the early cases and other
materials and argued that judges at the time thought judicial review
would be limited to "the concededly unconstitutional act."[18] One of
the leading historians of the Founding Era, Gordon Wood, found that
judicial review was "invoked only on the rare occasions of flagrant and
unequivocal violations of the Constitution."[19] In addition, the scholar
most associated with the view that the Supreme Court should be highly
deferential to acts of Congress, James Bradley Thayer, writing in the
late nineteenth century, justified his conclusions with historical evidence from the founding period.[20]

This consensus, however, has been somewhat challenged by Dean
William Michael Treanor of Georgetown University Law School.[21] Dean
Treanor collected and analyzed what appears to be the entire set of cases
from 1781–1803 (the year the Court decided *Marbury*), where state and
federal judges exercised judicial review to strike down laws or seriously
considered doing so. According to Treanor, prior to *Marbury*, there were
thirty-one cases where a state or federal court ruled a law unconstitutional, and seven more where one judge on a multimember court

thought a law unconstitutional.[22] After a careful analysis of these cases, Treanor concluded that judicial review was well accepted before *Marbury*, and that judges were not as reluctant to invalidate all laws as other scholars such as Kramer and Wood contend. Treanor also observed that most of the laws struck down by judges involved matters affecting courts and juries. Outside of these types of cases, according to Treanor, judges were "strikingly deferential" to state and federal laws.[23]

My review of these cases, the work of other scholars, and other materials from the time lead me to significant agreement with Treanor. Before setting forth why, it is important to remember that recreating what people who lived centuries ago thought about something as important, new, and controversial as the proper occasion for judicial invalidation of laws passed by legislatures is a task fraught with doubt and uncertainty. Moreover, brilliant scholars of different political leanings have looked at the same materials and come away with different conclusions. Nevertheless, some genuinely persuasive observations are possible.

First, despite the Constitution's silence on the subject, there is strong evidence that the founding fathers intended judges to exercise judicial review. This evidence includes the early cases relied on by Treanor striking down state laws as well as Hamilton's "Federalist No. 78," which argues that as a matter of logic and structure judicial review was necessary to the workings of the new Constitution. Additionally, in *Marbury*, Justice Marshall said that whether judges should strike down laws that are inconsistent with the Constitution is a "question ... deeply interesting to the United States; but, happily, not of an intricacy proportioned to its interest. It seems only necessary to recognize certain principles, supposed to have been long and well established, to decide it."[24]

Second, judges were more willing to strike down laws than some scholars suggest, but that stance was true only for a limited and narrow category of cases. Most of the decisions Treanor cites involved laws directly affecting courts such as the right to jury trials or the admissibility of evidence. These cases are complicated, and I recommend Treanor's work to readers interested in the specifics. For present purposes, it is enough to note that these decisions make clear that in the years between independence and *Marbury*, courts were willing to second-guess legislative judgments, even absent clear inconsistency with constitutional commands, only when the judicial process itself was at issue. In other cases, judges were extremely deferential to state and then federal laws.

One early state case discussed by Treanor is crucial to early understandings of judicial review because of the people involved in the case and their discussion of the proper exercise of judicial invalidation of state laws contrary to state constitutions. The issue in the *Case of the Prisoners*[25] was whether three people who had cooperated with the Crown during the Revolutionary War and convicted of treason were entitled to pardons.[26] The state's treason law did not allow the governor to pardon people for that crime, but it did allow him to suspend the sentence until the general assembly could meet and decide whether a pardon was appropriate. This law required the agreement of both houses of the legislature before a prisoner could receive a pardon. The lower house of the Virginia Assembly (the House of Delegates) had pardoned the prisoners, but the state senate (the Upper House) did not agree. The prisoners' lawyers argued that the statute requiring both houses to agree to a pardon was inconsistent with the state constitution, which seemed to allow the House of Delegates alone to grant pardons. The court ruled against the prisoners and upheld the law on several different grounds.

The state's attorney general was none other than Edmund Randolph, who would later be the attorney general of the United States and the secretary of state, as well as an influential figure at the constitutional convention. Although he defended the statute's validity, he accepted the idea of judicial review a full twenty-one years before *Marbury v. Madison*. Crucially, however, he also argued that the only proper occasion for its exercise by judges would be in the case of an irreconcilable conflict.[27] He advanced numerous arguments to support the idea that the state constitution did not allow one house pardons, but even he recognized, in a later letter to James Madison, that to most lawyers his efforts to reconcile the statute and the constitution "would appear unintelligible."[28]

Because of the importance of the *Case of the Prisoners*, the court invited other lawyers to appear and make arguments. One attorney who accepted was St. George Tucker, who would later be a William & Mary law professor, a federal judge, and the author of a leading constitutional law treatise. He also accepted the notion of judicial review and, like Randolph, expressed the idea that only laws that are "found absolutely and irreconcilably contradictory to the Constitution" shall be "null and void."[29] He went on to say that the statute requiring the consent of the Senate for a pardon was invalid because it was inconsistent with the "spirit" of the state constitution that "the power of pardoning in all cases where it is not given to the Executive is vested in the House of Delegates alone."[30]

Treanor relies on Tucker's use of the word *spirit* to argue that this important founding father and legal expert did not believe that a clear inconsistency between a law and a constitution was a prerequisite for judicial invalidation of statutes. But even Treanor observes that Tucker concluded his argument by saying that "we may trace an *absolute Contradiction* – For the Law declared that to be insufficient which the Constitution had before declared fully sufficient..."[31] Although Tucker did not require an absolute contradiction between a law and *constitutional text*, he did require that kind of contradiction between a law and the constitution even if the plaintiffs' proof could be supplied by a combination of text and extrinsic evidence. Treanor seems to be confusing the appropriate sources of constitutional meaning with what level of certainty a judge should possess before striking down a law. To Tucker, judges must be sure there is what Hamilton called an "irreconcilable variance" between a statute and the Constitution before judges exercise judicial review, even if that variance can be established by the plaintiff through a combination of text and "spirit."

This reading of Tucker is consistent with what one of the judges who ruled on the case said about judicial review. Chancellor Edmund Pendleton did not explicitly embrace the idea of judicial review, although he did state that if the legislature went beyond the limits in the state constitution, "it would seem their Act would be void."[32] He did not resolve the issue in this case because he accepted one of the relatively strained arguments made by Edmund Randolph in favor of finding no inconsistency between the pardon law and the state Constitution. However, Pendleton did say the following:

> But how far this court, in whom the judiciary powers may in some
> sort be said to be concentrated, shall have power to declare the

nullity of a law passed in its forms by the legislative power, without exercising the power of that branch, contrary to the *plain terms* of that constitution, is indeed a deep, important, and I will add, a tremendous question ... from which ... I will not shrink, if ever it shall become my duty to decide it: at present, I am happy in having no occasion to make the decision.[33]

This is important evidence showing an important founding father believed that, if judges were going to strike down state laws, there must be evidence that the statutes violated the "plain terms" of the state constitution. Moreover, it is not a large leap to conclude that a judge who is not even sure whether judicial review is appropriate in the first place, and says that in any event a law would have to violate the "plain terms" of the Constitution to be declared void, would require strong evidence of absolute inconsistency before invalidating a law.

Treanor observed that Pendleton indicated that the "spirit" of the Constitution, not just its text, may be consulted by judges exercising judicial review.[34] Again, Treanor is confusing the relevant sources of judicial review with the quantum of proof a plaintiff must establish before successfully challenging a law as being inconsistent with the Constitution. Even Alexander Hamilton, who articulated the "irreconcilable variance" standard in "Federalist No. 78," observed that judges had a duty to strike down laws that were inconsistent with the "manifest tenor" of the Constitution.[35] This "manifest tenor" could, consistent with prevailing views of statutory interpretation at the time, be established in extreme cases of ambiguity not just by plain text but also by the context of constitutional language. No matter the evidence, however, a judge would need to be convinced of obvious and clear illegality before he could properly exercise the power of judicial review.

Much of Treanor's lengthy study of these early state court opinions is devoted to establishing that in cases involving judicial power, judges did not require proof of an "irreconcilable variance" between a law and the Constitution. In the one case where the challenged statute did not fall into these categories, the law "was upheld, despite a strong tension between the statute and the relevant constitutional provisions."[36] He then turned to twenty-one federal cases decided between 1787 and 1803. Of the twenty-one decided cases, eighteen involved the power of courts or juries, while two implicated the federal Constitution's

Contracts Clause, and one involved a state constitutional provision. Treanor concluded that the pattern replicated the pre-1787 cases. When the dispute concerned matters involving "the province of the judiciary,"[37] courts did not require an irreconcilable variance between the law and the constitution before invalidating the statute. In the cases involving the federal Contract Clause, however, "the challenged statutes were clearly unconstitutional,"[38] and in the third case, the court upheld the law. Looking at the same cases, Professor John McGinnis concluded that "there is a very large number of statements that suggest that the obligation of deference was not confined to a particular set of cases and that this obligation was widely known."[39]

Dean Treanor's study suggests that when faced with laws diluting or affecting judicial power, early courts did not exercise deferential judicial review. This pattern is consistent with *Marbury v. Madison*, the first Supreme Court case to strike down an act of Congress, as the law at issue in that case regulated the original jurisdiction of the Supreme Court. On the other hand, except for only a few cases where state laws clearly transcended federal authority, early courts were strongly deferential to laws that did not pertain to the courts. In sum, as to the universe of state and federal decisions prior to *Marbury*, I agree with Treanor's conclusion that "there is evidence . . . of general deference to a coequal legislature's substantive constitutional decision making but close scrutiny of that body's decision making where it affected the judiciary."[40]

Do these early cases tell us anything helpful about how the Supreme Court should exercise judicial review today? As a predictive matter, they do not. The Supreme Court has struck down hundreds of state and federal laws over the years. In few of those cases could anyone make a straight-faced argument that the challenged statutes were obviously inconsistent with clear constitutional commands.

An originalist truly concerned with modern judges acting consistently with the original idea of judicial review, however, should be in favor of strong judicial deference to state and federal laws that do not directly involve the judiciary's power or authority. As discussed in Chapter 4, many Original Originalists such as Raoul Berger and Lino Graglia did favor that form of limited judicial review, but only a minority of modern originalists embrace that approach.

From the middle of the nineteenth century to the early part of the twentieth century, the Court transitioned from the limited type of judicial review exercised by judges in the early cases to the aggressive judicial review practiced by the modern Court. The next section examines how judges and scholars began that slow transformation.

B. NINETEENTH-CENTURY JUDICIAL REVIEW

The standard account of the Court's exercise of judicial review from 1803–1857 is that, although the Court invalidated state laws during this period, it did not strike down a single federal law. If this were true, it would support the idea that, at least as to federal laws, for the first seventy years of our country's history, the Court exhibited great deference to federal statutes.

Professor Keith Whittington, however, has challenged this traditional account and argued that the Justices were more actively exercising judicial review over federal laws during this period than most historians have suggested.[41] One myth he is trying to debunk is that the landmark, and infamous case, *Dred Scott v. Sandford*,[42] decided by the Court in 1857, was not a "bolt from the blue" but instead the result of the Court "gradually over the course of the first half of the nineteenth century, facilitating the goals of national political actors and consolidating the Court's claim to be able to define the constitutional limits of congressional power.... [T]he power of judicial review [was] politically constructed through the over-time, back-and-forth dialogue between the branches, rather than through one-time, unilateral doctrinal assertions by the Court."[43]

Professor Whittington's evidence that the Court actively reviewed federal laws between *Marbury* and *Dred Scott* consists mostly of cases where the justices discussed judicial review but upheld acts of Congress and cases where the Court reviewed laws dealing with the judicial power. The first class of cases are consistent with a deferential approach to judicial review, while the second dovetails with the early cases where judges exercised aggressive review over cases dealing with their own authority. Whittington agrees that *Dred Scott* was *unusual* "[i]n that... the Court ruled against congressional power in a high-profile

and politically salient case."[44] That observation is crucial to the historical point that *Dred Scott*, decided 54 years after *Marbury*, marked the
first time that the Supreme Court struck down an important act of
Congress unrelated (in part) to the federal judicial power. That it took
more than a half-century after *Marbury* to reach that point is indicative
that the founding fathers, and the generation after them, did not believe
the Court should play a prominent role in keeping Congress within
constitutional bounds absent a clear constitutional violation.

The United States in the 1850s was a bitterly divided country.
The Southern states cherished slavery in all its dimensions: political,
civil, cultural, and of course, economic. The Northern states were
largely, though not completely, in favor of abolition and firmly
opposed to allowing slavery in the newly acquired territories. A series
of compromises in the preceding decades stalled total unrest, but the
1854 Kansas–Nebraska Act, which allowed settlers to choose slavery
or not, undercut those agreements and led to the formation of the new
Republican Party and, eventually, the Civil War.[45]

Between the signing of the Kansas–Nebraska Act and the start of
the Civil War, the Supreme Court decided a case that many historians
and legal scholars believe to be the "worst atrocity in the Supreme
Court's history" and a "self-inflicted wound that almost destroyed
the Supreme Court."[46] The case also generated the first originalist
Supreme Court decision overturning an important federal law, though
many originalists today believe the opinion misapplied originalism to
achieve that result.

The facts giving rise to *Dred Scott* were not in dispute. Scott was a
slave whose master took him to, among other places, the Northwest
Territories, a place where the Missouri Compromise had made slavery
illegal. The master and slave eventually returned to Missouri, where
slavery was legal. Scott argued that he was now a free man because he
had visited places where slavery had been abolished.

Scott brought his lawsuit in federal court, where his new owner
made two major arguments – one jurisdictional and one substantive.
Scott's suit depended on diversity jurisdiction, which allows citizens of
one state to sue citizens of another state. Sandford argued that, Scott
being the descendant of slaves, never was and never could be a citizen
of Missouri. Sandford also argued that the Missouri Compromise,

which outlawed slavery in the Northwest Territories, was unconstitutional because it went beyond Congress's enumerated federal powers and deprived slave owners of their property (slaves) without due process of law in contravention of the Fifth Amendment.[47]

In a 7–2 opinion, Justice Taney agreed with Sandford on both counts. He held that Scott never was and never could be a citizen of Missouri because African Americans and their descendants were not considered part of "We the "People" by the ratifiers of the Constitution.[48] The Court also held that Congress had taken Sandford's property without due process of law because Congress lacked the power to prohibit slavery in the new territories.

Although the Court's holdings have been almost universally criticized by legal scholars,[49] for our purposes it is how Justice Taney explained the proper method of judicial review that is most significant. He began by noting that the pursuit of "justice" is not the judicial task:

> It is not the province of the court to decide upon the justice or injustice, the policy or impolicy, of these laws. The decision of that question belonged to the political or law-making power; to those who formed the sovereignty and framed the Constitution. The duty of the court is to interpret the instrument they have framed with the best lights we can obtain on the subject, and to administer it as we find it, according to its true intent and meaning when it was adopted.[50]

Taney tried to establish that, at the time of the founding, African Americans did not have constitutional rights protected by the Constitution. As to the Declaration of Independence's statement that "all men are created equal," Taney responded that "it is too clear for dispute that the enslaved African race were not intended to be included, and formed no part of the people who framed and adopted this declaration, for if the language, as understood in that day, would embrace them, the conduct of the distinguished men who framed the Declaration of Independence would have been utterly and flagrantly inconsistent with the principles they asserted. . . ."[51]

At the end of his long historical analysis, Taney described an originalist method of judicial review:

> No one, we presume, supposes that any change in public opinion or feeling, in relation to this unfortunate race . . . should induce the

court to give to the words of the Constitution a more liberal
construction in their favor than they were intended to bear when
the instrument was framed and adopted. Such an argument would
be altogether inadmissible in any tribunal called on to interpret it. If
any of its provisions are deemed unjust, there is a mode prescribed
in the instrument itself by which it may be amended; *but while it
remains unaltered, it must be construed now as it was understood at the
time of its adoption* ... Any other rule of construction would abro-
gate the judicial character of this court, and make it the mere reflex
of the popular opinion or passion of the day. This court was not
created by the Constitution for such purposes.[52]

Taney's intent was reasonably clear. Even if, by 1857, there was
significant sentiment among white Americans that excluding African-
Americans from citizenship was immoral and unjust, the Court should
not look past the Constitution's original intent. If that led to injustice,
Article 5 provided procedures for amending the document.

Many modern originalists do not take issue with Taney's method
or his description of the proper judicial role. Instead, they argue that
he misapplied originalism.[53] They point to Justice Curtis, who also
applied an originalist approach but reached different conclusions on
both of the major issues in the case. Those who believe originalism is
the only proper method of constitutional interpretation avoid
the stigma of Taney's originalism by arguing that judges can misapply any theory of interpretation. The problem with *Dred Scott*,
according to originalists, is not that originalism is improper but that
in the wrong hands, like any theory, it can be used by judges to reach
bad results.

These theorists have a valid point. As Professor Mark Graber has
argued, no "prominent approach to the judicial function compels any
result" in *Dred Scott*.[54] Regarding both of the major issues in the case,
the facts and history were contested enough at the time to justify both
the majority and dissenting opinions. The almost universal condemnation of the case flows from originalists claiming that Taney misapplied
history and from living constitutionalists that Taney did not properly
consider contemporary standards of morality and humanity.[55] Today,
all we can agree on is that the result in *Dred Scott* is horrific by our
modern standards.

Still, *Dred Scott* provides important lessons about today's originalism debates. First, Taney's description of the judicial role as being
separate from issues of justice, like all such statements, is misleading.
Although Taney may not have been a strong proponent of slavery, his
personal views on property rights, American politics, and the difficult
regional conflicts at the time, certainly played a major role in his
decision.

Second, one of the important critiques leveled by non-originalists
against originalism is that in most litigated cases historical sources
cannot constrain judicial decision making.[56] *Dred Scott* starkly makes
that point. Even though the litigation developed only about seventy-
five years after the founding, the justices and the people at the time
strongly disagreed about the best reading of history. In other words, a
judge concerned exclusively with text and history could have ruled
for either party under the legal standards and historical accounts of the
day.

Finally, *Dred Scott* dramatically illustrates an important theme
about constitutional litigation that runs throughout this book. Whether
the constitutional issue is abortion, affirmative action, campaign
finance reform, free speech, freedom of religion, federalism, separation
of powers, or any other frequently litigated constitutional law issue, the
applicable text is usually so imprecise, and the history of the relevant
provisions so unclear, that no theory of constitutional interpretation,
with the exception discussed later, can meaningfully restrain Supreme
Court justices from imposing their unique perspectives on constitutional law.[57] As I have previously documented at length, in virtually
every corner of litigated constitutional law, the imposition of the justices' personal values has been more important than application of text,
history, and original meaning.[58] The only theory of interpretation that
could significantly limit judicial discretion is one of extreme deference
to the elected branches. Only by employing such deference can words
and phrases like "free exercise," "equal protection," and "due process" lead judges to a principled method of constitutional interpretation where in many, if not most, cases, preexisting law plays a primary
role. Only with such deference does originalism even make sense given
the grave difficulties historians, much less judges, have in trying to
recreate the past. Those difficulties get harder, not easier, as time

moves on, and society changes in dramatic ways the founders never anticipated. How to apply a fixed Constitution to such changes, as discussed later, is one of our most difficult and controversial constitutional law problems.

C. CONSTITUTIONAL CHANGE

In the second half of the nineteenth century, the US population moved west as new forms of transportation and technology triggered economic expansion. Congress legislated at an accelerated rate creating new national agencies with regulatory power. With the new economy and laws came legal and constitutional challenges brought by plaintiffs representing diverse economic interests. In 1900, just a little more than a century after the ratification of the Constitution, Professor Arthur W. Machen wrote a two-part law review article discussing the relationship between a fixed Constitution and an ever-changing society.[59] He began his groundbreaking article this way:

> As the period of the formation of the American Union becomes more and more remote, it becomes constantly more important to inquire to what extent the decision of a question of federal constitutional law may properly be affected by the many changes in language, customs, morals, and in individual and national environment which have taken place since the adoption of our fundamental law. ... Commerce, instead of being conducted by stage-coaches and sail-boats, is carried on by railways, telegraphs, and ocean liners. Ideas of morality have changed: lotteries and dueling, once regarded as praiseworthy, are now thought pernicious and immoral. The effect of all these changes upon our system of constitutional law is surely an interesting and important matter for legal inquiry... *The present paper deals with the problems which arise when a constitution, the letter of which remains unchanged, is to be applied by the courts to an altered state of facts.*[60]

After framing the issue so starkly, Professor Machen asked whether "it [is] ever possible to justify a departure from the original intention? Can the Constitution be changed, silently and without formal amendments?"[61] He addressed this question by distinguishing between two different schools of constitutional interpretation. One school, the "strict and literal constructionists," generally looked only to the "dictionary meaning" of the Constitution's words to discover the intentions of the framers, while the other school, the "broad constructionists," advocated looking for the "actual intent" of the framers in whatever way possible, sometimes giving a "forced or ungrammatical" meaning to the Constitution's words.[62] Although they employed different means, both schools agreed that, if ascertainable, the framers' intentions, as manifested in the original text, were controlling.

Professor Machen considered whether there were any exceptions to the general rule that the framers' intentions, if discoverable, must govern constitutional interpretation. He summarized the views of those who believed that significant societal change justified evolving constitutional meanings. According to these scholars, "[t]o follow out precisely in all cases the will of men who lived over a century ago may, in certain contingencies, from the standpoint of policy, be extremely undesirable."[63] The Constitution, the supporters of this view argued, was intended by the framers to be "elastic and adaptable to changed conditions," and it must be "a living, growing organism, capable of adapting itself to all the multiplex conditions in which the nation may be involved."[64] The framers could not have intended that a political instrument designed to "endure through all time should always bear the same construction."[65] The Constitution "is not dead but living."[66] Machen appears to be the first person to use the terminology "living" and "dead" constitutions in a law review article.

Professor Machen at first rejected these arguments for a living Constitution. He argued that if judges could evade the intent of the framers for reasons of policy and expediency, the Constitution would no longer be binding law. He claimed that there is no "middle ground" between following the framers' intentions and deviating from those intentions for policy reasons. Although judges following the original meaning of the Constitution might hamper the operations of the government, the alternative would allow the judiciary to alter the Constitution and place the courts above the Constitution. That result would jeopardize our system of government and threaten the advantages of being governed by a "fixed organic law."[67]

Machen conceded that his discussion assumed that judges could ascertain the framers' intentions. He knew that in many cases those intentions would be unclear because "imperfection and vagueness of

human language [and] the difficulty of placing ourselves in the position
of men who lived so long ago" causes great difficulty for "the interpreter of the Constitution."[68] In such cases, Machen suggested, judges
should rely on practical rules of construction, and legislative and
administrative practice, to decide constitutional issues. Even though
he did not specifically identify such practices, Machen nevertheless
warned judges not to use notions of expediency to decide difficult legal
questions. Although he recognized a judge will "almost inevitably be
unconsciously influenced by his knowledge of the immediate ill effects
which a theoretically correct judgment might produce," he hoped that
judges would ignore policy considerations that the framers would not
have accepted.[69] Otherwise, judges might reach a different interpretation of the language than would a court sitting immediately after the
founding, and that Machen argued, judges should never do.[70]

   In the first part of his article, Machen sounds like many modern
originalists. He urged judges to use all available tools to discover what
the words of the Constitution meant at the time they were written and
argued that judges should ignore contemporary policy considerations
when determining those intentions. If those intentions were undiscov-
erable, standard rules of construction should guide constitutional decision making. Contemporary originalists would find little to complain
about in this advice to judges.[71] As we will see, however, Part II of
Professor Machen's article undercuts much of his reliance on originalism and shows that he embraced living constitutionalism as his
preferred method of constitutional interpretation.

   Professor Machen began the second part of his article with the
acknowledgment that, even when judges apply the rule that the original
intentions of the framers control constitutional interpretation, it "does
not follow that an act which was unconstitutional one hundred years
ago must necessarily be so held today."[72] Although the identification of
the Constitution's meaning by judges must not change, the validity of
legislative acts often turns on the specific factual context of the case,
which may vary from one generation to the next. According to Professor Machen:

   The separation of the law from the facts is a difficult but tran-
   scendently important task. For while denying in the most

unqualified terms the notion that the Constitution is capable of a varying construction, *we may often be swayed by the same arguments advanced in favor of that heresy, and even reach the same results, but in a perfectly legitimate way, simply by a careful discrimination between matters of law and fact. The law of the Constitution remains forever unchanging: the facts to which it must be applied are infinitely various.*[73]

Professor Machen provided as an example of this thesis the case of margarine. He suggested that a law passed at the behest of margarine sellers in the year 1900 forbidding the sale of butter might well be struck down by the courts as an arbitrary denial of due process of law. But if the facts changed and people began to prefer margarine to butter, and people were now concerned that sellers of butter were trying to pass off that product as margarine, then on "those facts . . . the legislature might constitutionally prohibit the manufacture and sale of butter . . . just as acts absolutely forbidding the sale or manufacture of oleomargarine are now . . . upheld."[74] In that circumstance, "the construction of the Constitution would not have varied. The same rule of constitutional law would be applied, the same definition of 'due process' would be given. It is the facts which would have changed – the interpretation of the Constitution – would be still unaltered."[75]

Machen's suggestion that judges in different eras might reach inconsistent results in similar or even identical cases by carefully parsing facts from law suggests that his reliance on the original intentions of the framers is stylistic not substantive. In his example given earlier, the application of the phrase "due process of law" to a statute prohibiting the sale of butter leads to a legal result in one case but a contrary outcome in another because society changes. Whether we label that a change in "meaning," which Machen denies, or a change in application of law to facts makes no difference to the litigants, the country, or the rule of law. The result is the same.

Machen's other example further illustrates the point. He questioned the Supreme Court's decision in *Brass v. Stoeser*,[76] where the Court held that a grain elevator in a small town was subject to reasonable regulation because of a prior case involving similar elevators in New York City and Buffalo. The Court rejected the plaintiff's argument that the facts of its case were different because of the small-town nature of its business, on the basis that the plaintiff's argument raised "purely legislative" considerations.[77] Machen disagreed with that reasoning, arguing that individual factual circumstances can and should control the constitutionality of laws like the one at issue in *Stoeser* because the "habits, manners, opinions and needs of the people of the several states are so widely divergent that what would be arbitrary in one state at one time may, at the same time in another state, or at another time in the same state, be harmless and even beneficent."[78]

Machen conceded that these kinds of factual distinctions are "more legislative than judicial," and that this kind of analysis "opens up to the courts many matters unsuited for judicial discussion."[79] Machen argued, however, that American judges must realize that many problems of government that other countries leave to legislatures and other elected officials are submitted here to federal judges.[80] Put differently, in many if not most constitutional cases, just looking for the original meaning of the relevant constitutional text will not provide clear enough guidance to judges for them to avoid close, fact-based inspection. Relying on original meaning is nice as a theoretical matter, but for real judges deciding actual cases, they must do much more work to resolve cases.

Professor Machen accepted the hard reality that changed circumstances and new technologies make constitutional decision making often dependent on difficult interpretative questions. For example, he asked whether the Eighth Amendment's prohibition on "cruel and unusual punishments" meant "unusual when the amendment was adopted [in 1791], or unusual when the punishment is inflicted."[81] Machen did not resolve this question. He noted that all of "the familiar arguments in favor of an 'elastic constitution' may be urged in support of that construction [which tests constitutionality as of the time the punishment is imposed]. The fact that the Constitution was intended to endure perpetually, the importance of leaving the legislature . . . free to adopt such measures as the sentiment of the people may permit or require – these are legitimate reasons for interpreting 'unusual' to mean unusual when the penalty is exacted."[82] Professor Machen noted that there were counterarguments, as well, and concluded "either interpretation is permissible, and that either may be adopted without conflicting with the sound theory of constitutional construction; and that the same thing is true in other similar cases."[83]

This concession from Machen, that the Eighth Amendment's original meaning was that judges might have to determine what are cruel and unusual punishments according to contemporary considerations, undercuts much of his originalist sounding rhetoric. If the meaning of "cruel and unusual" can change over time, why not the meaning of "freedom of speech," "free exercise of religion," "liberty," and "equal protection"? The framers were smart men who chose their words with care. When they wanted to be precise, such as mandating the president be thirty-five, or that there must be two senators from every state, they knew how to be precise. When they used vague and elastic language, they certainly must have known that judges would have great discretion applying that text to varying and changing circumstances. In fact, as we will see in Chapter 5, this method of constitutional interpretation is exactly the kind of "originalism" advocated by many twenty-first-century originalist scholars.[84] However, as we will also see, this form of "originalism" is not materially different in practice from non-originalism or what has been called "living constitutionalism."[85]

Professor Machen's extraordinary (for its time) article is still relevant to contemporary originalism debates. Many years later, Justice Scalia, Laurence Tribe, and Ronald Dworkin engaged in a similar debate about originalism generally and the Eighth Amendment specifically.[86] It is far from clear whether their discussion illuminated the issues any better than Machen, who wrote his two-part article three-quarters of a century earlier.[87]

3 ORIGINALISM'S PATH

> *Just what our forefathers did envision, or would have envisioned had they foreseen modern conditions, must be divined from materials almost as enigmatic as the dreams Joseph was called upon to interpret for Pharaoh.*
>
> Justice Robert Jackson[1]

A. JUDICIAL REVIEW: 1865–1950

From the end of the Civil War to the beginning of the twentieth century, the Supreme Court's most notable constitutional law cases, with a few exceptions, involved the rights of African Americans. Although the Court started down this path by interpreting the Fourteenth Amendment to invalidate a state's exclusion of blacks from juries,[2] the Justices soon reversed course and prevented Congress from ending segregation in places of public accommodations, and then rubber-stamping state-required segregation.[3] During this time, the Court did exercise judicial review in a few other notable cases such as striking down state laws that interfered with interstate commerce, invalidating the federal income tax (a decision eventually reversed by the Sixteenth Amendment), and as discussed in Chapter 9, first prohibiting and then allowing Congress to make paper money legal tender. Overall, however, the Supreme Court did not overturn legislation on a frequent basis during the second half of the nineteenth century.

The Court's deference to state and federal statutes began to change as our nation moved westward and new laws were enacted to govern the growing economy. Starting around the turn of the century, the Court started to exercise aggressive judicial review on a consistent basis for the first time. The case that symbolizes this period of American jurisprudence is *Lochner v. New York*.[4]

New York law comprehensively regulated the bakery industry, including limiting the number of hours bakery employees could work to sixty in a week and ten in a day.[5] Historians dispute exactly why the law was enacted, but most agree it was a combination of progressive sympathy for bakery workers and rent-seeking pressure from large bakeries and unions feeling competition from small bakeries in which immigrants were willing to work long hours for little pay.[6] The New York legislature passed the statute unanimously.

The majority struck down the maximum hours section of the law, holding that it had no reasonable relationship to the health or safety of either bakery employees or the public and because "clean and whole-some" bread "does not depend upon whether bakers work ten hours per day or only sixty hours per week."[7] The Court also worried about the slippery slope of this kind of protectionist legislation because if the hours of bakery workers could be limited, so could the hours of "doctors, lawyers, scientists, all professional men, as well as athletes and artisans."[8] The Court concluded by holding that New York's law was "an illegal interference with the rights of...both employers and employees, to make contracts regarding labor upon such terms as they may think best."[9] The constitutional provision the justices cited to strike down the law was the Fourteenth Amendment's command that no state deprive any person of "life, liberty or property without due process of law."[10]

Justices Harlan and Holmes dissented, arguing that the majority should have been much more deferential to the New York legislature. Holmes famously said that different economic experts might hold conflicting views concerning the benefits of the New York law and, more importantly, the Constitution "is not intended to embody a particular economic theory, whether of paternalism...or *laissez faire*."[11] Holmes concluded that "the word 'liberty,' in the Fourteenth Amendment, is perverted when it is held to prevent the natural outcome of a dominant opinion, unless it can be said that a rational and fair man necessarily would admit that the statute proposed would infringe fundamental principles as they have been understood by

the traditions of our people and our law."[12] Holmes did not think
the law violated such principles.

The most interesting aspect of *Lochner* for our purposes is that
the Court spent no time discussing the original meaning of the Fourteenth Amendment's Due Process Clause. Instead, the justices simply
reasoned that, given the importance of freedom of contract, New
York's justifications for the law were not constitutionally sufficient.
There is nothing originalist or textualist about the opinion.

Over the next thirty years, the Court struck down hundreds of
state and federal laws dealing with workers' rights, unions, and
safety conditions in factories and other places of employment. In
one of these cases, *Hammer v. Dagenhart*,[13] Congress used its power
to regulate "commerce among the states," to prohibit companies
who employed child labor to send their goods across state lines. At
the time, large numbers of children were working long hours in
terrible conditions throughout the United States. Although this federal law was literally a regulation of "commerce among the states,"
the Court struck it down without citing any evidence concerning
the original meaning of the commerce clause, other than taking out
of context snippets from a few of Chief Justice Marshall's early
opinions.

For roughly thirty years, the Supreme Court blocked progressive
state and federal laws while often failing to point to ratification-era
evidence to support their judgments.[14] During this same time, however, many of the justices paid lip service to their alleged responsibility
in constitutional cases to finding the original intent of the text at issue.
Statements like these by Justice Brewer were common: "To determine
the extent of the grants of power, we must, therefore, place ourselves in
the position of the men who framed and adopted the Constitution and
inquire what they must have understood to be the meaning and scope
of those grants."[15] Similarly, in a famous dissent, Justice Sutherland
argued that "the meaning of the Constitution does not change with the
ebb and flow of economic events."[16] Despite these protestations,
however, the justices rarely relied on originalist evidence to reach their
legal conclusions.[17]

After the Great Depression plunged the country into economic
turmoil, and the Court invalidated a few of President Franklin Delano

Roosevelt's early New Deal efforts to improve the economy, the Court entered a crisis stage leading the president to make his famous Court packing threats. Around the same time, Justice Owen Roberts changed his mind on several key issues, and after a few Justices retired or died, and Roosevelt appointed more justices, the Court stopped striking down economic legislation. How this dramatic shift occurred plays an important role in the history of the country and the Court,[18] but its relevance, for our purposes, is the direction the Court adopted after it stopped striking down economic legislation.

Once the Court abandoned any pretense of seriously reviewing economic laws governing the workplace, the justices issued a decision in 1937 that eventually formed the basis of a different kind of aggressive judicial review. The issue in *United States v. Carolene Products*[19] was whether Congress could prohibit the interstate shipment of "filled" milk. As the *Lochner* era had ended a few years earlier, the justices had no trouble holding (in a relatively short opinion) that the law easily passed the Court's now deferential "rational basis" test. The issue of whether the milk presented any safety issues for the public was "at least debatable" and therefore a "decision ... for Congress" not the Court.[20]

In what has become the most famous footnote in the history of the Supreme Court, the justices suggested that they might not apply the same degree of deference to all state and federal laws:

> There may be narrower scope for operation of the presumption of constitutionality when legislation appears on its face to be within a specific prohibition of the Constitution, such as those of the first ten amendments, which are deemed equally specific when held to be embraced within the Fourteenth ... It is unnecessary to consider now whether legislation which restricts those political processes which can ordinarily be expected to bring about repeal of undesirable legislation, is to be subjected to more exacting judicial scrutiny ... Nor need we enquire whether similar considerations enter into the review of statutes directed at religious ... or racial minorities ... [or] whether prejudice against discrete and insular minorities may be a special condition, which tends seriously to curtail the operation of those political processes ordinarily to be relied upon to protect minorities, and which may call for a correspondingly more searching judicial inquiry.[21]

In this footnote, the justices signaled that laws affecting the political process, religious and racial minorities, and specific rights enumerated in the first ten amendments might trigger more aggressive judicial review than ordinary economic legislation. Eventually, the justices of the Warren and early Burger Courts engaged in exactly that kind of decision making igniting political and legal disputes that are still with us today. Interestingly, the justices did not cite any originalist or historical evidence to justify the potentially more searching review of noneconomic rights mentioned in *Carolene's* famous footnote. Given this dramatic shift, it is important to take stock of the jurisprudential playing field that contributed to this radical change in legal philosophy.

Professor Jacob tenBroek, writing in 1938 and 1939, authored a five-part series of law review articles in the *California Law Review* comprehensively discussing the role original intent (what we now call original meaning) had played and should play in constitutional interpretation.[22] These articles shed light on the constitutional interpretation debates circa 1939 and provide valuable insight into how the Court's use of originalist materials was viewed by some scholars at that point in our country's history. These articles are also important because they are vintage pieces of "Legal Realism," a doctrine that emerged among some judges and scholars in the 1920s and 1930s. Before turning to tenBroek's analysis, a summary of Legal Realism is necessary to put his important work in the proper perspective.

Justice Oliver Wendell Holmes was one of the early intellectual leaders of the legal realist movement, believing that most difficult cases involve "a conflict between two social desires [where] judges are called upon to exercise the sovereign prerogative of choice."[23] Holmes didn't think that prior legal rules decided cases as much as the justices' personal, social, and political views. Along with leading academics such as Jerome Frank and Karl Llewellyn, the realists argued that Supreme Court decisions reflected judgment not logic. In his book, *Originalism in American Law and Politics*, Professor Jonathan O'Neil summed up the legal realist movement this way:

> The core claim of the realists was that in deciding cases judges responded primarily to the facts and reached a result based on what they thought was fair and right – decisions were not motivated or

constrained by the legal reasons or the constitutional text... Furthermore, analogical reasoning, statutory interpretation, and facts themselves were often too indeterminate to resolve a case.[24]

The legal realists disagreed with the constant assertions by Supreme Court justices that text, history, and precedent were the only appropriate sources of constitutional law. Karl Llewellyn wrote that the aggressive use of the due process clause to strike down economic laws was just the "enforcement of the majority's ideal of government-as-it-should-be."[25] Some scholars believe that the *Lochner* line of cases "gave birth to the realist movement."[26] Professor tenBroek, a realist himself, applied this mind-set to offer a devastating critique of historical and formalist based methodologies.[27]

In the first four parts of his series, tenBroek showed through a detailed historical analysis of judicial decisions from the founding through the New Deal that Supreme Court justices sometimes used ratification-era sources to support their legal conclusions, but often they didn't. TenBroek discussed the justices' use of the 1787 convention debates, *The Federalist Papers*, the decisions of the first few Congresses, and early Supreme Court decisions and observed that the Court's use or nonuse of these inherently elastic and mostly indeterminate historical sources depended on the specific results the justices wanted to reach.[28]

In his fifth article, tenBroek added to this detailed historical analysis two assumptions he said the Justices often *claimed* to adhere to when resolving constitutional questions: (1) judges should "abandon" contemporary perspectives in deference to the "vantage point" of the people living when the Constitution was adopted; and (2) the original meaning of the Constitution does not change.[29] To tenBroek, however, the idea that the Constitution has a fixed meaning that modern judges do not change was not an accurate description of constitutional law. He argued that originalism inverts how judges decide cases. Judges don't delve deeply into an array of historical sources "uninfluenced by outside considerations and entirely unprejudiced by predilections and biases."[30] In fact, "[n]othing could be further from the facts!"[31] Instead, the justices use "independent judgment" and "reasoning processes" to support the "conclusion the Court wishes to reach."[32]

Constitutional questions, tenBroek argued, are "as much studies in personnel and in judicial psychology as they are problems in law."[33]

Even if the justices looked in good faith for answers to hard cases in the original meaning of the Constitution, tenBroek argued, the search would be mostly fruitless. The convention and ratification debates are "too particular, ungeneralizable and superficial" to be truly helpful, and the "history of the times too vague" to resolve difficult modern problems.[34] Considering the difficulty of ascertaining what people who lived long ago thought about issues they could not foresee, the doctrine of originalism "falsely describes what the Court actually does."[35]

TenBroek also argued that the meaning of the Constitution changes all the time in the hands of judges and justices (as he thought it should to keep up with modern conditions). Pointing to the reversal of numerous *Lochner*-type cases by the post–New Deal Court, tenBroek observed that these "changes in the meaning of the Constitution did not result from altered judicial views as to the original intent; they came rather from a different prevailing attitude in the Court with respect to economic, social, and political policy."[36]

Although the search for the original meaning of the Constitution should, where possible, be one factor in hard cases, tenBroek suggested many other equally important considerations should be used by judges wrestling with difficult constitutional issues. These factors include the court's views as to "justice, expediency, policy, social need, economic and political theory, and ultimate consequences."[37] But, most important, "questions should be considered in the light of present day conditions as they actually exist, not in the near darkness of the world as it surrounded the framers ..."[38]

TenBroek also addressed the theory, often articulated by modern-day originalists, and employed back then by Supreme Court Justice Sutherland, that the "provisions of the Federal Constitution, undoubtedly, are pliable in the sense that in appropriate cases they have the capacity of bringing within their grasp every new condition which falls within their meaning. But, their meaning is changeless; it is only their application which [changes]."[39] TenBroek responded that the "meaning of terms cannot be changeless."[40] His point was that in determining what new conditions fall within the meaning of constitutional text, "the Court is defining [its] meaning, and by including or excluding new referents, changing [its] meaning."[41] The examples of these kinds of constitutional changes could fill a casebook, and I detail many of them in Chapters 8 and 9.

TenBroek ended his article by pointing out that written Constitutions, if they are to last, must adapt to changing times, and the justices, perhaps implicitly, know they must also keep up with those times. What justices shouldn't do is pretend answers to hard constitutional questions can be gleaned from centuries past: "[T]he very realism of the doctrine of constitutional adaptability makes the intent theory of constitutional interpretation, with its dogma of organic immutability and its retrogressive aspects, with its misapprehension of the facts of judicial operation and with its weakness of theory, one of the fundamental doctrinal fallacies of the Supreme Court of the United States."[42]

By the time tenBroek's articles were published in 1939, Legal Realism had taken hold among many judges and scholars, and just a few years later, the justices who had spent almost a quarter century striking down economic legislation (with barely a nod to originalist sources) were dead or retired. For the next fifteen years or so the Court did not strike down many state or federal laws. Two landmark cases in the early 1950s, however, would forever alter the history of the Court and the country, and one of them would help usher in another era of aggressive judicial review of state and federal laws.

B. JUDICIAL REVIEW – 1952–1972

1. The Steel Seizure Case[43]

In 1950, President Harry Truman ordered the US military into an armed conflict in support of South Korea's fight against North Korea. The Korean War was the first time an American president entered a major military conflict without congressional authorization (as seemingly required by Article I, Section 8).[44] Subsequently, Congress passed statutory initiatives supporting and funding the war, although it never passed a formal Declaration of War.[45]

In 1952, after efforts to settle a nationwide steel strike had failed, Truman issued an Executive Order directing the Secretary of Commerce to seize privately owned steel mills and keep them operating. This Executive Order was drafted as a "military imperative."[46] The Order emphasized that that (1) "American fighting men... are now engaged in deadly combat with the forces of aggression in Korea"; (2) needed weapons and materials "are produced to a great extent in this country, and steel is an indispensable component of substantially all of such weapons and materials"; and (3) a steel strike "would immediately jeopardize and imperil our national defense... and would add to the continuing danger of our soldiers, sailors, and airmen engaged in combat in the field."[47]

The Supreme Court expedited its hearing in the case after a lower court judge enjoined the Executive Order. The Solicitor General of the United States, arguing on behalf of the Order, made a passionate plea saying that the country was at war (even if undeclared), and the president was attempting to prevent a "national catastrophe."[48]

Truman argued that he had the authority to seize the mills under his Article II powers as commander-in-chief, the president's inherent executive authority, and the president's powers to deal with an emergency. The steel mill owners responded that there was no dire need for the seizure, and that Truman should have used the national labor laws to deal with the strike instead of seizing private property.

Just two weeks after the arguments, the justices issued their decision holding that the president did not have the authority to take over the steel mills.[49] Justice Black wrote the opinion of the Court, but there were five separate concurring opinions, and three justices dissented. Parsing all six of the justices' separate opinions holding that Truman acted illegally shows that the main points were that the Executive Order constituted lawmaking, which is the sole province of Congress; that the president doesn't have inherent executive powers other than those specifically enumerated in Article II; that the president's commander-in-chief authority did not apply outside the "theater of war"; and that the president's emergency powers, if any, did not reach this situation.

The three dissenting Justices argued that Congress had authorized the Korean military actions through laws funding it, that the president could seize the mills under his authority to faithfully execute those laws, and that the president had the authority to protect our troops under his powers as commander-in-chief. The dissent also noted that Truman explicitly said he would rescind the Order if Congress asked him to, which reduced fears of executive tyranny.[50]

Justice Jackson's concurring opinion, which is the one that has stood the test of time and is by far the most important, set up the now classic framework for evaluating the president's authority. If the president acts at Congress' behest, there is a strong presumption in favor of the president; if he acts in direct contravention of Congress, there is a strong presumption against his action; and if Congress has not spoken, the decision will depend on "the imperatives of events and contemporary imponderables."[51] Jackson decided that Truman's Order directly contravened the federal labor laws (a controversial opinion, given the text of those laws were silent on the issue), and that the president didn't have any statutory or constitutional authority to seize private property.

The Court's *Steel Seizure* decision was a dramatic and powerful exercise of judicial review. The president of the United States argued that there was a military emergency and that, absent his actions, our troops would face imminent harm. Truman also agreed to abide by any congressional action on the matter, reducing the risk of runaway presidential power. Nevertheless, the justices invalidated the Order and prevented the president from taking what he thought was necessary military action. Two leading scholars on separation of powers have observed that the fact that "the Justices went so decisively against presidential power, in the middle of a war, came as a surprise to many . . . After all, the Court was comprised of Roosevelt and Truman appointees and the entire decisional trend for fifteen years . . . had been in the direction of the aggrandizement of the powers of the president."[52]

The implications of *Steel Seizure* for constitutional law and the Court's power of judicial review are many. For the purposes of this book, however, there is one major aspect of the decision that is of overriding importance. In an important, if not the most important, judicial decision in American history overriding a presidential decision (in time of war, no less), there is little originalist discussion in the

opinions making up the majority's view that the president acted unlaw-
fully. One scholar has argued that "in Youngstown's shadow, there is
exceedingly little room for foreign affairs originalism in any form."[53]
Another commentator has argued that Justice Jackson's concurrence,
the most important of the six opinions in the case, is "among the most
anti-originalist opinions in the modern canon."[54] There is strong
evidence for this conclusion in Justice Jackson's clear rejection of the
idea that the issues in the case could be resolved by an originalist
approach:

> Just what our forefathers did envision, or would have envisioned
> had they foreseen modern conditions, must be divined from mater-
> ials almost as enigmatic as the dreams Joseph was called upon to
> interpret for Pharaoh. A century and a half of partisan debate and
> scholarly speculation yields no net result but only supplies more or
> less apt quotations from respected sources on each side of any
> question. They largely cancel each other.[55]

As Professor Steve Vladeck points out, Jackson's opinion was later
adopted by the Supreme Court as the "'the accepted framework for
evaluating executive action in this area.' Thus, the methodology
adopted by the Supreme Court to resolve separation-of powers conflicts, particularly in cases implicating 'foreign affairs,' was one hostile
to originalism in both its conceptualization and its implementation."[56]
When invalidating what the president thought was an essential
reaction to a military emergency, the Supreme Court of the United
States did not pause to reflect on the original meaning of the Constitution, even after fifteen years of quite limited judicial review. Just two
years later, the Court would hand down a historic civil rights decision
and would again reject the relevance of originalist evidence to the
resolution of hard constitutional questions.

2. Brown v. Board of Education

In 1954, there were two Americas, one white and one black. Racial
discrimination was prevalent throughout the nation. In many parts of
the country, not just the deep South, African Americans had to endure
not only the indignity of separate schools, hotels, and restaurants, but

also, depending on the state, separate parks, water fountains, sports fields, public libraries, prisons, and even telephone booths.[57] Although the word is not often associated with the United States, there was in much of our country a system of racial apartheid.

To fully understand how this evil came to an end, we must first see how it began. Both at the beginning, and at the end, of the period known as Jim Crow, the Supreme Court played a major role.

After the Civil War, the United States ratified the Thirteenth, Fourteenth, and Fifteenth Amendments to the Constitution. The Thirteenth ends slavery while the Fifteenth makes it illegal to deny anyone the right to vote on the basis of race. The Fourteenth Amendment prohibits the states from denying anyone "life, liberty or property without due process of law," the "equal protection of the laws," and the "privileges or immunities of citizenship." Congress was expressly given the power to enforce these provisions through "appropriate legislation." There is consensus among scholars, historians, and judges that the central purpose of all three Amendments was to reverse the *Dred Scott* decision and give African Americans full rights of citizenship, even if there were (and are) debates over which rights were intended to be protected.

Ten years after the Civil War ended, Congress passed a law purporting to end private racial discrimination in hotels, restaurants, and other places of public accommodations.[58] The statute was partly a reaction to the early efforts of white supremacists to create a segregated society in many parts of the country. The Supreme Court, however, in the unfortunately titled *Civil Rights Cases*,[59] overturned the law on the basis that the Fourteenth Amendment only allows Congress to restrict official state action and that "[i]ndividual invasion of individual rights is not the subject-matter of the amendment."[60] There was little originalist analysis in the opinion, though the majority did rely on the text of the Fourteenth Amendment to argue it was limited to correcting official government action. The decision was relatively brief, with only Justice Harlan dissenting. His main point was that "in every material sense... railroad corporations, keepers of inns and managers of places of public amusement are agents or instrumentalities of the State, because they are charged with duties to the public, and are amenable, in respect of their public duties and functions, to governmental regulation."[61]

One key to understanding the difference between the majority opinion and Justice Harlan's dissent is found in Justice Joseph Bradley's private diary (he wrote the majority opinion), which said that "depriving white people of the right of choosing their own company would be to introduce another kind of slavery."[62]

Historians generally agree that, even if the Court had upheld the Civil Rights Act, most of the South would have ignored the decision, and Congress would not have had either the resources or political will to enforce the Court's judgment. Although that account is likely true, even a largely symbolic Court decision against segregation could have had major effects later (as we will see is true with *Brown v. Board of Education*) and might have made it harder for Jim Crow to take effect so swiftly, so dramatically, and for so long.

After stopping Congress's efforts to *prevent* segregation, the Court eventually compounded the problem by rubber stamping state laws *requiring* segregation. In *Plessy v. Ferguson*,[63] decided in 1896, the Court upheld a Louisiana law requiring separate accommodations for white and black railroad passengers. The statute also said the compartments had to be "equal," but of course no one then or now believed that to be the case. The lawsuit was brought by Homer Plessy, who was 7/8 white, in association with the railroad, which also opposed the law.[64]

Justice Henry Billings Brown wrote for a 7–1 majority that the law did not violate the Fourteenth Amendment's equal protection clause because whites and blacks were treated equally by the law, which was not "unreasonable, or more obnoxious to the fourteenth amendment than the acts of congress requiring separate schools for colored children in the District of Columbia."[65] Just a few years before the Court would apply strict review to economic legislation in *Lochner* and other cases, the Court applied deferential review to a case involving racial classifications. To make matters worse, in language that would become infamous, the Court ruled that the required separation of whites and blacks did not "stamp the colored race with a badge of inferiority" and "if one race be inferior to another socially, the Constitution of the United States cannot put them upon the same plane."[66]

In one of the more famous dissents in Supreme Court history, Justice Harlan took issue with virtually the entire majority opinion.

The most important paragraph of his opinion would eventually form the basis for modern debates over affirmative action and other race-conscious remedies used by the states and federal government in modern times to overcome our country's racist past:

> [I]n view of the Constitution, in the eye of the law, there is in this country no superior, dominant, ruling class of citizens. There is no caste here. Our Constitution is color-blind, and neither knows nor tolerates classes among citizens. In respect of civil rights, all citizens are equal before the law ... It is therefore to be regretted that this high tribunal, the final expositor of the fundamental law of the land, has reached the conclusion that it is competent for a State to regulate the enjoyment by citizens of their civil rights solely upon the basis of race.[67]

Although few today would take issue with the egalitarian sentiments in Justice Harlan's opinion, two important caveats are in order. First, no other justice shared his dissent, and it is likely that his views represented a distinctively minority opinion in 1896, and not just in the Deep South. Second, Harlan's words immediately preceding this paragraph aren't quite as wonderful: "The white race deems itself to be the dominant race in this country. And so it is, in prestige, in achievements, in education, in wealth and in power. So, I doubt not, it will continue to be for all time, if it remains true to its great heritage and holds fast to the principles of constitutional liberty."[68]

Plessy had an almost immediate and terrible effect on race relations in America. Many states passed laws requiring separate facilities for whites and blacks.[69] After the decision, "segregation became even more ensconced through a battery of Southern laws and social customs known as 'Jim Crow.' Schools, theaters, restaurants, and transportation cars were segregated. Poll taxes, literacy requirements, and grandfather clauses not only prevented blacks from voting, but also made them ineligible to serve on jury pools or run for office."[70]

It was not until 1954 that the Supreme Court ruled legal segregation unconstitutional. The landmark case *Brown v. Board of Education*,[71] did not, however, come out of nowhere. Starting in the 1930s, the NAACP, led by Charles Hamilton Houston and Thurgood Marshall, came up with a strategy to challenge the "separate but equal" doctrine

in institutions of higher education.[72] From 1936 to 1950, the
NAACP successfully challenged several all-white law schools and
graduate programs.[73] Eventually the NAACP decided the time was
right to challenge segregated public elementary and secondary
schools, a much more daunting task. *Brown v. Board of Education*
was actually five separate challenges to segregated schools in different
parts of the country.[74] It was first argued in the 1952–1953 term, but
the justices couldn't reach a decision and held the case over until
the next year. They asked the parties to file further briefs on an
additional five questions relating to whether the ratifiers of the Fourteenth Amendment would have thought segregated schools violated
the Constitution. Before the case was re-argued, however, Chief
Justice Vinson passed away, and Earl Warren, the ex-governor of
California, was appointed chief justice. Many scholars believe
Warren was primarily responsible for the Court's eventual unanimity
in overturning "separate but equal."[75]

The Court's decision in *Brown* is only ten pages long. There were
no concurrences or dissents. The Court clearly, categorically, and
emphatically rejected an originalist approach to the case:

> Re-argument was largely devoted to the circumstances surround-
> ing the adoption of the Fourteenth Amendment in 1868. It covered
> exhaustive consideration of the Amendment in Congress, ratifica-
> tion by the states, then existing practices in racial segregation, and
> the views of proponents and opponents of the Amendment. This
> discussion and our own investigation convince us that, although
> these sources cast some light, it is not enough to resolve the
> problem with which we are faced. At best, they are inconclusive . . .
> In approaching this problem, we cannot turn the clock back to
> 1868 when the Amendment was adopted, or even to 1896 when
> *Plessy v. Ferguson* was written. We must consider public education
> in the light of its full development and its present place in American
> life throughout the Nation. Only in this way can it be determined if
> segregation in public schools deprives these plaintiffs of the equal
> protection of the laws.[76]

From there the Court held that public school education was an
essential function of state and local governments critical to the
success of children nationwide. The Court recounted that in several

cases it had already held that separate facilities for whites and blacks in graduate schools were unconstitutional. Relying on social science reports, the Court concluded that "in the field of public education the doctrine of 'separate but equal' has no place. Separate educational facilities are inherently unequal. Therefore, we hold that the plaintiffs and others similarly situated for whom the actions have been brought are, by reason of the segregation complained of, deprived of the equal protection of the laws guaranteed by the Fourteenth Amendment."[77]

The enormous backlash to the Court's unanimous decision is beyond the scope of this book as is the sad reality that public schools in the South remained almost completely segregated for another decade until Congress conditioned federal funds on state efforts to desegregate.[78] What is essential for our purposes is the Court's rejection of originalism and, as will be discussed in later chapters, herculean efforts by originalist scholars to claim *Brown* could have been justified by ratification-era evidence.

There can be little debate that *Brown* is one of the most important decisions in Supreme Court history. But like the landmark civil rights cases that came before it, the justices' decisions were not generated by originalist evidence. Professor Stephen Griffin summed up the relationship between *Brown* and originalism as follows:

[O]ne of the most celebrated Supreme Court decisions in U.S. history, a decision that helped underwrite the legitimacy of the contemporary constitutional order, especially for racial and ethnic minorities, was deliberately and unanimously not based on any version of original intent or meaning, despite the clear understanding of the justices that originalism was an option.[79]

The decision in *Brown* was technically reached during what is known as the Warren Court era, but the justices on the Court at the time did not habitually exercise aggressive judicial review. It would take almost ten more years before the Court dramatically exercised judicial review in areas of law not related to racial discrimination. When that time came, the Court rarely paused to consider whether its rulings had any basis in the original meaning of the US Constitution.

3. The Liberal Court

During the 1960s and the early 1970s, liberal justices dominated the Supreme Court who, in the words of Jonathan O'Neil, rejected "analytical reasoning" and "technical details"; "aimed 'to do justice and write moral ideas into the law'"; and had "a pragmatic conception of law" allowing them to pursue "empathy, compassion and justice."[80] Often reflecting the left-wing social movements of the day, these justices implemented the famous footnote in *Carolene Products* by siding with racial and other minorities, protecting the franchise, and for the first time in American history, issuing numerous rules to govern how states arrested, tried, and convicted criminal defendants. The justices also waded into highly controversial disputes concerning the separation of church and state. Most of these decisions did not rely on originalist evidence to support the holdings. It is beyond the scope of this book to survey these cases in detail, but a broad understanding is necessary to place the resulting originalism backlash among judges and legal scholars in the proper perspective.

In 1962, when President Kennedy appointed Justice Arthur Goldberg to the Court, liberals had a solid majority for the first time and started reshaping America. Over the next decade or so, the Court issued the following landmark decisions during both the Warren and Burger Courts (a partial but still breathtaking list):

Engle v. Vitale, Abington School District v. Schempp – school-led prayer and Bible readings in public schools violate the First Amendment.[81]

Gideon v. Wainwright – Indigent state criminal defendants have the right to a state-paid attorney.[82]

Reynolds v. Sims – When redistricting, states are bound by "one person, one vote."[83]

New York Times v. Sullivan – Public figures can sue the media for defamation only if they prove "actual malice."[84]

Griswold v. Connecticut – There is a constitutional "right to privacy," and Connecticut's anticontraception law is unconstitutional.[85]

Miranda v. Arizona – Defendants' confessions can only be used in court if the accused is told of the right to an attorney and right to remain silent.[86]

Loving v. Virginia – Virginia law banning interracial marriage violates the Fourteenth Amendment.[87]

Katz v. United States – Fourth Amendment applies to all areas where
people have a "reasonable expectation of privacy."[88]

Brandenburg v. Ohio – Inflammatory speech cannot be punished by the
government unless it was intended to and likely leads to imminent
lawless action.[89]

Roe v. Wade – Women have a constitutional right to terminate their
pregnancies.[90]

These are ten of the most important liberal decisions decided
during this time, but there are many more. Each decision likely would
have shocked those who wrote and ratified either the original Constitution or the Reconstruction Amendments. Many of them contained
little or no discussion of originalist evidence. For example, Justice
Douglas's plurality opinion in *Griswold* finding a constitutional right
to privacy, which would later be used by the Court in *Roe v. Wade*, is
only six pages long. Even though Douglas referenced the First, Third,
Fourth, Fifth, Ninth, and Fourteenth Amendments to support his
holding, and even though the word *privacy* is not in any of them,
there is not a syllable about the original meaning of the constitutional
text in the entire opinion. One scholar has noted that the result in
Griswold cannot be supported by "doctrinal, prudential, or structural
arguments – and was supported even less by historical or textual
arguments."[91]

Another glaring example of non-originalist analysis is *Reynolds
v. Sims*,[92] which established the fundamental principle of "one person,
one vote." For most of this country's history, the Supreme Court had
held that allegations that political districts were malapportioned were
nonjusticiable for several reasons, including that there were no man-
ageable standards for the justices to use to determine proper districting
principles. The Court changed its mind on the jurisdictional issue in
Baker v. Carr,[93] which Chief Justice Warren called the "most important case of [his] tenure on the Court."[94] Two years later, the justices
came up with the "one person, one vote" standard, which dramatically
altered the way many states performed the political task of dividing
themselves into voting districts. The Court relied on the Equal
Protection Clause of the Fourteenth Amendment for this principle
without any discussion of the original meaning of that Clause and little

legal analysis. Perhaps the most substantive portion of the decision is the famous paragraph that:

> Legislators represent people, not trees or acres. Legislators are elected by voters, not farms or cities or economic interests. As long as ours is a representative form of government, and our legislatures are those instruments of government elected directly by and directly representative of the people, the right to elect legislators in a free and unimpaired fashion is a bedrock of our political system.[95]

Nothing in those sentiments requires "one person, one vote" as the exclusive method of redistricting, nor does anything in the text or history of the Constitution. If *Sims* is correct as a matter of constitutional law (and maybe it is), it is not because text, history, original meaning, or prior case law supported the decision.

The third example is perhaps the most astounding. The Court's opinion in *Brandenburg v. Ohio*,[96] which articulated the fundamental test for determining whether inflammatory speech (in that case virulent racist epithets) is constitutionally protected is five pages long and contains not a syllable about the historical meaning of the First Amendment. Moreover, Justice Black, who some claim was the Court's first originalist, wrote a two-sentence concurrence without mentioning original meaning. *Brandenburg* is a landmark constitutional case advancing a free speech test applicable to myriad difficult and complicated factual circumstance that arise frequently throughout the country with virtually no legal, much less historical, analysis.

One scholar, Professor Frank Cross, has argued that the Warren Court used far more originalist sources than any previous Supreme Court.[97] His empirical work, however, does not distinguish between the landmark cases discussed earlier and less important constitutional law cases. In addition, he does not suggest that the Court was more originalist than subsequent courts, and more important, he concedes that it is likely that even when the justices pointed to ratification-era sources, it was more for window dressing than as a driver of results.[98]

In *Brown, Griswold, Reynolds, Roe,* and *Brandenburg,* the Supreme Court redefined this country's commitments to racial equality, sexual privacy, voting rights, abortion, and free speech, while either explicitly rejecting originalist evidence or ignoring it altogether. The Court did the same in other areas of constitutional law such as criminal procedure and defamation. Whether one agrees or disagrees with these aggressive decisions, it is hard to argue with one scholar's description of them as having "no coherent jurisprudence 'apart from the results reached.'"[99] This was a time when the justices were concerned with fairness, justice, and equality, as they understood those concepts, through their political and legal lens, not legal reasoning, formalism, or judicial restraint. No surprise, then, that toward the end of the era, a new conservative movement would arise to push back and combat what many politicians and scholars saw as the judicial excesses of the Warren and early Burger Courts.

4 THE ORIGINAL ORIGINALISTS AND THEIR CRITICS

For what is the point of drawing up ... laws, if anybody may attach a new meaning to the words to suit his own taste, find some remote interpretation, and twist the words to fit the situation and his own opinion?

John Locke[1]

A. THE ACADEMIC AND POLITICAL ATTACKS ON THE LIBERAL COURT

The Warren and early Burger Courts' decisions on privacy, voting rights, and criminal procedure, among many others, caused significant backlashes against the Court in both the political and academic spheres. Richard Nixon attacked the Court's liberal decisions in his 1968 and 1972 presidential campaigns.[2] He promised to nominate "strict constructionists" who would "interpret" not "make" the law.[3] These were code words for an antidefendant's rights, "law and order," conservative agenda.

In 1971, Nixon introduced his Supreme Court nominee, William Rehnquist, as a judge who would "not twist or bend the Constitution ... to perpetuate his personal ... views."[4] Nixon was appealing to conservatives fed up with the riots, social movements, and turbulence of the 1960s. Given Nixon's introduction of Rehnquist, it was no surprise when, at his confirmation hearing, Rehnquist said that he would not "disregard the intent of the framers of the Constitution and change it to achieve a result that [might] be more desirable for society."[5]

Meanwhile, prominent legal scholars began articulating a sustained argument for originalism combining attention to the framers' original intent with judicial deference to legislative majorities. This new movement provided the groundwork for what would eventually become President Ronald Reagan's legal agenda.

In the early 1970s, Robert Bork was a relatively young, conservative law professor at Yale Law School. Deeply troubled by the lack of historical grounding in the Warren Court decisions, he wrote in *Fortune* magazine that constitutional law was in a state of "intellectual chaos."[6] His first major attempt to bring order to the constitutional "chaos" became one of the most cited and important law review articles of his generation.

In an *Indiana Law Journal* essay,[7] Bork wrote that the question of the Court's legitimate authority had been made "acute" by the Warren Court's decisions.[8] He argued that a "Court that makes rather than implements value choices cannot be squared with the presuppositions of a democratic society. The man who... insists upon the rightness of the Warren Court's performance ought also ... to admit that he is prepared to sacrifice democratic process to his own moral views. He claims for the Supreme Court an institutionalized role as perpetrator of limited coups d'état."[9] Bork wondered, in language that Justice Scalia echoed years later in a number of important dissents, why "the Court, a committee of nine lawyers, [should] be the sole agent of change?"[10]

Bork suggested that the solution to the unwarranted and aggressive judicial review of the Warren Court was a "legitimate Court... controlled by principles exterior to the will of the justices."[11] These principles must be found in either the text or history of the Constitution and their "fair implications."[12] By limiting themselves to such sources, the justices' value choices will be "attributed to the Founding Fathers, not the Court."[13]

Bork presented an easily understandable hypothetical he claimed supported his thesis. He compared the facts of *Griswold v. Connecticut*[14] to a hypothetical dispute over an energy plant regulation. In *Griswold*, the people of Connecticut voted for an anticontraception law because they morally disapproved of birth control. Bork posited that the same people voted for a smoke pollution regulation, which led to more expensive energy bills. In *Griswold*, a married couple claims the law is unconstitutional because they want to use contraceptives. In the other case, the energy company claims the environmental law is unconstitutional because the company wants the freedom to produce cheaper energy for its customers and more profits for its shareholders. Bork argued that neither argument is answered by the text or history of the Constitution or its fair implications. He then wrote the following famous paragraph:

> Unless we can distinguish forms of gratification, the only course for a principled Court is to let the majority have its way in both cases ... There is no principled way to decide that one man's gratifications are more deserving of respect than another's or that one form of gratification is more worthy than another. Why is sexual gratification more worthy than moral gratification? Why is sexual gratification nobler than economic gratification? There is no way of deciding these matters other than by reference to some system of moral or ethical values that has no objective or intrinsic validity of its own and about which men can and do differ. Where the Constitution does not embody the moral or ethical choice, the judge has no basis other than his own values upon which to set aside the community judgment embodied in the statute. That, by definition, is an inadequate basis for judicial supremacy.[15]

Bork's insistence that the justices' personal moral views play little or no role in constitutional interpretation formed the basis for his originalist philosophy. The judge's exclusive job, according to Bork, is to enforce rights specifically mentioned in the text of the Constitution or ascertainable from its history.

Bork combined this approach with another aspect of judicial decision making that many modern originalists reject. Bork argued that judges "must accept any value choice the legislature makes unless it *clearly* runs contrary to a choice made in the framing of the Constitution. It follows, of course, that broad areas of constitutional law ought to be reformulated."[16] Bork's focus on judicial restraint unless the law "clearly runs contrary" to the Constitution is reminiscent of Alexander Hamilton's warning that judges should not strike down laws absent an "irreconcilable variance" between a statute and the Constitution.[17] For Bork, if judges didn't take deference seriously, even a focus on text, original meaning, and their fair implications could not constrain judicial choice.

In addition to Judge Bork, Raoul Berger, a leading academic, who was in no sense a conservative, helped jump-start the originalism movement. Berger was the son of Russian immigrants. He became a classically trained musician and a constitutional law professor.[18] He worked in the executive branch during the New Deal, then for years in private practice, and eventually spent his academic careers at Berkeley and Harvard. He wrote seven books and hundreds of law review articles and self-identified as a Democrat.

Berger's originalist views first formed during the *Lochner* and post-*Lochner* eras. He wrote an article in 1942 criticizing the recently decided *Bridges v. California*,[19] which held that the First Amendment prohibits state courts from issuing contempt citations for out-of-court statements pertaining to a pending case absent a "clear and present danger."[20] Berger believed that the decision contradicted the history of the First Amendment. He felt the evidence supporting that proposition was so clear that he compared *Bridges* to the aggressive judicial review of the *Lochner* Court. He asked rhetorically whether "liberals, after steadily criticizing the tendency of the [*Lochner*-era] court to read laissez-faire into the Constitution, [can] afford to sanctify by their own example an interpretive approach which for a generation was employed to block social legislation and may once again be turned against themselves?"[21]

Berger examined the history of both the First Amendment and the practice of contempt citations for out-of-court statements, concluding that one had nothing to do with the other. He criticized the Court's "willfulness" to reach a conclusion not justified by text or original intent and observed that the "costs of this willfulness in terms of a generation of sweated labor and unchecked industrial piracy should remind us that a Court which can read a beneficial power into the Constitution today can read out cherished rights tomorrow."[22] He ended his article by chiding the liberals on the Court: "Even advocates of a flexible Constitution recognize that judicial exercise of the vast power of adaptation can be tolerated only when tempered by self-restraint. It is the melancholy lesson of the *Bridges* case that it is easier to preach self-restraint to the opposition than to practice it oneself."[23]

Thirty years later, Berger played an important role during the Watergate scandal by arguing that there was no historical evidence supporting a presidential executive privilege to withhold papers and tapes relevant to either a criminal or congressional investigation. In making these arguments and others, he never wavered from his strong views about judicial restraint and original intent or meaning (he did not distinguish between the two). He believed that James Bradley Thayer's rule of "clear mistake" (that judges should only overturn federal laws when their constitutionality was not open to "rational question") was the proper stance for the judiciary.[24] Given these previous writings about the proper role of original intent in constitutional interpretation, when faced with the aggressive, antihistorical, judicial review practiced by the Warren Court, it came as no surprise that Berger argued strenuously against the Court's decisions.

In 1977, Berger's book, *Government by Judiciary*, became an originalism manifesto.[25] The essential thesis of his book, one that would be repeated by many originalist scholars, was that only a theory of interpretation based on the "original intentions" of the founders could negate the "judicial power to revise the Constitution."[26]

Much of Berger's book tried to demonstrate that the Supreme Court's interpretations of the Fourteenth Amendment ignored and/or distorted the original meaning of that Amendment. To Berger, the central purpose of Section 1 of the Amendment (the Equal Protection, Due Process and Privileges or Immunities Clauses) was to "insure that there would be no discrimination against the freedmen in respect of 'fundamental rights,' which had a clearly understood and narrow compass."[27] These rights were limited to making contracts, litigation, owning property, and enjoying the benefits of the law.[28] Berger believed that, as an original matter, the Fourteenth Amendment did not prohibit segregated schools among other rights the justices had found protected by the Amendment.[29]

Although Berger spent much of the book justifying this historical analysis of the Fourteenth Amendment, he also discussed the broader question of how judges should engage in constitutional interpretation. He argued that judges who transform vague constitutional text into open-ended repositories of rights "usurped the sovereign power" of elected institutions to make laws adapting to social change.[30] He believed that the founding fathers, although expecting judicial review, never intended the Court to go beyond the Constitution's specific text and original intent.

Thirty-five years after his first law review article on the topic, Berger had still not given up trying to convince liberals that if judges departed from original intent whenever they deemed it important enough, then judicial review will inevitably reflect the subjective value choices of the judiciary, which at times will be quite conservative. One reviewer of his book summed up this argument as follows: "If judges are not limited by some historically ascertainable legislative intent, they will have nothing to guide them but their own preferences. This result is inconsistent with democratic values and frequently leads, as during the *Lochner* era, to substantively undesirable decisions."[31]

Before discussing the impact of Berger's book, it is important to consider one important and self-contradictory aspect of his narrative. Berger defended originalism as the only basis for judicial review partly on his historical argument that exclusive reliance on text and original meaning was a "centuries-old canon of interpretation."[32] At the same time, however, Berger lamented that the Court had consistently failed to live up to that cannon.[33] That inconsistency can also be seen in Judge Bork's work responding, not just to the Warren Court, but also to the legal realists who argued that values writ large, not prior legal doctrine, inevitably generated judicial decisions.[34] For Bork and Berger, their faith in judicial review depended on judges applying a constrained and originalist brand of constitutional interpretation that they both (correctly) claimed the justices had all too rarely exercised throughout our history.[35] Neither man came to terms with this conflict.[36] For all their brilliance and legal acumen, both Berger and Bork were advancing an article of faith more than a realistic appraisal of the Court's past behavior or a pragmatic blueprint the justices would ever adopt.

Despite this disconnect between his theory and actual constitutional practice, Berger's book, according to Jonathan O'Neil, "had an explosive effect on constitutional debate in the late 1970's and 1980's ... Responding to Berger became 'somewhat of a cottage industry in constitutional scholarship.'"[37] Although most reviewers criticized Berger's dogmatic insistence that proper judicial review should focus only on text and original meaning, he did have a few allies.[38] More important, after Ronald Reagan won the 1980 election, Berger's outspoken and strident originalism, along with Judge Bork's writings, were used by the new administration to latch on to originalism as a political, legal, and social movement. As two leading Yale Law School scholars have observed, "[d]rawing on the work of pioneer conservative academics like Robert Bork and Raoul Berger, originalism became a central organizing principle for the Reagan Justice Department's assault on what it regarded as a liberal federal judiciary."[39] That "assault" transformed the originalism debate from a largely inside the legal academy hypothetical discussion to a much larger political conversation about the proper role of the Supreme Court in American society.

During his first presidential campaign, Ronald Reagan focused his attacks on the Supreme Court by lamenting "judicial activism" more than promoting originalism.[40] These criticisms were linked to the bourgeoning antiabortion, anti-*Roe v. Wade* political movement. His first attorney general, William French Smith, "worked to characterize Reagan's interest in anti-abortion judges as a desire to select only those judges who rejected what Smith saw as the judicial activism of the Warren and Burger Courts."[41]

The New Right, the Moral Majority, and religious leaders such as Jerry Falwell and Pat Robertson, become strong political forces in America in the 1970s, partly because of their vocal opposition to the Warren and Burger Courts' decisions, especially *Roe v. Wade*. Reagan saw great political value in attacking the Court through criticizing *Roe*.[42] His speeches were littered with statements describing Warren Court opinions as "fanciful readings of the Constitution that produce such decisions as *Roe v. Wade*."[43] Eventually, during Reagan's second term, his administration asked the Supreme Court to expressly overrule that decision. The legal basis supporting that plea was developed in large part by Reagan's second attorney general, Ed Meese, who advocated strongly for originalism and attacked those judges and scholars who he claimed believed in a "living Constitution."

Ed Meese had been Ronald Reagan's aide for many years before becoming his attorney general in 1985. Meese served as the unofficial go-between linking the administration and the Religious Right. He played a prominent role soothing the frazzled nerves of those opposed to *Roe* after Reagan nominated Sandra Day O'Connor to the Court in 1981 (because many on the right thought she might not be aggressively anti-*Roe*).[44] Beginning in 1985, Meese tried to bring his originalist message to the legal community and the public at large.[45]

In July of that year, Meese delivered the first of many speeches on constitutional interpretation. He emphasized the primacy of the original intentions of the framers in constitutional disputes.[46] Lamenting how "utterly unpredictable" the Court's decisions were, he advocated for the "text of the document and the original intention of those who framed it... [as] the judicial standard in giving effect to the Constitution."[47] Accusing the Supreme Court of "roam[ing] at large in a veritable constitutional forest," he concluded that a "jurisprudence seriously aimed at the explication of original intention would produce defensible principles of government that would not be tainted by ideological predilection."[48] He ended his speech this way:

> It is our belief that only "the sense in which the Constitution was accepted and ratified by the nation," and only the sense in which laws were drafted and passed provide a solid foundation for adjudication. Any other standard suffers the defect of pouring new meaning into old words, thus creating new powers and new rights totally at odds with the logic of our Constitution and its commitment to the rule of law.[49]

Meese's speech became, in the words of Professor Stephen Calabresi, "part of the originalist creed."[50] Just over a year later, Meese gave another speech where he questioned what had been a bedrock principle of constitutional law for at least several decades.[51] He argued that although a Supreme Court decision "binds the parties in a case and also the executive branch for whatever enforcement is necessary," the "decision does not establish the 'supreme Law of the Land' that is binding on all persons and parts of government, henceforth and forevermore."[52] He claimed that the idea that "constitutional law and the Constitution are not the same" may seem "obvious," but "there have been those down through our history – and especially, it seems, in our own time – who have denied the distinction between the Constitution and constitutional law."[53] Meese suggested that the decisions of the Warren Court that were not based on constitutional text and original intent were not the supreme law of the land because they were not supported by the Constitution. Criticizing famous dicta in

Cooper v. Aaron,[54] where the justices unanimously proclaimed that their decisions were the supreme law of the land, Meese boldly said that such a principle is at "war with the Constitution, at war with the basic principles of democratic government, and at war with the very meaning of the rule of law."[55]

Meese's message was not subtle. He urged people inside and outside government to question the validity of the justices' authority whenever they strayed too far from what Meese claimed was the actual Constitution. This was a startling message from the attorney general of the United States.

At about the same time, students at Yale and several other law schools tried to stoke the fires of Meese's originalism. These conservative and libertarian law students, a distinct minority at the time, enlisted several elite professors, including future Judge Ralph Winter at Yale and future Justice Antonin Scalia at Chicago, to help them start a new organization called The Federalist Society.[56] The society held its first organized academic conference in 1982, and just a year later, the group grew to seventeen law school chapters. The message was one of originalism, federalism (state's rights), separation of powers, and judicial restraint. The group went on to hold annual conferences whose articles were published in a specialty law review at Harvard. The overriding theme of these early symposia was "originalist attacks on legal liberalism" with the Warren Court decisions as the primary target.[57]

Today, the Federalist Society has lawyer, faculty, and student divisions and chapters at every accredited American law school.[58] It holds hundreds of events annually. Four current justices, Thomas, Roberts, Alito, and Gorsuch, are now or were members, and there are many lower-court judges who are also alumni of the organization. Although there are some real policy differences among the conservative and libertarian members (such as what level of deference judges should apply to economic legislation), commitments to originalism and federalism, as well as hostility to "living constitutionalism," are widely shared among the group's members.

The story of the phenomenal growth and influence of the Federalist Society is beyond the scope of this book, but its early influences on the Reagan Administration as well as Meese's, Bork's, and Berger's efforts to spread the originalism gospel cannot be overstated.[59] To the Reagan Administration, the Society was not only a "philosophical supporter and intellectual resource," but also a supplier of "personnel."[60] In fact, membership in the Society became almost a prerequisite for law students who wanted important clerkships with conservative federal judges appointed by Reagan, as well as for consideration for high-level positions in the Reagan White House and Justice Department.[61]

By the end of 1986, originalism as a method of constitutional interpretation was embraced by a presidential administration, a sprinkling of important lower court federal judges, and a new group of young conservative and libertarian law professors whose influence far exceeded their numbers. Moreover, the movement's political goals, opposition to abortion and affirmative action, as well as criticism of the Court's school prayer and parochial school funding decisions, appealed to the religious right who held a "reverential attitude" toward both the text of the Bible and the written Constitution.[62]

On the Supreme Court, however, only one justice out of nine, Antonin Scalia, was an avowed originalist. Moreover, his confirmation hearings were hardly a referendum on originalism as he sailed through by a 98–0 vote in the wake of a contentious Senate debate on the elevation of Associate Justice William Rehnquist to be Chief Justice. Just one year later, however, when Reagan nominated Robert Bork, now a federal appeals court judge, to replace swing vote Lewis F. Powell on the Court, originalism for the first time made a dramatic appearance on national television. To understand that historic battle and where it fits into the originalism debates, however, it is important to review the political, judicial, and academic responses to the jurisprudence of original intent championed by Meese, Bork, Berger, and the first generation of Federalist Society members.

B. THE ACADEMIC AND POLITICAL RESPONSE TO THE ORIGINAL ORIGINALISTS

Like today, liberal academics dominated the legal academy in the early 1980s, at least in terms of numbers. These left-leaning law professors mounted an impassioned attack on Bork's, Berger's, and Meese's original intent call to arms. The responses began in isolated law review articles, then large symposia, and eventually in full-length books. By the mid-1980s, even Justices Brennan and Stevens joined the fray. The first wave of serious pushback, however, came from inside the law schools.

The most important early response to the newly emerging originalism movement was Professor Paul Brest's article, "The Misperceived Quest for the Original Understanding."[63] Brest leveled numerous attacks arguing that: (1) determining the "intent" of institutions composed of many people is difficult in the best of situations; (2) ascertaining the intent of the members of the Philadelphia Ratifying Convention, as well as the state ratifying conventions, is well nigh impossible; (3) discovering the appropriate level of generality the framers intended with regard to vague constitutional phases is fraught with danger; (4) translating the framers' intent and values to modern conditions is quite difficult; (5) the fact that women and racial minorities were not allowed to take part in the drafting and ratification of the original Constitution and the Reconstruction Amendments creates serious problems of democratic legitimacy; and (6) there are strong normative objections to being ruled by people who lived centuries ago.[64]

Professor Brest illustrated these objections through specific examples of constitutional interpretation. The most accessible and persuasive of these involved the Fourteenth Amendment's instruction that no state shall deny to any person the "equal protection of the laws." There is a strong historical argument (made by Raoul Berger and others) that the original meaning or intent of this provision was only to guarantee a "limited formal racial equality" between the races as to narrowly defined civil rights.[65] Brest pointed out, however, that since 1868, our society's attitudes toward racial questions had changed dramatically. These changes include "the achievements of blacks in the face of a century of discrimination, changes in the economy with attendant changes in labor and migration patterns, and direct evidence of attitude change" toward African Americans.[66] Modern judges simply cannot determine how those who voted for the equal protection clause would have applied its vague command to contemporary racial problems given those dramatic changes. For that reason, Brest argued,

Chief Justice Earl Warren correctly determined in *Brown v. Board of Education* that the Court could not "turn the clock black to 1868" to determine the validity of state-required segregation.[67] Brest made similar arguments about other constitutional issues including those implicating free speech, freedom of religion, federalism, and gender discrimination.

Professor Brest's objections were eventually adopted and more fully explicated by other scholars writing in the early and mid-1980s. For example, Ronald Dworkin argued in a series of articles and books that the framers deliberately used vague and general language in the rights-creating provisions of the Constitution knowing that judges should and would identify fundamental values important to their own times.[68] Dworkin and others argued that it is not possible that the folks who wrote and voted for limitations phrased so nebulously imagined that judges would or could freeze the meaning of those phrases at the moment of ratification.

Professor Daniel Farber argued that historical analysis should not play a significant role in constitutional interpretation because judges are not trained as historians. He said the following:

> Historians learn to make sophisticated credibility judgments based not only on the documents themselves and their drafting, but also on a knowledge of the culture and politics of the period...But judges may be ill-prepared to make such judgments...While judges have fulsome experience in regard to the behavioral patterns of the sorts of people who typically appear before them, they know little about how people behaved in the distant past. Thus, they may reason anachronistically when they use their present-day behavioral assumptions to assess the accuracy of a particular interpretation of the past. After all, judges are not selected for office because they have special skill in reconstructing the intentions of individuals in the past.[69]

Farber's criticisms of what others have called "law office history"[70] presented a strong challenge to the originalism project. He suggested that judges and their clerks were not up to the task of conducting serious historical research. Another related attack came from Professor Jefferson Powell, who launched what many consider to be a serious offensive on originalism in his now-classic articles, "The Original

Understanding of Original Intent"[71] and "Rules for Originalists."[72] Although the former gathered more attention,[73] the latter is the more important critique of originalist constitutional interpretation. In that piece, Powell comprehensively described most of the weaknesses of originalism that other legal scholars had been advocating over the preceding ten years.

Powell began by noting that no "turn to history" can obviate the need for judicial value choices.[74] He argued that it is an "arduous" task for judges to use history as their guide.[75] Nevertheless, Powell believed that judges and lawyers will inevitably use history to support their preferred interpretations of the Constitution. Therefore, he set forth a set of "rules" he thought judges should adhere to when engaging in the "arduous task" of historical investigation. Although Powell labeled these suggestions "rules," they are really critiques of the originalist enterprise because most of his objections deny originalism's central claim that the use of text and history is the only viable method of cabining judicial discretion.

Powell devoted most of his article to arguing that "[h]istory itself cannot prove anything non-historical."[76] Powell's point was that, even if history provided clear answers to modern constitutional problems, which of course it doesn't, judges still must answer the question, "So what?"[77] Whether people today should accept as binding the wishes of people who lived two hundred years ago is a question of political theory, not historical investigation. Moreover, Powell argued that constitutional law and our culture have changed so dramatically since the time of the founding that no theory of history can tell judges what to do with prior cases and political practices that might be at odds with our best understanding of the original meaning of the Constitution. How judges should balance precedent, changed conditions, and interpretations of the Constitution by the other branches with original meaning simply cannot be struck through historical analysis.

Powell also contended that in many, if not most, cases, "constitutional disputes involve facts, practices, and problems that were not considered or even dreamt of by the founders . . . once it is conceded that the Constitution speaks to questions that those who adopted it did not answer, it becomes obvious that in such cases the interpreter must use some process of generalization or analogy to go beyond what

history can say. The inevitable disputes over whether a given interpretation overgeneralizes or is based on a faulty analogy are not resolvable
by historical means; at this point history, and originalism as a program
of obedience to history, have no more to add to constitutional
discourse."[78]

Powell used the question of whether discrimination against women
is prohibited by the equal protection clause to illustrate many of the
issues raised by originalist constitutional interpretation. Other than a
few scattered (and probably strategic) remarks about discrimination
based on sex, the issue of gender equality simply wasn't substantially
addressed by those who debated whether to pass the amendment. The
correct conclusions to be drawn from this silence, however, considering how broadly the amendment is worded, cannot be answered by
historical analysis. The people living in 1868, according to Powell,
simply can't help us work out gender issues today because most
modern questions of discrimination did not and could not have
occurred to them in any meaningful sense.[79]

Another problem for originalism that Powell (and many later
critics) pointed out was that it may well be the case that the founders
did not want historical investigation into original intent to play a
primary role in constitutional interpretation. In that sense, originalism
becomes inconsistent with itself and is self-defeating.

Powell used the Ninth Amendment to explore this position. Powell
argued that the Ninth Amendment shows that there are times when the
framers "chose to leave a question of constitutional meaning for later
interpreters. Turning to history to avoid ... interpretative freedom, in
these instances, the originalist finds history's message to be a flat
refusal to restrict that freedom."[80]

The Ninth Amendment provides that: "The enumeration in the
Constitution, of certain rights, shall not be construed to deny or disparage others retained by the people."[81] Powell argued that "scattered
throughout the records of the Philadelphia convention, the ratification campaign, and the discussion in the First Congress of James
Madison's proposed bill of rights, are expressions of an ongoing
concern on the part of many Americans that certain essential rights
be explicitly secured against federal interference and a somewhat
antagonistic fear that explicit enumeration of certain rights would

be taken by subsequent interpreters to 'deny or disparage' the existence of other rights."[82] The Ninth Amendment sought to reconcile these two concerns by prohibiting the inference that the only rights Americans held were those explicitly listed in the Constitution. The problem for originalism, "is that fidelity to this provision's probable historical meaning requires one not to look to history for answers on the question of unenumerated rights."[83]

Powell identified numerous other arguments against originalism. He suggested that drawing conclusions from silence is a perilous enterprise; assuming the founders shared many of our common assumptions is a mistake; separating out historical meanings from later practices is often quite difficult; at best historical analysis may yield probabilities not clear answers; and, most important, "[h]istory never obviates the necessity of choice."[84] Powell's main objective was to demonstrate that resort to history requires the originalist judge to make choices and interpretative decisions that cannot be objectified and that will inevitably be impacted by their own personal values and biases. To the extent that Bork, Berger, Meese, and others advocated for originalism on the basis that using history cabins the imposition of subjective judicial values, Powell thought they were flatly wrong.

Before moving on to other academic critiques of the Original Originalists, it is important to note that Powell's critique is persuasive only if he is addressing the right question. If the judicial task is defined as ascertaining the original meaning of vague constitutional text as applied to unforeseen modern problems, then his warnings about the use of history in constitutional interpretation are persuasive. Asking a judge to try to ascertain the original meaning of the Fourteenth Amendment as applied to affirmative action, for example, illustrates Powell's concerns. Our society has changed dramatically since 1868, the text of the Amendment is so vague, and the issue of affirmative action so remote to the concerns of the ratifiers of the Fourteenth Amendment, that trying to answer the question of the constitutionality of affirmative action through historical investigation is a fool's errand.[85]

But if the question is posed differently, then Powell's warnings aren't as important. We could say that the judicial task is limited to determining whether the plaintiff challenging an affirmative action program has demonstrated beyond any real doubt that using racial preferences in higher education or government programs clearly violates either the text or original meaning of the Fourteenth Amendment. Absent such proof, the plaintiff simply loses. Stated that way, the judge's job is not to come up with historical conclusions but only to answer whether the plaintiff has proven her case. This question may be difficult in some hard cases, but most of the time this type of "clear error" rule will yield relatively easy answers.

People may have legitimate normative objections to placing the burden of proof so squarely on the plaintiff, but the difficulties identified by Powell with historical investigation are mitigated when judges need only determine whether the evidence obviously points to the unconstitutionality of the challenged law or program. As Professor Richard Kay argues, judges should not be "asked to give a full account of the original meaning of a constitutional provision, but only to answer the binary question of whether original intent permitted or disallowed a challenged government action. "All [the judge] needs to do is decide which of the two possible answers in that case is more likely."[86] This task becomes even easier, and more law-like, if the plaintiffs bear a heavy burden of proof. In other words, adding strong deference to the originalist enterprise renders many of Powell's concerns less persuasive.

Returning to the critics responding to the Original Originalists, Professors Brest, Farber, Dworkin, and Powell all criticized originalism from the perspectives of traditional legal scholars. During the early and mid-1980s, other law professors critiqued originalism from the vantage point of a far-left political movement called Critical Legal Studies. These professors, led by Mark Tushnet, Roberto Mangabeira Unger, Duncan Kennedy, and Mark G. Kelman, adopted a wide-ranging platform that went far beyond a simple disavowal of originalism and argued more broadly that "meaningful adjudication [is] impossible as anything beyond the mere pronouncing of policy preferences of the judges."[87] As part of this overarching critique of formalism and the inability of prior legal rules to constrain judges, critical legal scholars found originalism a fairly easy target, arguing that looking to the past for guidance is "plagued with historical ambiguity and inference from limited evidence, and . . . requires judges 'to trace historical continuities between the institutions that the framers knew and those contemporary judges know.'...To understand original intent requires a 'creative re-creation of the past.' Because of the 'gulf that separates the framers' world from ours,' the past can be re-created in many different ways; such re-creation destroys the possibility of originalism being an effective restraint on judges."[88]

The story of the rise and fall of the critical legal studies movement is beyond the scope of this book. Their leaders' attacks on legal rules as generators of judicial decisions, however, echoed the legal realists' views that personal values, not legal doctrine, drive results in hard cases. This critique of formalism presents a strong challenge to the Original Originalists, who advocated for their theory primarily on the basis that judicial discretion can be effectively cabined by a strong reliance on text and history. Both the legal realists of the 1930s and the critical legal scholars of the 1980s argued that resort to legal materials will not deter judges from reaching the results they desire and will serve only to hide the real basis of decision from the American people. To the extent that critique is persuasive as to text and precedent, it is even more so regarding originalism given all the problems associated with historical investigation outlined by noncritical legal scholars such as Professors Powell, Farber, and Brest.

By the mid to late 1980s, there was a cottage industry of academic literature arguing that judicial reconstruction of the original intent of the founding generation to solve modern legal problems is a largely hopeless task. Professor Larry Solum, a so-called New Originalist, writing years later and with the benefit of hindsight, accurately summed up the problems with searching for the original intent of the framers of the Constitution:

> In the case of a single speaker, in face-to-face communication, the intentions of the speaker may be the meaning of what is said. But when there are multiple authors of a text that must function across decades and centuries, it is not clear that there is such a thing as the intention of the framers that could guide the application of the text to future cases. Instead, we find ourselves with fragmentary evidence of multiple and inconsistent intentions that fail to answer many of our constitutional questions.[89]

This critique of originalism became well accepted in the legal academy, which was dominated by liberal scholars. The imbalance would eventually change as the Federalist Society grew in numbers, and Ronald Reagan appointed more originalist judges. Before that occurred, however, and to the surprise of many, two Supreme Court justices stepped into the fray to respond specifically to Ed Meese's speeches advocating originalism.

As discussed earlier, in July 1985, Ed Meese gave an important public speech defending originalism and criticizing what he saw as the activist decisions of the Warren and early Burger Courts.[90] Meese later admitted that he was trying to "raise originalism's profile."[91] Just a few months later, liberal Supreme Court Justice William Brennan, who was starting his thirtieth year on the Court, appeared at a legal symposium at Georgetown University School of Law and responded directly to Meese's attacks.[92] This speech became a historic defense of what legal scholars have come to call "the living Constitution" approach to constitutional interpretation.

Brennan began his speech by talking about the important responsibilities of Supreme Court justices and how consequential their decisions are for the people and the country. He talked about how the justices should interpret the Constitution and observed there "are those who find legitimacy in fidelity to what they call 'the intentions of the Framers.' In its most doctrinaire incarnation, this view demands that Justices discern exactly what the Framers thought about the question under consideration and simply follow that intention in resolving the case before them. It is a view that feigns self-effacing deference to the specific judgments of those who forged our original social compact. But in truth it is little more than arrogance cloaked as humility."[93]

Justice Brennan also lamented this "arrogance" for many of the reasons legal academics thought a jurisprudence of original intention was unworkable. Brennan argued that judges should not "pretend that from our vantage we can gauge accurately the intent of the Framers on application of principle to specific, contemporary questions. All too often, sources of potential enlightenment such as records of the ratification debates provide sparse or ambiguous evidence of the original intention. Typically, all that can be gleaned is that the Framers themselves did not agree about the application or meaning of particular constitutional provisions, and hid their differences in cloaks of generality."[94]

The justice did not mince words while condemning what he labeled the "facile historicism" of those advocating for originalism.[95] He argued that, far from it being a method of "depoliticization of the judiciary, the political underpinnings of such a choice should not escape notice. A position that upholds constitutional claims only if they were within the specific contemplation of the Framers in effect establishes a presumption of resolving textual ambiguities against the claim of constitutional right... This is a choice no less political than any other; it expresses antipathy to claims of the minority rights against the majority. Those who would restrict claims of right to the values of 1789 specifically articulated in the Constitution turn a blind eye to social progress and eschew adaptation of overarching principles to changes of social circumstance."[96]

Justice Brennan emphasized that judges must make decisions for modern times and not limit themselves to historical investigation. They must "read the Constitution in the only way that we can: as Twentieth Century Americans. We look to the history of the time of framing and to the intervening history of interpretation. But the ultimate question must be, what do the words of the text mean in our time?"[97] For Brennan, "the genius of the Constitution" did not lie "in any static meaning it might have had in a world that is dead and gone, but in the adaptability of its great principles to cope with current problems and current needs. What the constitutional fundamentals meant to the wisdom of other times cannot be their measure to the vision of our time. Similarly, what those fundamentals mean for us, our descendants will learn, cannot be the measure to the vision of their time."[98]

Justice Brennan gave numerous examples of changed constitutional meanings that, in his view, led to greater dignity for all people, and he ended this section of his speech with a quote from *Weems v. United States:*

> Time works changes, brings into existence new conditions and
> purposes. Therefore, a principle to be vital must be capable of
> wider application than the mischief which gave it birth. This is

peculiarly true of constitutions. They are not ephemeral enactments, designed to meet passing occasions. They are, to use the words of Chief Justice John Marshall, "designed to approach immortality as nearly as human institutions can approach it" ... In the application of a constitution, therefore, our contemplation cannot be only of what has been, but of what may be.[99]

According to the authors of Justice Brennan's biography, his speech did not go unnoticed by the Reagan Justice Department. The head of the Office of Legal Counsel, William Bradford Reynolds, mentioned Brennan by name a few months later arguing that the justice turned "his back on text and historical context, and argues instead for a jurisprudence that rests, at bottom, on a faith in the idea of a living, evolving Constitution of uncertain and wholly uninhibited meaning."[100] Meese later said that Brennan's speech helped publicize his own speeches and furthered the emerging battle lines between originalists and non-originalists.[101] These fundamental disagreements between the Reagan Justice Department and the Supreme Court were also emphasized in a speech given by Justice John Paul Stevens in Chicago in October 1985.

At the time, Justice Stevens was not viewed by legal scholars as a strong liberal (he had been nominated by Republican Gerald Ford), and his jurisprudence was only moderately left-of-center. Thus, it likely surprised many that he directly engaged Meese by name in this speech. Stevens was concerned that Meese had suggested that he might not accept the incorporation doctrine, whereby the Bill of Rights applies to the states through the Fourteenth Amendment's Due Process Clause. Stevens said that Meese, "[i]n advocating what he described as a constitutional 'Jurisprudence of Original Intention,' placed great emphasis on the fact that the Bill of Rights, as debated, created and ratified was designed to apply only to the national government."[102]

Stevens argued, however, that Meese's argument, focused "on the original intention of the Framers of the Bill of Rights, overlooks the importance of subsequent events in the development of our law. In particular, it overlooks the profound importance of the Civil War and the post-war amendments on the structure of our government, and particularly upon the relationship between the Federal Government and the separate States."[103]

Stevens provided examples of constitutional change that were inconsistent with a jurisprudence of original intent. He cited James Madison, who famously changed his mind concerning the constitutionality of the national bank (as a congressman Madison had argued that Congress had no power to create the bank, but he signed a bill as president authorizing the bank). Stevens also took issue with Meese's position that the Warren Court's Establishment Clause jurisprudence, which required strict governmental neutrality between religion and nonreligion, would have struck the founding fathers as "bizarre." Stevens responded that the term "founding generation describes a rather broad and diverse class. It included apostles of intolerance as well as tolerance, advocates of differing points of view in religion as well as politics, and great minds in Virginia and Pennsylvania as well as Massachusetts. I am not at all sure that men like James Madison, Thomas Jefferson, Benjamin Franklin or the pamphleteer, Thomas Paine, would have regarded strict neutrality on the part of government between religion and irreligion as 'bizarre.'"[104] Stevens's agenda was to suggest, perhaps with tongue in cheek, that he might have misconstrued Meese's argument, but "if there is ambiguity in the message that was conveyed by an articulate contemporary lawyer last July, is it not possible that some uncertainty may attend an effort to identify the precise messages that equally articulate lawyers were attempting to convey almost two hundred years ago?"[105] It is unlikely that this chiding of Meese for his historical method was lost on the audience present for the speech.

C. REAGANS' NOMINATIONS AND ORIGINALISM

Less than a year after Brennan's and Stevens's speeches, President Ronald Reagan nominated Justice Antonin Scalia to the Supreme Court. He also nominated Justice Rehnquist to replace the retiring Warren Burger as Chief Justice. One would have thought that, given the back and forth over originalism between Meese and the justices, as well as the bourgeoning Federalist Society movement, the doctrine of originalism would play a major role in both confirmation hearings. However, such was not the case.

Justice Scalia was nominated in June of 1986 and confirmed just three months later. The Republican Party controlled the Senate, and the Iran-Contra scandal had not yet become a major story.[106] Moreover, the Democrats fought Rehnquist's elevation to chief justice and, after they lost, did not seem hungry for another pitched Supreme Court battle, especially because the justice leaving the Court, Warren Burger, was a reliable conservative vote, so Scalia did not alter the Court's political balance.

The Senate confirmed Scalia by a vote of 98–0. During his questioning, he only offered opinions on a couple of cases and, to the amazement of many, including Senator Arlen Specter, would not even say whether *Marbury v. Madison* was correctly decided.[107] When asked about his theory of constitutional interpretation, the person who would become a strong advocate for originalism said the following: "I am embarrassed to say this. I am 50 years old, grown up, and everything. I cannot say that I have a fully framed omnibus view of the Constitution ... I think it is fair to say you would not regard me as someone who would be likely to use the phrase, living Constitution. On the other hand, I am not sure you can say, he is pure and simply an original meaning ... [sic] [but I am] more inclined to the original meaning than I am to a phrase like 'living Constitution.'"[108]

When senators asked Scalia how he would interpret the Fourteenth Amendment, he responded that a "strict constructionist would use only the understanding at the time of the Fourteenth Amendment. The evolutionist would say no, the understanding today as well. Whichever of those two you use – and as I said in some earlier questioning, I am a little wishy-washy on that point."[109]

Throughout his hearing, Scalia referred to the text and original meaning (not intent) of the Constitution as his starting point for constitutional interpretation, but he was never challenged or pushed to explain his views in any detail. As far as confirmation hearings being a possible referendum on originalism, that type of discussion would have to wait until a year later when President Reagan nominated Robert Bork to the Supreme Court of the United States.

Bork served as a judge on the US Court of Appeals for the District of Columbia prior to his Supreme Court nomination. The story of Bork's failed selection has been told many times, so this recounting will be mostly limited to the relevance of the hearing to the debates over originalism and judicial review.

When Bork was nominated, two major facts had changed from the time the Senate unanimously approved Scalia. First, the Democrats now controlled the Senate. Second, whereas Scalia replaced a conservative justice, Bork was taking Justice Lewis Powell's seat. Powell was a moderate and often the swing vote. The Court's ideological balance was now at stake, and Reagan's promise to "unwind the work of the Warren Court" became a distinct possibility.[110]

Bork's selection came as no surprise. Liberal senators and left-wing public-interest groups were well prepared. On the day of his nomination, Senator Ted Kennedy famously said on the Senate floor that "Robert Bork's America is a land in which women would be forced into back-alley abortions, blacks would sit at segregated lunch counters, rogue police could break down citizens' doors in midnight raids, and schoolchildren could not be taught about evolution."[111] These were all vast overstatements, but the nomination wars had begun.

The White House knew how big a battle was on their hands. There were internal disputes among Bork's handlers as to whether he should openly embrace the originalist conservative philosophy that he had advocated so strongly in his articles and judicial opinions or whether he should be less combative and try to appeal to moderate senators.[112] The White House encouraged the moderate path, but Bork refused to adopt that strategy. Instead he adhered to his prior attacks on the Warren Court, setting up a national conversation on some of the Court's most important liberal precedents.

During his hearing, Bork took numerous positions that seemed out of step with popular opinion. He took issue with (1) the Court's decisions outlawing segregation in DC public schools; (2) cases outlawing poll taxes; (3) the one person, one vote rule; (4) opinions providing heightened scrutiny for gender discrimination; and even (5) *Griswold*'s overturning Connecticut's ban on contraception.[113] All these cases were legally incorrect according to Bork, though he repeatedly said he would respect them as precedents. That lip service, however, couldn't repair the damage. As two leading scholars of the confirmation process have observed, by the end of the hearing, Bork's "constitutional vision . . . was clear . . . [and] it was not, it turned out, the constitutional vision of the American people. Bork's nomination was defeated by a vote of 58–42. As importantly, it also was not the constitutional vision of the person who would ultimately succeed in becoming the Court's 104th justice: Anthony Kennedy."[114]

According to Professors Randy Barnett and Josh Blackman, "what went wrong for Robert Bork was that his 'original intent' approach appeared to threaten too many past 'precedents' and future results that the Democratic majority in the Senate cared deeply about."[115] This account seems accurate. Throughout his hearings, Bork tried to convince the Senate, and by extension the American people, that there was a significant difference between voting for the constitutionality of a law, such as one prohibiting contraceptives, and favoring that law. Bork claimed over and over that he favored equal rights for women and minorities, that he liked his privacy as much as anyone else, and that he supported voting rights. The problem, according to Bork, was that neither the text nor the original intent of the Constitution supported judicial overreaching to achieve those goals. For example, as to whether the Connecticut anticontraception law should have been invalidated by the Court under the doctrine of substantive due process, Bork argued that "if you say it is due process and we will do whatever is fair or good under due process, the court's powers are unlimited. That is the problem I have with substantive due process...which I have long thought is a pernicious constitutional idea."[116] As to a seminal case overturning a state law allowing women to buy beer at an age younger than men, Bork disagreed, and said that you "would have thought it was the steel seizure case the way [the justices] went at it. And I thought, as a matter of fact, the differential drinking age probably is justified ..."[117] And, in a response to an exasperated Senator Biden asking Bork whether a married couple has a right to "engage in the decision of having a child or not having a child," Bork's answer was he had been unable to find such a right in the Constitution.[118] It is unlikely that this answer played well with a majority of senators or the American people.

Justice Scalia likely shared most of the same legal opinions offered by Judge Bork during the latter's confirmation hearings. Scalia argued throughout his career against the judicially created right to privacy, that women were not entitled to heightened scrutiny under the Equal

Protection Clause, and that the Court had gone too far protecting voting rights. Scalia also consistently gave speeches and wrote dissents arguing that when judges stray from the text and original meaning of the Constitution, they wrongfully interfere with the authority of more accountable governmental officials. Scalia's hypocrisy on these questions will be examined in Chapter 7, but the relevant question here is, why did Congress unanimously approve Scalia and reject Bork? After all, their views on the Constitution were virtually identical.

One factor may have been that Justice Scalia refused to answer questions about specific cases and was not pushed to reconcile his views with Warren Court decisions that were well accepted by the American people. It is likely he received this free pass from Senate Democrats because they knew they couldn't defeat him because the GOP controlled the Senate. Furthermore, Scalia's vote was not going to change the partisan balance on the Court. Neither of these two conditions were true for Judge Bork. Had Bork been nominated in 1986, and Scalia in 1987, it is almost certain that we would have had a Justice Bork but no Justice Scalia (at least during that time).

There are two lessons from the Bork hearings that are relevant to the transition from the Original Originalists of the 1970s and 1980s to the New Originalists of the 1990s and today. First, throughout his hearings, Bork made it clear that the original meaning of the text, not the original intent of the founders, was what he thought judges should examine where resolving constitutional issues not resolved by text or precedent. Although he did not see a big difference between the two ideas, the difference would become quite important to later originalists, especially when, in the years after the hearing, Justice Scalia repeatedly and explicitly affirmed this distinction. Today, most originalists use the vocabulary of original meaning not intent. Chapter 6 discusses whether there is a meaningful difference between the two forms of originalism.

Another lesson that some important originalists took from Bork's failed nomination, and the successful appointment of Justice Anthony Kennedy, who explicitly adopted a "living constitution" approach to the right to privacy in his hearings, was that certain key constitutional cases and ideas could not be relitigated in the political arena. Soon after Bork's hearings, it became difficult to find prominent academic originalists arguing that *Griswold* was wrongly decided or that the Equal

Protection Clause doesn't protect women from gender discrimination. As Professors Ringhand and Collins point out in their comprehensive study of Supreme Court confirmation hearings, Bork's defeated nomination "served primarily to reveal a new constitutional consensus, one so broadly accepted that no nominee in the two decades following Bork would refute it."[119]

That epilogue is ironic for one of the most important, if not the most important, Original Originalist. And, as we will see, although originalism, of course, did not die with Bork, its new adherents would eventually favor a completely different type of judicial review from the one advocated by Bork, Berger, Meese, and the other Original Originalists, who first articulated the doctrine in the hopes it would persuade judges to be more deferential to more accountable political officials. This transformation began with Justice Scalia and then morphed into a movement that, while paying lip service to Bork's emphasis on text and original meaning, ended up being indistinguishable from Justice Brennan's theory of the living Constitution.

5 **THE NEW ORIGINALISTS**

*If non-originalist constitutional law is objectionable for its
undermining of authority and rationality, originalist
constitutional law seems objectionable for exactly the same reasons.*
                                             Professor Steven D. Smith[1]

A. THE PASSING OF THE TORCH

By 1992, Justices Anthony Kennedy and Clarence Thomas had
replaced Lewis Powell and Thurgood Marshall on the Supreme Court.
These justices joined with Rehnquist, O'Connor, and Scalia to form a
five-person majority that reached, if not consistently conservative
results (as some might argue), at least decisions substantially less liberal
than those of the Warren and early Burger Courts. In the areas of
federalism and criminal procedure, especially, the Rehnquist Court
moved the law far to the right. This new conservative Court was
followed by a different brand of academic originalism that had little
in common with the Original Originalists.

The theoretical and political shifts in originalism were so dramatic
that Professor Keith Whittington, a leading New Originalist, wrote in
2004 that, by the 1990s, "the 'old originalism' largely passed from the
scene."[2] The form of originalism championed by Meese, Bork, and
Berger, which "arose as a response to the perceived abuses of the
Warren and Burger Courts," had been made "largely irrelevant" by
the Rehnquist Court.[3] The justices' politics had changed dramatically,
and so would the originalism theories propounded by one influential
group of conservative and libertarian law professors.

The Original Originalists criticized liberal decisions for straying too
far from text and original meaning, but did not provide sophisticated

theoretical alternatives. Professor Larry Solum described the Bork, Berger, and Meese forms of originalism as only "partially theorized."[4] The old originalist critique, according to Whittington, worked well in dissents but did not provide much of a guide for majority opinions.[5]

The new political climate created by a more conservative Court generated intellectual demands for conservative academics to create an interpretative approach justifying aggressively conservative judicial review. That is exactly what some, though certainly not all, New Originalists set out to do.[6] At the same time, however, these academics understood what a powerful political symbol originalism had become, and they did not want to lose that mantle. Their difficult job was to justify strong judicial review without being vulnerable to the legal realist critique that Supreme Court decisions reflected mostly judicial values and ideology.[7] The New Originalists wanted to maintain the law/ politics distinction that the Original Originalists claimed was so important to the rule of law, while at the same time justifying more aggressive judicial review than the Original Originalists would have tolerated.

In addition to the political reasons for transforming originalist theory in the 1990s, there were also intellectual adjustments triggered by liberal critiques of originalism set forth by scholars and judges in the decades before. The most important of those criticisms included (1) the problem that many of the Founding Fathers were opposed to judges searching for original intent when deciding legal and/or constitutional questions; (2) the indeterminacy problem that arises when judges try to ascertain the intent of many different framers as well as the intent of the people at the state ratifying conventions; (3) the difficulties judges face figuring out the appropriate level of generality for imprecisely worded constitutional provisions; and (4) the "dead hand" problem created by judges deferring to the values of people who lived centuries ago.[8]

Eventually, New Originalist scholars addressed each of these critiques, but their responses converted this form of originalism to a doctrine largely indistinguishable from the type of pluralistic judicial review practiced by the Warren and early Burger Courts and advocated by non-originalist scholars such as Laurence Tribe, Philip Bobbitt, and Michael Dorf. Although there are originalists today such as Professors Michael Rappaport and John McGinnis (whose work is discussed in the next chapter), Mike Ramsey, and Richard Kay, among others, who don't share many of the precepts of the New Originalists, this chapter is concerned primarily with what most academics refer to as the New Originalism. Although it is not clear whether the New Originalists have affected judges on the ground, there can be little debate that their work is influencing law students, other academics, and the originalism debates inside and outside the legal academy.

B. ORIGINAL INTENT OR ORIGINAL MEANING

In 1986, just three days before President Ronald Reagan nominated him to become a Supreme Court justice, Antonin Scalia gave an important speech urging originalists to focus on the "original meaning" of the constitutional text, not the original intent of the people who wrote and ratified that text.[9] Scalia said that he "ought to campaign to change the label from the Doctrine of Original Intent to the Doctrine of Original Meaning."[10] He argued that originalists should try to ascertain "the most plausible meaning of the words of the Constitution to the society that adopted it – regardless of what the framers might secretly have intended."[11] It is the objective legal meaning of the text that was ratified, not the secret or even public views of those who did the ratifying, that Scalia said was the appropriate focus of constitutional interpretation.

Four years later, in his famous book, *The Tempting of America*, Judge Bork explicitly agreed with Scalia's reinterpretation. He wrote the following:

> Though I have written of the understanding of the ratifiers of the Constitution, since they enacted it and made it law, that is actually a shorthand formulation, because what the ratifiers understood themselves to be enacting must be taken to be what the public of that time would have understood the words to mean ... The search is not for a subjective intention. If someone found a letter from George Washington to Martha telling her that what he meant by the power to lay taxes was not what other people meant, that would not change our reading of the Constitution in the slightest ... When lawmakers use words, the law that results is what those words ordinarily mean.[12]

Over the next few years, Scalia's and Bork's reframing of the appropriate originalist stance became a well-accepted and integral part of the New Originalism.[13] Professor Gary Lawson wrote that "the Constitution's meaning is its original public meaning. Other approaches to interpretation are simply wrong."[14] Professor Michael Paulsen insisted that the constitutional text itself demands that judges give it "the objective, original meaning of its . . . language."[15] Professor Randy Barnett argued that the shift from intent to meaning "obviates some, but not all, of the most telling practical objections to originalism and can be very disappointing for critics of originalism – and especially for historians – when they read original meaning analysis."[16] Barnett argued that originalism was no longer concerned with the subjective intentions or expectations of the framers but rather with "objective" evidence of what the text meant. Originalists should use "dictionaries, common meanings, and formal structural analysis" to discern the "objective original meaning that a reasonable listener would place on the words used in the constitutional provision at the time of its enactment."[17]

Barnett justified this new approach by relying on, of all people, the decidedly non-originalist, liberal legal philosopher Ronald Dworkin. Barnett embraced Dworkin's distinction between "semantic" and "expectations" originalism. That "crucial distinction [is] between what some officials *intended to say* in enacting the language they used, and what they intended – or expected or hoped – would be *the consequence* of their saying it."[18] Barnett argued that the difference between "expectations" and "semantic" originalism "helps to "clarify the movement from original intentions originalism to original meaning originalism. It is not only a movement from subjective to objective meaning. Depending on the textual provision being interpreted – for some at least – it is also a movement, to employ another Dworkinian distinction, from relatively specific rule-like commands to more abstract principle-like injunctions, the approximate meaning of which we must still look to the past to discover."[19]

Barnett used Dworkin's distinction between what the framers meant to say and what they expected to happen, as well as the move from original intent to original meaning, to claim that New Originalism survived the critiques of both Paul Brest and Jefferson Powell, the two

most prominent critics of originalism discussed in Chapter 4. Brest
criticized originalism on the basis that trying to discover the intentions
of people who lived centuries ago was a difficult task not suited for
judges and lawyers. Barnett did not disagree: "since intentions exist in
people's minds, it is difficult to discern what those intentions are. But
it is especially problematic to hypothesize a "collective intent" of
multiple minds. This deep incoherence . . . [is] a valid criticism."[20]

Barnett also pointed out that while Brest criticized what he called
the "strict intentionalism" of the Original Originalists, Brest also suggested that moderate originalism, as defined in the following quote, was
"a perfectly sensible strategy" for constitutional decision making:[21]

> A moderate textualist takes account of the open-textured quality of
> language and reads the language of provisions in their social and
> linguistic contexts. A moderate intentionalist applies a provision
> consistent with the adopters' intent at a relatively high level of
> generality, consistent with what is sometimes called the "purpose
> of the provision." Where the strict intentionalist tries to determine
> the adopters' actual subjective purposes, the moderate intentional-
> ist [or original meaning originalist] attempts to understand what the
> adopters' purposes might plausibly have been, an aim far more
> readily achieved than a precise understanding of the adopters'
> intentions.[22]

Barnett also agreed with Professor Powell, who argued that the
framers would have rejected judicial efforts to ascertain the original
subjective intentions of the ratifiers, and thus original intent originalism
was inconsistent with itself. But Powell also argued that the framers
approved the search for the text's "original meaning" through judicial
examination of relevant legal sources.[23] Thus, Barnett argued, one of
the standard critiques of originalism, that it is inconsistent with itself, is
at least partially cured by the movement away from subjective intentions and toward objective original meaning.

Professor Stephen Griffin helpfully summarized Barnett's strategy
to resurrect originalism in the wake of Brest's and Powell's famous
critiques:

> As Barnett tells the story, originalism was thought to have been
> refuted in the 1980s, chiefly by criticisms offered by Paul Brest and

Jefferson Powell. Brest focused most of his fire on the implausibility of relying on subjective intentions, while Powell argued that the framers did not themselves resort to original intent to interpret the Constitution. According to Barnett, a turn to original meaning, understood as public original meaning, solves most of the problems identified by Brest and Powell. Problems caused by the search for subjective private intentions are no longer relevant, and Powell's evidence of the framer's interpretive intent did not invalidate reliance on public meaning, especially the meaning of the ratifiers of the Constitution.[24]

There is no doubt that a "central feature" of the New Originalism is an emphasis on objective meaning, not subjective intent.[25] In Keith Whittington's words, what "is at issue in interpreting the Constitution is the textual meaning of the document, not the private subjective intentions, motivations or expectations of its authors."[26]

New Originalists don't agree on which historical sources count when judges are trying to ascertain original meaning. Some "originalists focus on the understanding of the drafters; others on the understanding of the ratifiers; and still others on the understanding of the public."[27] Some New Originalists don't even search for the actual or real original understandings of the people living during ratification but instead posit what a hypothetical, reasonable observer at the time would have understood the text to mean.[28]

Although original meaning originalism in all these forms does, to some degree, suggest a different historical examination than does original intent originalism, the shift does not materially alter the standard debates between originalists and non-originalists. As Larry Solum has pointed out, often the best evidence of the original public meaning of the constitutional text will be evidence showing what the framers intended to say through their use of words (and the context of those words).[29] Solum argues that in "normal circumstances, the intentions of the Framers will be reflected in the public meaning of the constitutional text: as competent speakers and writers of ... English, the Framers are likely to have understood that the best way to convey their intentions would be to state them clearly in language that would be grasped by the officials and citizens to whom the constitutional text was addressed."[30] Thus, although the "theoretical grounds" for original intention and original meaning inquiries might be somewhat different, "as a practical matter, originalists are likely to agree on midlevel principles of constitutional interpretation."[31] Similarly, Professor Mark Tushnet has observed that what "a drafter believed a constitutional provision to mean is evidence of what at least one reasonably well-informed contemporary understood the provision to mean. Further, what a drafter believed a constitutional provision would do is similar evidence, to the extent that meaning resides at least in part in use."[32]

The move from intention to meaning does not address some substantial objections to originalism leveled by the doctrine's critics. The objections to "law office history" apply with equal, if not more, force to the search for the "objective original meaning" of the constitutional text. The judge who tries to ascertain the original meaning of vague constitutional language must review and evaluate voluminous and conflicting historical evidence. As others have pointed out, determining what the people who wrote and ratified constitutional text in fact intended is at least an empirical question requiring investigation into the words, minds, and actions of the people in the relevant groups. The search for original objective meaning, by contrast, is a theoretical inquiry requiring the judge to don the mantle of a hypothetical objective person living centuries ago.[33] Although tort and contact law at times require an investigation into an "objective person," the judges in those areas of the law are painting a picture of a person living today who holds modern beliefs and values. Asking judges to ascertain what the text meant to hypothetical people living centuries ago is a much more difficult, if not impossible, task.

Another standard objection to originalism that the move to original meaning does not address is the democratic legitimacy problem. Women and people of color were excluded from the constitutional decision making of the 1780s and the 1860s. The hypothetical "objective meaning" of much of the constitutional text at the time of ratification if looked at fairly runs directly through the racist and sexist values, perspectives, and actions of the people living at the time. For example, there can be little debate that a woman's choice to terminate her pregnancy was not part of the original public meaning of the word *liberty* in the Fourteenth Amendment. But many, perhaps most, of the men who wrote, voted for, and understood what *liberty* meant in 1868, believed women didn't have the right to vote or have substantial legal identities separate from their husbands. Why should judges today be beholden to people living in such a sexist society? There may or may not be satisfactory answers to that question, but the differences between original intentions and original meaning originalism do not suggest that answer.

Third, as Professor Griffin also argued, a major objection to originalism, whether phrased in the language of intentions or meaning, is that it does not remotely describe how the Supreme Court has ever consistently acted.[34] Although Barnett and other originalists might argue that their theory is prescriptive not descriptive, their scholarship suggests that the search for original meaning is so integral to the constitutional enterprise that non-originalists have the burden of justifying other techniques. But, if in fact, originalism is not the status quo, or even close to the status quo, "the adoption of originalism as the sole or primary method of constitutional interpretation would ... be a significant departure ... [and] originalists must assume a heavy normative burden. They must show why such a departure would be justified."[35]

Griffin makes a strong case that the Supreme Court, since the beginning of this country's history, has not used originalism in any form as the primary element of constitutional interpretation. Instead, the Court uses what Griffin and other scholars such as Professors Phillip Bobbitt and Mike Dorf have called a "pluralistic theory," where the justices examine text, ratification-era evidence, history, precedent, tradition, political practices, and pragmatic evaluations of consequences to reach decisions in constitutional cases.[36] Chapter 8 explores these Supreme Court practices and its non-originalist decisions, but for now it is enough to suggest that the differences between original meaning and original intent originalism do not address the problem that the Supreme Court has never consistently used either method.

C. CONSTRUCTION, INTERPRETATION, AND JUDICIAL REVIEW

New Originalism's other defining element is the distinction these scholars draw between interpretation and construction. These concepts are difficult to describe because they are what makes New Originalism in practice virtually indistinguishable from "living constitutionalism," or what scholars such as Griffin and Dorf call "pluralistic theories" of constitutional interpretation.

The difference between interpretation and construction predates New Originalism, but many of the theory's proponents accept Professor Larry Solum's description: "We ... use the term 'interpretation' to refer to the activity of discovering the linguistic meaning or communicative content of the constitutional text. The term 'construction' then can be used to refer to the activity of determining the legal effect given to the text."[37] The text's "communicative content" is simply what it meant at the time. Sometimes, what the text meant, and its legal effect, are the same. Solum uses Article I's requirement that each state must have two Senators as an example. He says that "[e]veryone understands that 'state' refers to each of the fifty states, that 'two' refers to the whole number two, and that 'Senate' refers to a particular political institution, the U.S. Senate, which holds formal meetings in the U.S. Capitol building. Once we grasp the communicative content of the text, the legal effect follows directly."[38] Other constitutional commands where the communicative content and the legal effect are the same are that the president must be thirty-five, and all impeachments must begin in the House of Representatives, and then be tried in the Senate.

When the meaning of constitutional text is clear, and its legal effect mirrors the language, judges have little discretion when conducting "constitutional construction." In most litigation, however, there is a gap between meaning and effect, and then construction with substantial discretion comes into play. For example, the phrases "establishment of religion," "free exercise of religion," "unreasonable search and seizure," and "cruel and unusual punishment" are all word clusters that in a variety of settings are likely to lead to litigation that will not give clear directions to judges. In Solum's words, "constitutional questions that cannot be resolved simply by giving direct effect to the rule of constitutional law that directly corresponds to the communicative content of the constitutional text ... are in the construction zone."[39]

How New Originalists describe the judicial task in the "construction zone" is the most mystifying element of their jurisprudence.

They might have said that when clear text does not point to an answer, judges should review and evaluate the text's original meaning to derive the best result. Or, they might have agreed with Bork, Berger, and Meese that unless the plaintiff can demonstrate the challenged law or practice violates clear original understandings of the text, she loses her case. Both of those approaches would rely heavily on original and ratification-era evidence and would be true to the label New Originalism.

Many New Originalists, however, choose a different path. They argued that once a judge is in the "construction zone," ratification-era sources are no longer particularly helpful defining vague constitutional text, and judges must employ other methods of constitutional construction. The problem with this approach is that, if originalism often runs out when the communicative content of the text is unclear, then originalism is largely irrelevant to judges deciding actual cases. One could reasonably ask, therefore, why would a person who believes all that identify as an originalist? As Professor Steven Smith has so cogently argued:

> *Indeed, there turns out to be not much practical difference between non-originalism and originalism.* Non-originalists all along maintained that judges are constrained by the words of the Constitution – the original words – but may depart from the enactors' understandings of what those words meant. Originalists now insist that judges are constrained by the meanings of the words, but may depart from the enactors' understanding of what those meanings would entail or require. How much practical difference is there, honestly, between these accounts?[40]

Keith Whittington describes constitutional construction "as a supplemental theory of constitutional elaboration" because "originalism is incomplete as a theory of how the Constitution is elaborated and applied over time."[41] Randy Barnett says that "[o]riginalism is not a theory of what to do when original meaning runs out. This is not a bug; it is a feature ... Unless there is something in the text that favors one construction over the other, it is not originalism that is doing the work when one selects a theory of construction to employ when original meaning runs out, but one's underlying *normative commitments*."[42]

Professor Jack Balkin, a liberal New Originalist, describes constitutional construction as follows: "When the Constitution ... uses
vague language, standards, or principles, an inquiry into original
meaning will not be sufficient to decide most contested questions.
Hence there is a second activity of constitutional interpretation, called
constitutional construction. Constitutional construction builds out the
'Constitution-in-practice,' fleshing out and implementing vague and
abstract language through doctrine, and creating institutions to further
constitutional values. All three branches of government engage in
constitutional construction, responding to each other and to continu-
ous waves of social and political mobilizations in politics and civil
society."[43]

The crucial admission in these descriptions of the interpretation/
construction distinction, is that, while original meaning may cabin
some extreme choices in the construction zone, original meaning will
run out as a useful tool for judges needing to resolve the case. When
that happens, the judge's other "normative commitments" will have to
do most of the work.

This construction zone/living constitutionalism approach is implicit
in the New Originalist notion that what the people living in 1787 or
1868 expected to happen is not the important question for an originalist. Judges should not try to glean the framers' intent or what the
people at the time expected the text to mean. Instead, the crucial issue
is, what was the objective, public meaning of the text at the time? But if
that meaning does not resolve the question at hand, and it usually will
not, then judges most look to non-originalist sources. In most cases,
that move takes virtually all the "originalism" out of "New Originalism." Or, as another scholar has said about New Originalism, "it is not
clear what is left of originalism, other than the name."[44]

There are many specific examples of New Originalists using this
broad "construction zone" theory to reach what appear to most people
decidedly non-originalist conclusions (while simultaneously donning
the originalist label). For example, Originalist Professors Steven
Calabresi and Ilya Somin argue that bans on same-sex marriage violate
the Fourteenth Amendment's original meaning because the bans con-
stitute unlawful gender discrimination.[45] Somin says that under these
laws a man couldn't marry a man or a woman a woman because both

were men, or both were women, not because of their sexual orientation.[46] In fact, gay men could marry gay women under these laws.
Therefore, Somin argues these bans constituted gender discrimination
violative of the Fourteenth Amendment.

The problem is not that Somin is wrong about his description of the
same-sex marriage bans, but rather that he concedes the people living
in 1868 when the Fourteenth Amendment was adopted would never
have thought those bans, even if based on gender, were unconstitutional. Somin suggests that is not the right question because "the
Framers' view that this form of sex discrimination is constitutionally
permissible hinged on dubious factual assumptions that we are not
bound by today."[47] We are not "bound by" those assumptions today
because the Fourteenth Amendment's text does not resolve the issue of
gender discrimination and, in the construction zone, originalism runs
out, and judges may use other tools to reach the right results.

Somin relies on a broader argument previously advanced by Professor Calabresi to argue that that the "original public meaning" of the
Fourteenth Amendment prohibits most forms of gender discrimination – an idea many originalists such as Judge Bork and Justice Scalia,
denied.[48] Calabresi first claims that the original meaning of the Fourteenth Amendment prohibits all "caste" legislation and then argues
that discrimination based on gender is certainly a form of "caste"
legislation. Calabresi concedes that "the Framers and ratifiers of the
Fourteenth Amendment [did not] understand sex discrimination to be
a form of caste or of special-interest class legislation ... [but] sometimes legislators misapply or misunderstand their own rules. For this
reason, although the Framers' expected applications of the constitutional text are worth knowing, they are not the last word on the
Fourteenth Amendment's reach."[49]

There are several important problems with Somin's and Calabresi's
arguments. First, both take the words of the Amendment, that "no
state shall deny to any person ... the equal protection of the laws" and
glean a broad anticaste principle. Many scholars, like Raoul Berger,
who have studied this history at length, disagree, arguing that the
clause simply was meant to provide African Americans equal civil
and political rights.[50] That disagreement, however, by itself, only
shows that people studying a vague constitutional provision might

disagree over the best interpretation of that text's history. That problem alone does not necessarily undercut originalism.

But in the case of state bans on same-sex marriage, we do not have to guess how the framers of the Fourteenth Amendment, or the people who voted for the Amendment, would have thought the language applied to same-sex marriage bans. Everyone, everywhere, agrees that they never, maybe not even a single person alive at the time, nor a hypothetical observer, would have thought the Amendment provided gays and lesbians a right to marry. Furthermore, as Calabresi and Somin admit, the Fourteenth Amendment was enacted at a time when women were denied many civil and political rights, and few at the time thought the Amendment changed that inequality. Given that reality, how can an "originalist" argue that today's same-sex marriage bans violate the "original public meaning" of the Fourteenth Amendment? Whose meaning or what meaning are they talking about?

The answer is that they can come to that conclusion only by first reading the language of the Constitution at a broad level of generality (not equal protection but anticaste) and then replacing the values and assumptions of the people living at the time with their own values and assumptions. There is nothing wrong with that method of constitutional interpretation, but it is also how a "living constitutionalist" or someone who believes in "pluralistic theories" of constitutional interpretation, would try to figure out the problem. It is not how someone who believes that original meaning should play a primary role in constitutional interpretation engages in constitutional interpretation, unless that phrase is drained of all relevant meaning.

Once we raise the level of generality of a constitutional provision to a high enough level and discard what we know the enactors thought about specific applications of that provision, judges can reach any decision they want without regard to original meaning. Professor Orin Kerr pointed this out specifically with regard to Somin's and Calabresi's same-sex marriage arguments:

> As far as I can tell, there is no serious originalist case for a right to same-sex marriage ... what are being described as originalist arguments may just be products of the Level of Generality Game with

the word 'originalist' tacked on. Most students of constitutional law will be familiar with the Level of Generality Game, as it's a common way to argue for counterintuitive outcomes. The basic idea is that any legal rule can be understood as a specific application of a set of broad principles. If you need to argue that a particular practice is unconstitutional, but the text and/or history are against you, the standard move is to raise the level of generality.[51]

Professor Kerr is right. We can play this "Level of Generality Game" for any number of modern disputes. For example, we know that a woman's right to terminate her pregnancy was not considered by the people at the time a "liberty" protected by the Fourteenth Amendment. There is no historical uncertainty about that question. Therefore, one would expect an originalist to believe that *Roe v. Wade* was wrongly decided. But here is Professor Jack Balkin:

> The right to abortion . . . is in fact based on the constitutional text of the Fourteenth Amendment and the principles that underlie it. That is so even though the framers and adopters of the Fourteenth Amendment did not expect or intend that it would apply to abortion. In this essay I offer an argument for the right to abortion based on the original meaning of the constitutional text as opposed to its original expected application.[52]

What is that argument? Professor Balkin argues that his form of originalism takes seriously both constitutional text and principle, but not the people's expected applications of the text. He says that "constitutional interpretation requires fidelity to the original meaning of the Constitution and to the principles that underlie the text. The task of interpretation is to look to original meaning and underlying principle *and decide how best to apply them in current circumstances.*"[53] This method of constitutional interpretation "is faithful to the original meaning of the constitutional text . . . [and] is also consistent with a basic law whose reach and application evolve over time, a basic law that leaves to each generation the task of how to make sense of the Constitution's words and principles. Although the constitutional text and principles do not change without subsequent amendment, their application and implementation can."[54]

Professor Balkin goes on to explain that some constitutional provisions are specific and don't need additional legal doctrines to flesh them out while others, such as the Fourteenth Amendment's equal protection and due process clauses, stand for broader principles that will change over time according to societal values and other factors. Most constitutional cases, of course, are based on the vague provisions that require construction to give them meaning. All of this sounds just like a "living constitutionalism" approach to those parts of the Constitution that are not specific, and Balkin, to his credit, does not deny the similarities. He concedes that "original meaning originalism and living constitutionalism are not only not at odds, but are actually flip sides of the same coin."[55] Eventually, Balkin even wrote a book called *Living Originalism*.[56] He expressly adopted the "construction zone" concept and wrote "in constitutional construction, 'originalist' argument is not a single form of argument; it involves many different kinds of argument, and it often appeals to ethos, tradition, or culture heroes."[57] This analysis is descriptively accurate and normatively smart, but it puts a new, and quite unusual, gloss on the term *originalist*.

As to abortion, Balkin argues that once judges are not bound by the people's "expected applications" of the constitutional text, it is not difficult to build arguments based on liberty, equality, "ethos," and "tradition," that women need to have the ability to control their own reproductive futures. Balkin chooses equality from the list and characterizes the Fourteenth Amendment as prohibiting "class legislation, caste legislation, and subordinating legislation."[58] Then, by making policy arguments that certainly make sense to this reader, as well as an historical evaluation of the evolving role of women in our society, Balkin constructs Fourteenth Amendment doctrine to protect a woman's right to have an abortion, even though we know for certain that neither the drafters nor the ratifiers of the Fourteenth Amendment expected that result.[59]

In the conclusion to his abortion article, Balkin makes transparent his updated notion of originalism. After pointing out that *Roe* has been the target of originalists for years, Balkin argues that his originalism is different:

> The Constitution, and particularly the Fourteenth Amendment, was written with the future in mind. Its drafters deliberately chose

broad language embracing broad principles of liberty and equality. Fidelity to the Constitution means applying its text and its principles to our present circumstances.[60]

Although Professor Balkin's method of text and principle does at times place substantial emphasis on historical evidence in constitutional cases, he does not argue that such evidence displaces or should displace the judgments and modern values of today's judges. Moreover, like Professor Barry Friedman, Balkin believes postratification historical events, even events far removed from the founding and the Reconstruction Amendments, play an important role in constitutional interpretation.[61] So maybe we are wrong to treat him as an originalist like the other scholars discussed in this book. Yet, Randy Barnett said a few years ago that it is "newsworthy . . . that Jack Balkin has adopted originalism as his own." Many self-styled New Originalist scholars also agree with Balkin that the meaning of broadly or vaguely worded constitutional provisions will change over time and allow courts to protect personal rights, like abortion, when there is no plausible argument that the people living at the time would have expected that provision to have that consequence. For example, Chapter 6 discusses the work of Professor Will Baude, who calls himself an originalist. He agrees with Balkin's method of "text and principle," as applied to many modern cases, including the same-sex marriage decisions. Barnett, in an article responding to Balkin's essay on abortion and originalism, said that "I am in agreement with nearly everything Balkin says about original meaning originalism . . . [and] I am also sympathetic with his conclusions about the unconstitutionality of prohibitions on abortion."[62]

Many New Originalist scholars, whether though the interpretation/construction distinction set forth by Professors Barnett, Whittington, and Solum or through Balkin's text and principle approach, advocate a form of constitutional interpretation that allows judges to take the broad constitutional principles of due process, equal protection, and freedom of speech, as well as other unclear constitutional text, and construct implementing doctrines based on historical evaluation, political practices, modern conditions, values, and apparently, "ethos" and "cultural heroes." That approach may also employ original meaning as one factor to consider but so does the model of living constitutionalism, which the New Originalists so frequently criticize. As Professor Steven Smith has argued, Balkin's text and principle approach is as living a theory as one can imagine and leads to the question what "is the point of all of the deliberation and debate ... and the crafting and drafting and redrafting of constitutional provisions, if those provisions will shortly be interpreted in terms of lofty principles with implications (to be enforced, by judges, against democratic majorities) that the enactors never intended, imagined, or desired? Why would sensible citizens and legislators engage in this peculiar exercise, bind themselves and their descendants in this profoundly unpredictable way?"[63] There may be persuasive answers to Smith's questions, but none of them are based in any serious originalist methodology, especially because people in the eighteenth century "would not have contemplated – nor can they be presumed to have consented to – an evolving Constitution that safeguards an ever expanding set of individual rights against the government."[64]

The construction zone that the New Originalists advocate is a place where the original meaning and historical evidence play at most limited roles. In addition, the judicial restraint that was such a crucial aspect of the old originalism, is virtually ignored by New Originalists probably because, other than Professors Balkin, Solum, and a few others, an important aspect of their scholarship is devoted to furthering specific conservative and libertarian objectives. As one scholar has observed, the use of "original public meaning [enables] originalists to argue that the abstract language of the ... [Constitution] warranted judicial protection of a host of economic liberties, either as a matter of constitutional interpretation or construction. Here was the beginning of originalism as a sword, an offensive justification for judges to advance conservative values against a hostile democratic process."[65]

Professor Larry Solum has argued that originalists, old and new, are "united by two core ideas."[66] The first is the "Fixation Thesis," which means that the original meaning or "communicative content" of the constitutional text "is fixed at the time each provision is framed and ratified."[67] The second idea is the "Constraint Principle" that says that "constitutional actors (e.g., judges, officials, and citizens) ought to be constrained by the original meaning when they engage in constitutional practice."[68] He then says what distinguishes Old and New Originalists is mostly the interpretation and construction distinction advocated by Barnett, Whittington, and others. But in the construction zone, as this chapter has shown, original meaning plays a limited role, and other normative modalities play a significant role. Judges who accept the New Originalism would not be constrained by original meaning in any significant sense nor would the alleged "fixed" nature of text at the time of ratification tilt either side to victory in most litigated constitutional cases. In other words, the two "core ideas" Solum claims are accepted by all originalists are in fact unhelpful to judges deciding most constitutional law cases.

Professor Solum himself has identified these problems with New Originalism. In a book-length debate with Professor Robert Bennett, Solum summarized how the interpretation-construction distinction poses a major challenge for originalists:

> [W]hat should an originalist say about decision making within the construction zone? . . . It might be argued that the construction of [vague] provisions requires judges to rely on their own values or beliefs about political morality and justice. If this were the case, then it might follow that much of the originalists critique of living constitutionalism would lose its force . . . if originalists allow judges to make law in the construction zone, it might be argued that the difference between originalists and living constitutionalism is only a matter of degree. Given the practical importance of the abstract, general and vague provisions [of the Constitution] living constitutionalists might well claim that the originalist endorsement of the interpretation-construction distinction effectively concedes the most important constitutional questions to non-originalists.[69]

Solum's responses to his own questions identify three possible options for originalists. One option for originalists is to advocate for great deference to other political decision makers when judges are in the construction zone.[70] This is a coherent response consistent with the Original Originalists and the framers' view of the proper judicial role. However, few New Originalists adopt it, and the post-nineteenth-century Supreme Court has not embraced such deference on a consistent basis outside of a few isolated areas of constitutional litigation. Another choice is to apply an approach where judges "attempt to

derive guiding purposes or principles ... to search for the values that
are immanent in the specific provisions and overall structure of the
Constitution."[71] It is far from clear how this search could possibly limit
judicial discretion in actual litigated cases. Without more specific ideas
or examples, this second option does not rebut the charge that modern
judicial values, not original meaning, will reign supreme in the construction zone. His final option is for judges to adopt a "model of
construction by original methods."[72] He does not explain what he
means by this option, but presumably he is referring to the theory of
original methods originalism advocated by Professors Rappaport and
McGinnis and discussed at length in Chapter 6. Solum himself, however, does not detail how this theory constrains judges, given the many
conflicting methods of interpretation a judge can select from among
those that were approved by the framers (as discussed in Chapter 6).

Solum fails to distinguish how judges act in the construction zone
from living constitutionalism. Professor Andrew Coan summarized
this idea as follows: The New Originalism "fails to meaningfully constrain judges because it licenses free-wheeling constitutional construction of open-ended constitutional text without reference to original
meaning. It also severs the content of contemporary constitutional
law from the democratic will of those who ratified it, whose expectations and intentions New Originalist judges are fully permitted to
ignore."[73] Remember the Original Originalists criticized the Warren
Court "for interpreting the Constitution's provisions to do things that
the provisions' enactors had never intended or contemplated."[74] The
same critique is applicable to the New Originalists.

This method of constitutional construction does not constrain
judges in any meaningful sense, and its theoretical foundations are
similar to those of living constitutionalism. Although Whittington
argues that "[f]ixing constitutional principles in a written text against
the transient shifts in the public mood or social condition becomes
tantamount to an originalist jurisprudence," Professors Tom Colby
and Peter Smith have detailed extensively how New Originalism, like
living constitutionalism, is in fact based on "transient shifts" and
"social condition[s]."[75] Randy Barnett, Ilya Somin, and numerous
other New Originalists, for example, argue for a type of "judicial
engagement" of licensing and takings laws, as well as numerous other

forms of economic legislation, that represent titanic departures from the originalism of Bork and Berger.[76] In their article, "Living Originalism," Colby and Smith detail numerous other ways originalists old, new, and very new[77] have responded to changed social conditions, court decisions, and even public opinion. These "originalists" formulate new jurisprudential strategies based not just on originalist values but also on the spirit of vague text, prior cases, structural values, political practices, and overall normative values, just like the "living constitutionalism" bundle of theories originalist scholars so often attack. The list of scholars who have made similar arguments about the lack of "originalism" in New Originalism is quite long.[78]

These critiques of New Originalism are substantiated by one of the most recent books attempting to defend originalism as a primary method of constitutional interpretation. Ilan Wurman's *A Debt Against the Living: An Introduction to Originalism*[79] explicitly adopts the interpretation/construction distinction and adds to it the ideas of "liquidation" and the "sense-reference" distinction. According to Wurman, the "first few times" a judge must resolve hard constitutional issues where construction is necessary, she will choose "among the competing plausible options."[80] This choice will "in some sense be arbitrary."[81] Over time, however, after "a series of mature deliberations made by many constitutional actors," similar "cases within that same context will presumably accord such collective decisions determinative weight and the matter will be settled."[82] In other words, the meaning will be "liquidated." Notice, however, that the original decision may not be based on originalist sources, and non-originalist holdings eventually may become the law of the land. Living constitutionalists like David Strauss would agree with this description of how judges over time give meaning to vague constitutional phrases.[83]

Wurman also adopts Professor Christopher Green's summary of the "sense-reference" theory of constitutional meaning. An originalist is not bound by what the people living in 1787 or 1868 expected the text to mean in concrete factual situations, except for those provisions where the text is clear beyond doubt, such as the president must be thirty-five. For the vague provisions (the ones that lead to litigation), the Constitution "enshrine[s] a sense that does not change with time. But the facts and conditions to which the sense applies – the referents of the constitutional provisions – can change."[84] Wurman argues that "we are not bound by [the framers'] factual errors."[85] For example, the "sense" of the Fourteenth Amendment is equality. The people in 1868 made the factual error of thinking racial segregation in public facilities was consistent with equality. Judges in 1954 may correct that "error" consistent with originalism.

Wurman's originalism allows judges to look to prior judicial doctrines and decisions to see if the meaning of the text has been liquidated. If not, judges may determine the "sense" of constitutional provisions, which in the case of the Fourteenth Amendment basically means equality and fairness. This method of constitutionalism is barely related, if at all, to the original public meaning of the constitutional text unless we assume that meaning is broad enough to apply to any inequality modern judges deem legally unwarranted. In Wurman's own words: "Originalists recognize that original meaning often requires that the application of the text *evolves* as modern circumstances *evolve*."[86] Just so, as virtually all living constitutionalists would agree.

Why do scholars like Wurman who quite obviously feel it is appropriate for judges to constantly update the applications of vague constitutional provisions to meet new conditions refer to themselves as Originalists? This discussion needs to be put off until Chapter 10 so that we can analyze two other recent schools of originalist thought and then examine substantial evidence that originalism has not, in practice, played a consistent role in the Supreme Court's constitutional decisions.

6 THE NEW, NEW ORIGINALISTS

Originalism is our Law.

Will Baude[1]

Interpretative theory has too long been under the grip of a nirvana fallacy.

Mike Rappaport and John McGinnis[2]

Many of the originalists discussed so far, whether from the Bork and Berger era or from the later Barnett, Whittington, and Somin era, were writing critically and prescriptively. They argued that the Court over time has not taken originalism, in any of its forms, as seriously as these scholars would like. They would also concur with Justice Scalia who once said that it "would be hard to count on the fingers of both hands and the toes of both feet, yea, even on the hairs of one's youthful head, the opinions that have in fact been rendered not on the basis of what the Constitution originally meant, but on the basis of what the judges currently thought it desirable for it to mean."[3] In other words, even Scalia recognized that originalist decision making was rare among contemporary judges.

Two of the newest voices in the originalism debate, however, Professors Will Baude and Stephen Sachs, have taken a different approach arguing that originalism properly conceived, is in fact, and has been for a long time, "our law."[4] To the extent that New Originalism and Living Constitutionalism are, as Balkin claims, "flip sides of the same coin," this thesis needs to be seriously considered by originalists and non-originalists alike. The first part of this chapter addresses and criticizes the claim that "originalism is our law."

The second half examines another relatively new perspective on originalism advocated by Professors John McGinnis and Michael

Rappaport. Their theory, which they label "original methods originalism," argues that judges today should only use the interpretive techniques that judges used at the time of the ratification of the Constitution.[5] Their work suggests that originalism isn't how judges decide cases today, but it should be.

A. "INCLUSIVE ORIGINALISM"

In an important and much cited article in the *Columbia Law Review*, Professor Will Baude asked a provocative question: "Is Originalism Our Law?"[6] His affirmative answer likely surprised many Court observers and other originalists, who believe that most Supreme Court decisions concerning free speech, criminal defendants, abortion, sovereign immunity, and the rights of gays and lesbians to marry, among many other cases, cannot be justified through historical analysis. For example, as Professor David Strauss argued in a recent Foreword to the *Harvard Law Review*,[7] neither text nor history can adequately support or justify most of the Court's constitutional law cases. Rather, Strauss argued, Supreme Court constitutional law is most accurately seen as common law where prior decisions reflecting the justices' personal values generate the decisions. In contrast, Professor Baude boldly argues that "inclusive originalism" has been and is the law of the land.[8]

Professor Baude's thesis, which is a branch or outgrowth of the "New Originalist" scholarship discussed in the previous chapter, tries to connect Court decisions to the various relevant ratification eras by using the interpretation/construction framework advanced by Professors Barnett, Whittington, and Solum. Baude's definition of originalism, however, is virtually indistinguishable from the non-originalist, "living constitution" approach that supported the liberal Warren Court decisions that the Original Originalists criticized. In a sense, then, originalism as a theory, in the hands of Professor Baude, and other scholars like Professor Stephen Sachs, has come full circle to mean almost the exact opposite of what the theory meant to Judge Bork and Professors Graglia, Berger, Kay, and others.

To understand and appreciate Professor Baude's novel thesis, it is necessary to understand what he means by "our law."[9] Baude does not specifically indicate whether he is writing for philosophers or judges or both when referring to "our law." He does say that "[i]f I'm right... originalist judging can potentially be justified on a... plausible normative ground – that judges have a duty to apply the law, and our current law... is this form of originalism."[10] He also wrote that his article "relies on lawyers' assumptions rather than technical jurisprudence."[11] Therefore, it appears that Baude's originalist approach is directed primarily at judges and lawyers, not theorists, and this book evaluates his "inclusive originalism" as it affects our legal practices on the ground.[12]

Professor Baude admits that what he calls "inclusive originalism" "may be frustrating to those who knew originalism in its unruly youth."[13] He dramatically understates that case. Judge Bork, Ed Meese, and the other originalists of the 1980s would likely not recognize as originalism many of the theories now claiming that mantle, including Baude's "inclusive originalism."

Professor Baude argues that his definition of "inclusive originalism" is "coherent, consistent with much modern originalist scholarship, and most important, consistent with our practice."[14] Interestingly and revealingly, he cites Justices Kagan and Alito, who are not exactly paragons of originalist decision making, to support his claim that "inclusive originalism" is "our law."[15]

Professor Baude defines his "inclusive originalism" as follows: "Under inclusive originalism, the original meaning of the Constitution is the ultimate criterion for constitutional law... This means that judges can look to precedent, policy, or practice, but only to the extent that the original meaning incorporates or permits them."[16] Professor Baude suggests that it is perfectly consistent with "inclusive originalism" for judges to interpret the open-ended phrases of the Constitution in ways that were "unforeseeable at the time of enactment."[17] This is so "because a word can have a fixed abstract meaning even if the specific facts that meaning points to change over time."[18] Other New Originalists, such as Randy Barnett and Jack Balkin, agree that the application of vague constitutional provisions may evolve over time as facts and circumstances also change.[19]

What does it mean for words to be simultaneously "fixed" and "abstract"? The answer shows why "inclusive originalism" is either inaccurate or indistinguishable from living constitutionalism, and why Professor Baude is correct that his version of originalism would mystify, to say the least, those "who knew originalism in its unruly youth."

According to Professor Baude, one "policy" and "practice" that is consistent with "inclusive originalism" recognizes that many constitutional terms are "ambiguous" or "vague," and judges must use devices like "construction" and "presumptions" to give those words meaning.[20] These methods of constitutional interpretation are consistent with "our law" as long as they are permitted by the "many versions of originalism."[21] Not only are such creative methods of judicial interpretation consistent with inclusive originalism but "[a] method like the use of evolving language is likely an example of a sub-method that is *required* by originalism. Giving evolving terms, their intended evolving meaning is necessary to be faithful to their original sense."[22]

Professor Baude's "inclusive originalism" allows judges to give the vague constitutional phrases that trigger most constitutional litigation different meanings as facts and society evolve. In his words, "fixed texts can harness what seems to be changing meanings."[23] So defined, originalism is indistinguishable from "living constitutionalism" because most cases that end up in front of judges implicate imprecise phrases like "equal protection," "due process," "establishment of religion," and "cruel and unusual punishment."

For Professor Baude to support his claim that "inclusive originalism" is "our law," he tries to fit a wide variety of landmark Supreme Court decisions, considered by most scholars to have little originalist content, into his definition. His explanations for these cases indicate that he believes that Barnett's and Solum's "construction zone" originalism is, in fact, originalism. But if he is right about these cases, his originalism isn't originalism in any serious sense. If he is wrong that these cases are originalist, he needs a new descriptive label for his theory.

Professor Baude claims that cases like *Brown v. Board of Education*,[24] *Obergefell v. Hodges*,[25] and *Home Building & Loan Ass'n v. Blaisdell*[26] are consistent with his inclusive originalism. His efforts to fit these cases into his model reveal a lot about both his inclusive originalism and other New Originalist scholarship.

The Court in *Blaisdell* allowed Minnesota to put a temporary stop on the obligations of mortgagees to comply with the terms of their mortgages despite the Constitution's express prohibition on states passing any "Law impairing the Obligation of Contracts."[27] The Court allowed Minnesota to violate what appears to be the clear meaning of this provision on the basis that the Great Depression caused an emergency. The justices said that although an "emergency does not create power, emergency may furnish the occasion for the exercise of power," and while "an emergency may not call into life a power which has never lived, nevertheless emergency may afford a reason for the exertion of a living power already enjoyed."[28]

After these somewhat arcane suggestions, the Court went on to say that there are two types of constitutional provisions, specific and general. Specific provisions are "so particularized as not to admit of construction," but general ones "afford a broad outline" and the "process of construction is essential to fill in the details. That is true of the contract clause."[29] This language, of course, is similar to the vocabulary used by New Originalists to describe constitutional interpretation. Which constitutional provisions are "specific" so that they do not "admit of construction"? The *Blaisdell* Court said that no emergency would allow "a state to have more than two Senators . . . or permit the States to 'coin money,'" among a few other examples of clear constitutional text.[30]

Professor Baude argues that "there is some reason to believe that Founding-era lawyers would have expected a mortgage moratorium to violate the Contract Clause. But originalism often requires one to read the constitutional text beyond its specific expectations."[31] Although the Court may have mistakenly read the Contracts Clause as "general," not "specific," the justices asked "precisely the kinds of question [sic] about the original meaning of the Contract Clause that . . . originalism ought to embrace."[32] Professor Baude approvingly quotes Professor Thomas Colby (a prominent critic of New Originalism), who said that the reasoning in Blaisdell "actually appears to be a paragon of the New Originalism . . ."[33]

As his analysis of *Blaisdell* demonstrates, Professor Baude's "inclusive originalism" allows Supreme Court justices to ignore clear constitutional commands and well-documented original expectations about

those demands, if modern circumstances so require.[34] This type of constitutional interpretation is no different than the form embraced by living
constitutionalists (and liberals) such as Professors Erwin Chemerinsky
and Laurence Tribe as well as Justices William Brennan and Thurgood
Marshall. The fact that so-called originalists might pause and ask whether
the provision at issue is "specific" or "general" before embarking on their
"construction zone" constitutionalism cannot matter given that "specific"
provisions are almost never litigated, and even when they are, like the
Eleventh Amendment, the justices often give the plain meaning a different
interpretation if policy concerns are important enough.[35] In the case of the
Eleventh Amendment, the justices (including Scalia and Thomas) interpreted state immunity from suit by citizens of "another" state to mean
citizens of the "same" state, despite the clarity of the word *another*.[36]

Professor Baude's analysis also mistakenly assumes that the justices'
answers to hard constitutional questions – such as whether emergencies
can override clear constitutional commands – come *after* they ask their
originalist questions as opposed to *after* a decision about how the case
should be resolved.[37] One does not have to be a core legal realist to think
that Professor Baude's sequencing here is quite unlikely. It is far more
probable that the justices settled on a result and then justified it by labeling
the Contract Clause a general provision that may be constructed as times
and circumstances change. And, once they made that move, the originalist language in the opinion is mere window dressing. Legal realists and
living constitutionalists do not deny that the justices often use the rhetoric
of originalism to create a symbolic (and important) link to the past.[38]
They just deny that the rhetoric drives their decisions.

Professor Baude also argues that *Obergefell v. Hodges*,[39] is an
example of "inclusive originalism." He says that the Court's decision
that the "Fourteenth Amendment required states to license same-sex
marriages . . . seemed to pick the originalist route."[40] As discussed in the
previous chapter, this claim, that gays and lesbians have a constitutionally protected right to marry under an originalist interpretation of the
Fourteenth Amendment, is quite extraordinary given that we know for
certain that virtually no one alive in 1868 would have felt that way.[41]

Professor Baude supports this argument with two points. First,
he maintains that Justice Kennedy's opinion explicitly identified the
Fourteenth Amendment as a constitutional provision setting "forth broad

principles rather than specific requirements," consistent with the "new originalism."[42] Baude argues that the "Fourteenth Amendment's meaning was an anti-discrimination principle that was broader than race and might include sexual orientation ... The thrust of the original meaning argument is that the Fourteenth Amendment ratifiers decided to empower ... the courts to recognize and *invalidate new forms* of discrimination, potentially including this one (bans on same-sex marriage)."[43] For Baude, the judicial recognition that some constitutional provisions allow judges to embrace a decidedly non-originalist method of judicial review is tantamount to originalism "being our law." If he is right, there is no substantial difference between originalism and non-originalism for most litigated cases.

Second, Professor Baude cites the following paragraph from Justice Kennedy's opinion:

> The generations that wrote and ratified the Bill of Rights and the Fourteenth Amendment did not presume to know the extent of freedom in all of its dimensions, and so they entrusted to future generations a charter protecting the right of all persons to enjoy liberty as we learn its meaning. When new insight reveals discord between the Constitution's central protections and a received legal stricture, a claim to liberty must be addressed.[44]

Professor Baude takes Justice Kennedy's rather obvious homage to living constitutionalism and suggests "this sort of living originalism" amounts to the Court asking the right questions and doing "what an inclusive originalist would do."[45] Thus, "even in one of its most potentially anti-originalist moments, the Court ultimately claimed fidelity to the Amendment's original authors."[46]

Professor Baude's explanation for why *Obergefell* is an originalist opinion is unpersuasive because Justice Kennedy is obviously applying living constitutionalism, as he often did. In *Lawrence v. Texas*, for example, an important gay rights case, Justice Kennedy did not try to hide his choice between originalism and the living Constitution. He ended that opinion as follows:

> Had those who drew and ratified the Due Process Clauses of the Fifth Amendment or the Fourteenth Amendment known the components of liberty in its manifold possibilities, they might have

been more specific. They did not presume to have this insight. *They knew times can blind us to certain truths and later generations can see that laws once thought necessary and proper in fact serve only to oppress. As the Constitution endures, persons in every generation can invoke its principles in their own search for greater freedom.* [47]

A clearer choice to reject originalism is hard to imagine. If by "inclusive originalism," Professor Baude means that the Supreme Court may identify vague constitutional provisions, ignore what we know the people who ratified those provisions expected them to mean, and then "construct" the best modern meaning of those provisions, with the only originalist move being to first label the provision "general" and not "specific," then there is no difference between "inclusive originalism" and non-originalist methods. Either these gay rights cases are examples of living constitutionalism, or they are a form of originalism indistinguishable from living constitutionalism. The only other possible explanation is that cases like *Obergefell* and *Lawrence*, where the justices employ modern values to resolve cases, are outliers. Professor Baude does not make that argument (nor could he) considering the Court's long historical practice of using similar living constitutionalism methods of interpretation. [48]

Like most academics discussing constitutional interpretation, Professor Baude tries to fit *Brown v. Board of Education* into his descriptive theory. He concedes that "[i]f *Brown* does repudiate the original meaning of the Fourteenth Amendment, that is a big problem for the positive-law theory of originalism."[49]

Professor Baude begins his analysis by noting that the *Brown* Court held the case over one term and asked the parties to brief questions relating to the history of the Fourteenth Amendment as applied to segregated schools.[50] The Court's request does suggest an originalist analysis. But then, as Professor Baude relates, in its final opinion, the Court specifically said that the history was "inconclusive" and that historical "sources" are not clear enough "to resolve the problem with which we are faced."[51] The Brown Court went on to famously hold, based in part on modern social science reports, that separate schools could not be equal.[52]

Once again, Professor Baude uses the "Court asked the right question" justification to conclude that nothing in *Brown* contradicts originalism's legal status.[53] It is difficult to figure out how a Court that specifically rejected relying on historical sources somehow evidences "inclusive originalism," unless we define "inclusive originalism" to mean "not relying on originalism." To the extent that the justices' *rejection of originalism is consistent with originalism because the framers expected them to reject originalism* in Professor Baude's descriptive account, "originalism" and "not originalism" are the same thing. There is no other choice.

Professor Stephen Griffin once wrote the following about *Brown*:

> [O]ne of the most celebrated Supreme Court decisions in U.S. history, a decision that helped underwrite the legitimacy of the contemporary constitutional order, especially for racial and ethnic minorities, was *deliberately and unanimously* not based on any version of original intent or meaning, despite the clear understanding of the justices that originalism was an option.[54]

As Griffin points out, *Brown* is not the only example of obviously non-originalist judicial decisions:

> The problem for originalism posed by equal protection law goes far beyond *Brown*. The development of vast tributaries of equal protection law owes little to historical or originalist argument. We can examine basic ... precedents concerning school desegregation, interracial marriage and adoption, voting rights, racially disproportionate impact, affirmative action, and gender discrimination without finding any significant use of originalist argument. Equal protection law is a good demonstration of how doctrines can evolve legitimately without recourse to historical argument. This celebrated branch of law thus demonstrates that originalism is not the status quo.[55]

Why is it so important to Professor Baude to label non-originalist decisions originalist? The answer may lie in his uncritical acceptance of New Originalism as a distinct form of constitutional method different from living constitutionalism. What Baude adds to the conversation, however, is taking New Originalism to its logical end through his attempts to bring obviously anti-originalist Court decisions into the originalist fold. As Baude admits, Judge Bork's originalism would not have deemed any of the gay rights cases or most of the cases cited by

Baude acceptable nor would Bork ever have believed that the originalism he was espousing was already "our law."[56] Bork, along with Ed
Meese, Raoul Berger, and others espoused their originalist methodology because they strongly believed "our law" needed to be changed,
not because the Supreme Court was already using originalism.[57]

Although Professor Baude does cite a few cases, like the famous
Second Amendment case *District of Columbia v. Heller*, which he says
evidence a more authentic originalist analysis, he does not suggest
that those kinds of cases, where the justices admittedly devoted
considerable sections of their opinions to ratification-era evidence,
make up a significant portion of "our law."[58] Rather, his argument
depends on the assumption that the legion of Court cases interpreting vague constitutional text in a living constitutional manner are
consistent with his "inclusive originalism."[59] If he is right, there is no
meaningful difference between originalism and living constitutionalism (at least to judges). If he is wrong, then his descriptive account is
inaccurate.

Most legal realists, including this author, agree with Baude's
descriptive account that the Court continually updates its interpretation of unclear constitutional text according to the justices' perspectives on modern conditions and favored consequences. In Chapter 1,
however, we defined an originalist as someone who believes that the
meaning of the constitutional text is fixed at the time of ratification,
that judges should give that meaning a primary role in constitutional
interpretation, and pragmatic modern concerns are not allowed to
trump discoverable original meaning.[60] This definition is well accepted
by both originalists and non-originalists. Moreover, Professor Solum's
definition of originalism, one that is also generally accepted by both
originalist and non-originalist scholars, suggests that all originalists (old
and new) accept that the original meaning or "communicative content" of the constitutional text "is fixed at the time each provision is
framed and ratified," and that "constitutional actors (e.g., judges,
officials, and citizens) ought to be constrained by the original meaning
when they engage in constitutional practice."[61] In contrast, Baude's
inclusive originalism simply requires that the Court ask whether the
text at issue is general or specific. If it is general, his originalism does
not meet the criteria for originalism listed earlier.

Professor Baude seems to have no quarrel with the methods (not necessarily the results) of most of the decisions he uses to explain why "inclusive originalism" is indeed "our law."[62] But these cases all used various methods of constitutional interpretation that go much further than, and sometimes ignore, historical evaluations of the original meaning of constitutional text. These methods include the Justices not only considering prior Court decisions and the text and structure of the US Constitution, but also contemporary consequences.[63] In most of these cases, the justices do not privilege original meaning other than perhaps with a wink and a nod to the relevant text as being "general" not "specific."

What Professor Baude is describing is a pluralistic method of constitutional decision making that sounds a lot like the interpretative theories of such decidedly non-originalist scholars as Phillip Bobbitt, Richard Fallon, Michael Dorf, and Stephen Griffin (there are differences among the theories of these scholars, but they are not significant for the purpose of this point).[64] So why doesn't Professor Baude expressly align his "inclusive originalism" with these pluralistic theories? After all, to the extent that his descriptive account embraces the New Originalism of scholars like Barnett and Whittington, this critique has been made before. As Saul Cornell has written about New Originalism: "For right-wing scholars and judges, new originalism serves as a type of constitutional camouflage. It allows 'conservatives' to create their own living constitution and advance a form of judicial activism, while claiming to be simply engaged in an act of constitutional redemption."[65]

Similarly, and perhaps less pejoratively, but no less accurately, Professor James Fleming summed up in one sentence why New Originalism is not originalism at all: "the inclusiveness of the new originalism shows that it will require the very judgments that proponents of the moral reading have argued are necessary in constitutional interpretation and construction."[66] By the "moral reading," Fleming is referring expressly to Ronald Dworkin, who was not in any material sense an originalist scholar.[67]

A leading constitutional law theorist at one of the nation's elite law schools who teaches a seminar on originalism is advocating a theory of originalism that is quite similar to the work of the liberal, non-originalist

Ronald Dworkin. And he is not the only one. Professor Stephen Sachs, who Baude cites admiringly, believes that originalism is a theory of legal change that reveals that the law (including the Constitution) must stay the same until it is legally amended.[68] In other words, according to Sachs, "[o]ur law is still the Founders' law, as it's been lawfully changed."[69]

He is right. But Sachs also suggests that valid changes may be brought about by judges taking vague constitutional text and constructing modern meanings to address changed circumstances.[70] Is it really an originalist methodology to adapt vague text to contemporary values and developments even when we have a strong idea that the interpretation is not how the ratifiers would have thought about the problem (like the same-sex marriage cases)? Again, this is living constitutionalism disguised as originalism.

Both Professors Baude and Sachs offer interesting descriptive and normative accounts of constitutional decision making. Neither, however, takes original meaning or even history seriously as a constraint or even a significant factor in generating results in litigated cases.[71] If *Brown, Blaisdell,* and *Obergefell* are originalist cases, then the term has lost all meaning.

Why are these scholars so invested in characterizing "our law" as originalist? The answer lies, I think, with a great need or hope among many academics to believe that the justices are doing something other than imposing their personal values, writ large, on the rest of us. Judge Bork did not have that need. He constantly criticized Supreme Court justices for imposing their personal values on reluctant majorities unrelated to any relevant law.[72] Michael McConnell, another Original Originalist, also thought that the sin of non-originalist methods of constitutional interpretation lay in the unlawfulness of judges mistaking their personal values for legal values.[73] These scholars and judges saw constitutional law as practiced on the ground by the Supreme Court for what it is; an all-things-considered approach based primarily on the justices' values writ large. They offered a solution: strict adherence to original meaning along with a strong presumption in favor of legislation, and a large dose of judicial modesty.

Professor Baude does not advocate strict adherence to original meaning or strong deference to the elected branches. Yet, he must account for society-changing decisions such as *Brown, Obergefell,* and *Heller,* without simply conceding the legal realist critique that values not text and history drive Supreme Court decision. It appears Professors Baude and Sachs need to maintain the faith that judging, especially the form of judging embodied by front page, landmark decisions, is separate from ordinary politics. For them, constitutional decision making must remain special, otherwise their faith in constitutional law will be shaken. They are resisting the antitheory and antiformalism of the Legal Realists of the 1930s, the Critical Legal Scholars of the 1980s, Judge Richard Posner,[74] and this author,[75] among many others.

Professors Baude and Sachs have combined theory with antitheory. A doctrine of "inclusive originalism" that allows for significant "judicial construction," or a theory of constitutional change that allows meaning to evolve with changed facts, can be used by scholars to justify virtually every aggressive act of judicial review of the last two hundred years. But they also argue that justices aren't simply applying their own values and perspectives; they are originalists doing what the Founding Fathers would have wanted them to do all along. "Our law" is their law, and what Bork would have called judicial activism is to Baude and Sachs fidelity to the Constitution. This is "originalism" for everyone, and for every purpose. In other words, it is not "originalism" at all.

B. ORIGINAL METHODS ORIGINALISM

Unlike Professors Baude and Sachs, and other New Originalists, Professors John McGinnis and Michael Rappaport have recently advocated a form of originalism that places primary emphasis on historical understandings and originalist sources. Their book, *Originalism and the Good Constitution,*[76] adds a new and important form of originalism to those advocated by the Original Originalists and the New Originalists.

On the first page of their book, McGinnis and Rappaport distance themselves from New Originalists like Professors Baude, Balkin, Barnett, and Sachs by asking how "can an originalist jurisprudence address the *hundreds of judicial decisions* inconsistent with original meaning that are now deemed the law of the land?"[77] The authors

criticize the New Originalist "construction zone" method on the basis
that it "significantly reduces the scope of originalism" and might even
"largely collapse originalism into living constitutionalism."[78] They
even concede that "contemporary originalism . . . has substantial meth-
odological controversies at its heart."[79]

McGinnis and Rappaport's "Good Constitution" Originalism is
based on the argument that originalism "advances the welfare of the
present-day citizens of the United States because it promotes constitutional interpretations that are likely to have better consequences
today than those of non-originalist theories."[80] The original Constitution and its Amendments were adopted through "stringent supermajority rules [that] are likely . . . to generate good constitutional
provisions. Thus, the beneficence of the Constitution is connected to
the super-majoritarian process from which it arose . . . Consequently,
the results generated by originalism are likely to be beneficial."[81] In
other words, the understandings of the people at the time of the
ratification of the Constitution should govern us today because ratification required far more consensus and agreement than ordinary
legislation.

The authors sum up their arguments as follows:

> First, desirable constitutional provisions (or as we also call them,
> entrenched laws) should take priority over ordinary legislation
> because such entrenchments establish a structure of government
> that preserves democratic decision making, individual rights, and
> other beneficial goals. Second, appropriate supermajority rules are
> a sound method of producing legitimate and desirable entrench-
> ments and no superior method is available. Third, the Constitution
> and its amendments have been passed in the main under appropri-
> ate supermajority rules, and thus the norms entrenched in the
> Constitution tend to be desirable.[82]

McGinnis and Rappaport argue that our society can reap the
benefits of this super-majoritarian process *only* if judges embrace
originalism as the exclusive method of constitutional interpretation
(unless well-established and important prior cases require adherence as
a matter of stare decisis). Originalism is the only method of interpretation
that "captures the meaning that passed through the super-majoritarian
process."[83] When judges update or change what the Constitution

originally meant, not only are the benefits of the super-majoritarian process lost, but also the people will cease to use the Article V amendment process to alter the Constitution's meaning, losing the most effective mechanism for making major changes to ourselves and our country. Moreover, judicial correction of the Constitution is much less stable than using the Article 5 process.

To support this argument, the authors blame the Supreme Court's living constitution "correction" approach to gender discrimination for the failure of the states to pass the Equal Rights Amendment in the 1970s.[84] They argue that by the time the ERA was being considered by many states, legislators rationally believed (1) that the amendment was no longer necessary because of the Court's anti-originalist gender-discrimination decisions, but also (2) the Amendment would be subject to that same approach leading to bad results like courts mandating same-sex bathrooms.[85] The authors conclude that "had the Court not already updated the Constitution and had it been clear that the amendment would not be creatively interpreted, it is likely the Equal Rights Amendment would have been enacted."[86] The authors may be right (though I doubt it), but it seems an odd example to use as the Court's decisions protecting women from gender discrimination have been relatively stable now for almost forty years, and those protections are quite unlikely to prove erratic ever again.

Perhaps the major contribution made by *The Good Constitution* is its insistence that an indispensable part of the original meaning of the Constitution is the "original interpretative methods" that were used during the ratification era. Using the "enactors' interpretative methods ensures that the provisions have the meaning that the enactors expected and thereby reflects the costs and benefits of the provisions that the enactors would have calculated."[87] In the words of one reviewer as well as the authors, if "the 'supermajority' that ratified the Constitution 'employed those interpretive rules, then giving effect to the document they approved requires using those same rules.' The interpretive rules are thus as much a part of the Constitution as the original text."[88]

Although the authors spend some time on what these interpretative methods were, there is surprisingly little discussion in the book how such methods or rules of interpretation should be applied by judges faced with difficult constitutional questions. Throughout the book, the authors claim that these original methods will reduce the vagueness and imprecision of much of the constitutional text, but nowhere do they show how that would work in practice. Their project suffers from the absence of applying theory to facts because simply alleging that originalist rules and methods will make the judicial case deciding function easier, without showing how that is true, makes their claim hard to evaluate.

Some critics of *The Good Constitution* have taken the authors to task for failing to identify with more precision what constitutes the "good society" they claim is furthered by strict adherence to originalist methods and originalist interpretation.[89] The authors adopt a theory of "welfare consequentialism" to argue that clear, stable rules are better for a good society than more ad hoc, cost-benefit analysis, and that originalism will produce such stability better than other interpretative methods. Although these assertions are indeed quite controversial,[90] for our purposes it is their claim that originalism produces the best results in constitutional cases that is most relevant.

There are several problems with McGinnis's and Rappaport's defense of Original Methods Originalism. First, the authors concede that the exclusion of people of color and women from both the ratification of the original Constitution and the Reconstruction Amendments are serious flaws in the super-majoritarian processes. However, they claim that those flaws have "largely been rectified" by the constitutional amendments giving women and African Americans the right to vote, and by the Thirteenth and Fourteenth Amendments abolishing slavery and prohibiting the states from denying anyone the equal protection of the laws.[91] The authors acknowledge that state required segregation and racial apartheid lasted long after the Reconstruction Amendments but blame those evils on what they allege are non-originalist Court decisions like *Plessy v. Ferguson*, which upheld segregated trains in Louisiana. If only the Court had enforced the original meaning of the Reconstruction Amendments, that super-majoritarian process would have done its job.[92]

The authors' arguments concerning the exclusion of well over half the population from the original and Reconstruction ratification processes is unsatisfactory. As legal scholar Kurt Lash has pointed out, the authors assume what are quite "disputed assertions about the original meaning of the Fourteenth Amendment ... McGinnis and Rappaport blame ... *Plessy v. Ferguson* for failing to recognize that the Privileges or Immunities Clause protected equal, if unenumerated, rights of contract. The Supreme Court's decision in *Plessy* to uphold racial segregation, of course, is not generally criticized because it failed to enforce fundamental economic rights. Nor is there anything approaching a scholarly consensus about the original meaning of the Privileges or Immunities Clause of the Fourteenth Amendment."[93]

The majority view, in fact, is that it was the Court's decision in *Brown* that reversed *Plessy*, not *Plessy* itself that got original meaning wrong.[94] If it is true that the most accurate original meaning of the Reconstruction Amendments would have allowed segregated schools, as Raoul Berger and others have argued, it is unlikely we could call that super-majoritarian process superior to the judicial correction in *Brown* that finally secured formal equality for African Americans.

As to both people of color and women, McGinnis and Rappaport argue that they have had the right to vote for a long time, and it is unlikely that the Constitution would look significantly different had they been included in those ratification processes.[95] The authors claim that we don't know whether affirmative action or abortion, for example, would have been secured by the Constitution even had women and people of color not been excluded from participating in the ratification process.

This argument is strained at best. The authors support originalism on the basis that the super-majoritarian ratification process produces better results than ordinary legislation, and therefore both the substance and methods used in 1787 and 1868 should be used by judges today. This hypothesis is interesting and may even be right when the ratification conditions are optimal. But the thesis ignores the fact that in this country the ratification norms and procedures were adopted entirely by white men. The counterfactual argument that nothing of significance would have changed if over half the population had not been excluded cannot make up for the reality that the experiences and values of people of color and women were completely absent from the process. To take just one of an infinite number of possible examples, the original Constitution's protections for private property might have been significantly watered down had the people who couldn't own such property been included. In any event, imagine the reaction from people today if the authors suggested that a process for constitutional amendment that excluded all women and all African Americans would not result in different outcomes than one that doesn't exclude those groups. The reality is that the authors are claiming that the values of less than half the people living in two extraordinary periods of American history should be privileged over the values of all the people today.

Even if we assume, as the authors argue, that the super-majoritarian ratification processes did produce beneficial provisions, for their second argument to succeed, they must show that it is possible to discover and apply the interpretative methods the ratifiers expected judges to employ. This is not an easy task. What methods would the framers have used to determine whether lethal injections, which sometimes fail to act quickly, are cruel and unusual punishments; or whether public colleges can use limited racial preferences to make up for our racist past; or whether the commandeer-in-chief power in Article II allows the president, without any prior judicial approval or due process, to execute an American citizen who is an alleged terrorist while he is eating lunch in Yemen? Whatever the answers to these questions, you won't find them anywhere in *The Good Constitution*. The book's largest failing is its refusal to apply its suggested originalist methods theory to contemporary constitutional disputes.

There may be a good reason why the book fails to apply its recommendations to real cases. The people living in 1787 and in 1868 did not agree about how to interpret the open-ended text that they enacted. Scholars such as Jack Balkin have made compelling arguments that the framers would have expected the broad aspirational provisions of the Constitution, such as the First and Fourth Amendments, to be interpreted by judges with an eye toward modern conditions and consequences.[96] If those arguments are true, then the originalism arguments put forth by McGinnis and Rappaport are not only inherently contradictory, but they also would support the living originalism and constitutional construction theories the authors so strongly reject.

The framers and ratifiers in 1787 were not of one mind when it came to how they expected future judges to apply and enforce the brand-new Constitution. That uncertainty undercuts the authors' argument that "the reader of the US Constitution would recognize that its meaning depends on interpretive rules that were generally deemed applicable to written constitutions of this type."[97] As Professor Lash pointed out, "there were no other written constitutions of 'this type.' The very idea of a written judicially enforceable constitution was something new under the sun in post-Revolutionary America."[98] Lash described in his review of *The Good Constitution* many of the uncertain questions the framers had concerning the new document such as which legal rules would apply to its interpretation, how much, if any, the experiences under state constitutions would matter, and whether the old debates about statutory interpretation, such as the differences between intentional and strict construction approaches, would reproduce themselves when constitutional provisions led to litigation.[99] Lash concluded that what McGinnis and Rappaport "fail to recognize ... is that the proper methods of constitutional interpretation were not only under-resolved at the time of the Founding, they were the subject of heated and on-going debate ... Different founders proposed different methods of constitutional construction ... This dispute cannot be resolved by ... interpretive methodology ... it requires the application of normative theory. This is not the result of a temporary gap in our historical knowledge. It is history itself that tells us that originalism cannot go all the way down."[100]

McGinnis's and Rappaport's *The Good Constitution* fails to persuade mostly because it cannot make a strong historical case that the framers and ratifiers themselves would have privileged originalism as a primary interpretative method and because, as a normative matter, America in both 1787 and 1868 was a racist, sexist society promoting some fundamental values that are largely rejected by people living today. This disconnect, between the world of the founders and our world today, may explain why even those contemporary justices who self-identify as originalists have failed to consistently vote in an originalist manner. As the next chapter shows, the most persuasive evidence that originalism does not and cannot work as an interpretative theory (absent a strong clear error rule) is that originalism has in fact never consistently worked in practice as an interpretative theory.

7 THE NON-ORIGINALISM OF JUSTICES SCALIA AND THOMAS

Thomas will use originalism where it provides support for a politically conservative result, even if that support is weak... But where history provides no support, he's likely to ignore it altogether.

Doug Kendall and Jim Ryan[1]

I would conclude from his Taft Lecture and his behavior on the Court that Justice Scalia is simply not an originalist.

Randy Barnett[2]

Chapter 3 summarized a series of law review articles written by Professor Jacob tenBroek, who argued that as of his writing (1939), the justices' personal values and life experiences, not fidelity to text or ratification-era evidence, drove Supreme Court decisions.[3] He supported his descriptive account in a five-part series that described how often the Court issued decisions irreconcilable with constitutional text and history. For the next few decades, there was little substantial academic debate about the relationship between originalism and constitutional decision making. As Professor Jamal Greene has observed, "originalism remained firmly on the margins of constitutional law for [these] ... decades."[4]

After the Warren Court's aggressive liberal activism, however, came a renewed scholarly and judicial interest in using a rigorous text and originalist approach to cabin judicial discretion. Chapter 4 recounted the work of Judge Bork, Professor Raoul Berger, and others, who ignited what is today's much broader originalism debate. Even with the spread of originalism throughout the legal academy, the political world, and the citizenry, however, there has never been a modern Supreme Court Justice who voted consistently in an originalist manner.

The two justices (before Neil Gorsuch) who consistently self-identified as originalist, and who advocated for the doctrine on and off the Court, are Antonin Scalia and Clarence Thomas.[5] A careful examination of their voting records and opinions, however, demonstrates that neither Justice practiced what they preached. This failure is emblematic of how impractical and unworkable originalism is as a method of constitutional interpretation unless it is attached to a strong presumption of validity for state and federal laws – a presumption neither justice consistently applied.[6]

Although Justices Scalia and Thomas both claimed the mantle of originalist,[7] their ideologies have nuanced differences such as their use of precedent, tradition, and what evidence counts toward original meaning. However, both justices, in their opinions and in their off-the-Court writings, argued that judges should leave their personal values out of constitutional interpretation and only overturn the decisions of more accountable political officials when required to by text or history.[8] For example, Justice Thomas has said that a judge must try hard to push away his "racial, social, or religious background" when interpreting the Constitution and that a judge "must become almost pure, in the way that fire purifies metal, before he can decide a case. Otherwise, he is not a judge, but a legislator, for whom it is entirely appropriate to consider personal and group interests."[9]

Similarly, Justice Scalia has on many occasions argued that a judge's only job in constitutional cases is to interpret text and original meaning and not to consider policy, consequences, or a judge's own values.[10] For example, during the oral argument in one of the Court's landmark Second Amendment cases, Scalia suggested that it is the legislature's job to study gun control statistics and policies, but a judge should only be concerned with text and history.[11] Before his death, Scalia routinely toured the country giving talks where he loudly exclaimed that the Constitution is "Dead, Dead, Dead, Dead."[12] During these speeches, he also explicitly criticized living constitutionalism identifying himself as an originalist who "adheres to the text of the Constitution, but – more importantly – gives the text the meaning that it had when the American people adopted it."[13]

Despite these many claims rejecting anything but a textualist and originalist approach to constitutional interpretation, Scalia's and Thomas's jurisprudence, together and alone, is replete with aggressive acts of judicial review that they did not justify by reference to the

Constitution's text or its original meaning. It would take a stand-alone book to discuss the many examples where Scalia and Thomas rather obviously veered from their alleged disdain for the "living Constitution," but the following cases are representative and reflect broad and important swaths of constitutional law where these two justices prevented elected officials from implementing important legislative objectives. First, I broadly summarize those areas of law and then discuss why each one reflects "living constitutionalism" much more than originalism.

Justice Thomas wrote a concurring opinion in the Court's most recent campaign finance case arguing that virtually all laws limiting the spending of money on or for political campaigns are unconstitutional under the First Amendment.[14] Although Justice Scalia did not join that particular opinion, with the exception of disclosure requirements, Scalia has voted to strike down every campaign finance law that he has been called upon to review while sitting on the Court.[15]

Both justices have said they would prohibit Congress, the president, and every level of state and local government from employing any and all racial preferences.[16] Both justices would also prevent Congress from using state governments to help implement federal laws enacted pursuant to Congress's enumerated powers, and they would stop most plaintiffs from suing any state for money damages because of the doctrine of sovereign immunity.[17] In none of these examples, and a few others discussed in this chapter, where the justices voted to significantly alter the ways both federal and state governments are allowed to conduct their business, did either justice make persuasive arguments from either text or original meaning.

Before discussing these examples specifically, one argument that has previously been made by scholars responding to my work on Justices Scalia and Thomas must be addressed. Some originalists have argued in many of the areas of law where Scalia and Thomas voted in what appear to be a non-originalist manner, there are plausible, even if not persuasive, originalist arguments in support of their votes (arguments excavated by extremely motivated law professors, not the justices).[18] Even if there are persuasive arguments as to some of the non-originalist doctrines I identify, which I doubt, such speculations were not used by the justices and, more important, are unavailable to

Scalia and Thomas, who have argued that life-tenured federal judges should not invalidate decisions by other political actors absent clear constitutional text or strong historical evidence. For New Originalists like Randy Barnett and Ilya Somin, who openly admit that they believe in strong judicial review by what Scalia called "a committee of nine unelected lawyers,"[19] maybe reasonable historical evidence is enough to sustain aggressive judicial review. But neither Scalia nor Thomas ever argued for that position. Instead, in most of the areas of law discussed here, they simply ignored or mischaracterized originalist-era evidence while often stridently and hypocritically accusing other Justices of playing fast and loose with the rules of the constitutional game. In short, although the results in some of these cases might be justified by originalist theories advanced by dedicated and creative law professors, those arguments did not appear in the opinions, and there is no evidence that either Justice Scalia or Thomas were aware of them. In other words, I take the opinions as they were written, not as they might be re-imagined by originalist scholars.

A. CAMPAIGN FINANCE REFORM

Justices Scalia and Thomas, concluding that spending money on political campaigns is core political speech, consistently voted to strike down state and federal laws regulating the effects of money on our election system.[20] They also argued that corporations have the same speech rights as individuals to spend money on elections.[21] Neither justice, however, made a serious effort to harmonize these strong exercises of judicial review with the text or original meaning of the First Amendment. As many scholars have argued, even if spending money is the equivalent of speech, it is highly unlikely that the Founding Fathers would have privileged the corporate right to free speech over the government's compelling interests in fair elections and fighting corruption to prohibit reasonable campaign finance reform.[22] In any event, neither Scalia nor Thomas tried to justify the Court's hostility to campaign finance laws with historical evidence.

In Justice Stevens' dissent in the landmark *Citizens United* decision, he said that the "[t]he Framers thus took it as given that corporations could be comprehensively regulated in the public welfare."[23] In response, Justice Scalia briefly attempted to show that the Founding Fathers *might* have deemed corporations to have free speech rights (leaving the issue of balancing aside), though he also concluded that, even if the framers did not hold that belief, corporations play a different role today than in yesteryear.[24] This is a clear example of the living Constitution approach. If changes in the legal significance of the corporate form can result in legal outcomes the framers would not have accepted, why isn't the same true for other societal and cultural changes such as our fundamental views concerning the roles of women and minority groups in our democracy, the methods of carrying out the death penalty, or the increased acceptance by many of same-sex marriage. As one scholar noted, Scalia "repeatedly relied on constitutional protection for the media in arguing that the Constitution gives the same rights to corporations and the people, ignoring that the press was the only private business given explicit constitutional protection in the Constitution. Justice Scalia even goes so far as to suggest that the framers would have liked modern corporations if they only they had the chance to see them in action. Those who take constitutional text and history seriously should be appalled that this is what passes for legitimate argument by the leading originalist on the Court."[25]

In *McCutcheon v. FEC*,[26] Justice Thomas repeated his familiar refrain that the Founding Fathers viewed political speech as vitally important needing special protection under the First Amendment. Fair enough, but that determination tells us nothing about whether the people alive in 1791 would have equated the sending of a campaign check to a politician (the facts of *McCutcheon*) as the equivalent of constitutionally protected political speech. Of course, even if writing a check is the equivalent of political speech pursuant to the original meaning of the First Amendment, the question remains whether such speech can be regulated to further the vital governmental interest in preventing corruption. Neither justice has ever addressed that key issue as a historical matter, though Professor Lawrence Lessig has and concluded that the framers' view of corruption would have been broad enough to justify most campaign finance laws.[27]

Striking down state and federal campaign finance laws has significant effects on our representative democracy. Yet, neither Scalia nor

Thomas provided significant historical analysis of the issue. This failure stands in stark contrast to their harsh critiques of other justices, who they claimed ignored text and original meaning in other cases, such as the Court's abortion and same-sex marriage decisions, where Scalia and Thomas argued passionately against judges finding new (living) principles to limit legislative choices.[28]

B. AFFIRMATIVE ACTION

Adopting a firm "color-blind" interpretation of the Equal Protection clause of the Fourteenth Amendment, which in its text says nothing about race, Justices Scalia and Thomas voted against every affirmative action program they ever reviewed. Both justices argued that the Fourteenth Amendment prohibits state and federal governments, as well as all public universities, from using any racial criteria or preferences to remedy the formalized, legal racial discrimination (slavery and segregation) that plagued our country for most of its history.[29] Neither justice has ever shown, or tried to show, that the original meaning of that Amendment justifies such a far-reaching legal conclusion.[30]

The Fourteenth Amendment prohibits the government from denying to any person the "equal protection of the laws." It is plausible for judges to read the text to prohibit all racial preferences, even those designed to foster racial equality and diversity. However, it is at least equally plausible to read the text to justify the government's use of limited race-based remedies to further the equality promised by the Fourteenth Amendment but sabotaged by almost 100 years of segregation, Jim Crow, and other governmental programs designed for the express purpose of denying equality to African Americans (such as the federal government backing billions of dollars of private mortgages from the 1940s to the early 1960s with well over 90 percent of the money going to white families).[31]

The use of legacy admissions by state universities is constitutional but largely benefits whites because of historical discrimination. If universities routinely take alumni status into account, why can't they also use limited racial preferences to build a diverse class? The Fourteenth

Amendment's text, by itself, simply cannot resolve the difficult issues surrounding affirmative action when race-based measures are enacted to prevent the kind of caste-based society that the Amendment was intended to abolish.

Because the text of the Equal Protection clause does not resolve the issue of race-based preferences, both Justices Scalia and Thomas would normally say a judge should turn to the original meaning of that amendment. The original meaning of the amendment, however, does not come close to justifying a strict color-blind rule. When it was ratified, the drafters of the amendment were aware that schools in the District of Columbia were officially segregated.[32] There were also federal laws providing important benefits to blacks and only blacks.[33] Although this historical context might not conclusively justify today's affirmative action programs, it quite obviously does not preclude such programs. A sincere originalist, desiring to strike down limited racial preferences designed by the government to benefit traditionally disadvantaged minorities, would have to wrestle with these historical facts.

Instead, neither Justice Scalia nor Justice Thomas ever addressed this specific history or even the original meaning of the Fourteenth Amendment as applied to limited racial preferences. Moreover, not long after the Amendment was ratified, the Supreme Court embraced an interpretation of "equal" that was as far from color blind as possible when in *Plessy v. Ferguson*, it upheld a Louisiana law (7–1) requiring the separation of the races on public transportation.[34] Although Scalia and Thomas would likely argue that *Plessy* was wrong, there is a huge gap between interpreting the Fourteenth Amendment to prohibit racial apartheid and construing it to include a rigid color-blind principle forbidding any and all uses of race to make up for centuries of injustice. Most scholars who have examined the original meaning of the Four- teenth Amendment have concluded that it does not preclude affirma- tive action programs.[35]

The only real history either Justice Thomas or Scalia ever discussed in their affirmative action opinions came in Thomas's dissenting opinion in *Grutter v. Bollinger*.[36] In that opinion, Thomas discussed the views of Frederick Douglass, a famous abolitionist. The problem (in addition to the fact that Douglass's remarks came after ratification) is that Justice Thomas misrepresented Douglass's views. Thomas quoted Douglass as follows:

> In regard to the colored people, there is always more that is benevolent, I perceive, than just, manifested towards us. What I ask for the negro is not benevolence, not pity, not sympathy, but simply justice. The American people have always been anxious to know what they shall do with us ... I have had but one answer from the beginning. Do nothing with us! Your doing with us has already played the mischief with us. Do nothing with us![37]

Justice Thomas argued, based on this quote, that Douglass would have opposed racial preferences and just wanted formal equality for all Americans regardless of race (which is conveniently Justice Thomas's view). The problem is that Thomas took Douglass's words out of context, omitted relevant parts of the quote he relied on for his color-blind argument, and failed to review much of Douglass's life work, some of which strongly leads to the opposite conclusion about affirmative action than the one asserted by Justice Thomas.

Justice Thomas left out from the preceding quoted language the next part of Douglass's speech:

> If you see him (a black person) on his way to school, let him alone, don't disturb him! If you see him going to the dinner table at a hotel, let him go! If you see him going to the ballot box, let him alone, don't disturb him! If you see him going into a work-shop, just let him alone, – your interference is doing him positive injury.[38]

Douglass was obviously angry at the racial discrimination faced by black citizens at the time he was writing, not making any argument for or against government preferences to make their lives easier. More important, at other times in his life and in other speeches, Douglass clearly felt that the government had not done nearly enough for the newly freed slaves. In 1875, he said the following:

> [T]he world has never seen any people turned loose to such destitution as were the four million slaves of the South. ... They were ... free to hunger, free to the winds and the rains ... free without bread to eat, or land to cultivate. ... We gave them freedom and famine at the same time. The marvel is that they still live. What the negro wants is, first, protection of the rights already conceded by

law and, secondly, education. Talk of having done enough for these people after two hundred years of enforced ignorance and stripes is absurd, cruel, and heartless.[39]

Frederick Douglass gave many public speeches on different aspects of the plight of the freed slaves, and it is difficult, if not impossible, to know how he, or anyone else living at the time, would have felt about racial preferences today. What we do know is that the original meaning of the Fourteenth Amendment, to the extent that it is relevant to affirmative action, does not preclude such programs.

Given the national importance of this issue, and the many statements by Justices Scalia and Thomas that judges should not impose their personal policy preferences on the rest of us, they should have provided a persuasive historical justification for the invalidation of all racial preferences and tried to rebut the evidence many scholars have put forward concerning affirmative action programs used by the federal government at the time of the adoption of the Fourteenth Amendment. But they simply never addressed these arguments.[40]

C. COMMANDEERING

The Tenth Amendment to the Constitution provides that the federal government is limited to those powers that are specifically enumerated in the Constitution, and all remaining powers are reserved to the states or the people.[41] Even when the national government exercises one of its powers, such as the Commerce Clause, it is of course limited by other parts of the Constitution's text. Thus, pursuant to its power to regulate "commerce among the states," Congress could regulate shipping newspapers across state lines for profit, but the First Amendment would render unconstitutional a law favoring liberal newspapers over conservative newspapers. Assuming no other textual constitutional limitation applies, however, federal laws enacted pursuant to an enumerated power are the supreme law of the land under Article VI's Supremacy Clause.[42]

In 1936, California sued the federal government arguing that its operation of a state railroad could not be regulated by Congress because it would interfere with and impede state sovereignty. In a unanimous and short opinion, the Court rejected this argument as being inconsistent with the clear text of the Constitution.[43] Justice Stone said that the "sovereign power of the states is necessarily diminished to the extent of the grants of power to the federal government in the Constitution. The power of a state to fix intrastate railroad rates must yield to the power of the national government when their regulation is appropriate to the regulation of interstate commerce."[44] In other words, if Congress passes a valid law under the commerce clause, the states have no right to object on the grounds of state immunity.

The ruling in *United States v. California* remained the law of the land until 1976 when the Court ruled in *National League of Cities v. Usery*,[45] that Congress did not have the power to regulate a state's traditional governmental functions even when Congress was exercising an enumerated power. There is not a sentence in the entire opinion, however, concerning the original meaning of the Constitution. *Usery* was highly controversial both because it reversed a long-standing decision, and it seemed inconsistent with the clear texts of the Tenth Amendment and the Supremacy Clause.

Just a few years later, in *Garcia v. San Antonio Transit Authority*,[46] the Court explicitly reversed *Usery*. In clear language, the Court rejected the idea that principles of state sovereignty trump Congress's enumerated powers. Justice Blackmun quoted James Madison, who said that "[i]nterference with the power of the States was no constitutional criterion for the power of Congress. If the power was not given, Congress could not exercise it; if given, they might exercise it, although it should interfere with the laws, or even the Constitution of the States."[47]

Garcia, however, would not be the Court's last word on the subject. After Justice Thomas replaced Justice Marshall in 1991, and the Court had a new conservative majority, it reversed course once again. In two cases, the Court held that when Congress exercises enumerated powers under Article I, it may not require states to assist in the implementation of federal law.[48] In the first case, *New York v. United States*, Justice O'Connor presented a general overview of what the framers thought about federal and state powers but did not refer to any specific evidence helpful to this question. Instead, her opinion simply assumed that there was a rule against commandeering as a matter of constitutional structure, implicit deductions from general historical sources, and her policy preferences concerning the appropriate state-federal balance.

In the second case, *Printz v. United States*, after saying that that "there is no constitutional text speaking to this precise question,"[49] Justice Scalia did turn to specific historical materials relevant to the question of whether Congress had the authority to commandeer the states pursuant to its enumerated powers. Any objective review of those materials, however, leads to the conclusion Scalia did not favor – that Congress could, when exercising its enumerated powers, require the states to help implement federal laws.

As the dissent in *Printz* pointed out, Alexander Hamilton addressed the commandeering issue directly in the Federalist papers and wrote that "the legislatures, courts, and magistrates, of the respective members, will be incorporated into the operations of the national government as far as its just and constitutional authority extends; and will be rendered auxiliary to the enforcement of its laws."[50] Scalia's response to this piece of historical evidence was singularly unpersuasive. He suggested that if this quote meant what it seems to say about the commandeering issue, then states would have to help implement federal laws even when not asked, an absurd result.[51] No one, however, not the federal government nor the dissenting Justices nor any scholar, made that absurd, antitextual argument. Scalia's response to this clear historical approval of the government's power to commandeer the states was simply an irrelevant ipse dixit.

Scalia also suggested that Hamilton's rule would be inconsistent with the Court's holding in *New York v. United States*, a truly circular argument given that many believe *New York* was wrongly decided. Justice Stevens was far more persuasive when he pointed out, "it is hard to imagine a more unequivocal statement that state judicial and executive branch officials may be required to implement federal law where the National Government acts within the scope of its affirmative powers."[52] This one statement by Hamilton, of course, does not resolve the issue, but it is the most relevant history on point and should have shifted the burden of proof to those justices who reached the contrary conclusion, at least for those judges who profess to abide by the dictates of originalism. Moreover, as the Supreme Court pointed out almost fifty years earlier, the structure and text of the Constitution both indicate that the states gave up their sovereignty when they ratified the Constitution to the extent they gave Congress enumerated powers.[53]

Justices Scalia and Thomas might believe that federalism policy is best served by their anticommandeering rule, but despite three Supreme Court cases on the subject during their tenure, neither justice presented a shred of persuasive historical evidence that contradicts the clear meaning of the Tenth Amendment and the Supremacy Clause that, when Congress exercises its enumerated powers, its authority is supreme unless contradicted by another textual limitation. In other words, even if these anticommandeering holdings are the best normative rule governing the relationship between state and federal power, as several other conservative justices also believed, it is a living constitutionalism rule with no basis in text or original meaning.

D. THE ELEVENTH AMENDMENT

There is no better example of how Justices Scalia and Thomas ignored clear text and relevant history when it suited their policy preferences than their interpretations of the Eleventh Amendment, which says the following: "The Judicial power of the United States shall not be construed to extend to any suit in law or equity, commenced or prosecuted against one of the United States by Citizens of *another* State, or by Citizens or Subjects of any Foreign State."[54]

The Eleventh Amendment by its clear terms bars any suit, whether for damages or an injunction, against a state by citizens of "another" state. Both Justices Scalia and Thomas, however, have interpreted this language to bar lawsuits by citizens of a state against their home state.[55] They have taken the word *another* and twisted it to mean "the same." They engaged in this fancy word play despite the beliefs of four dissenting justices,[56] and the views of most scholars,[57] that the Amendment only bars suits against states by citizens of a different state, consistent with the clear text.

Justice Thomas has never written an opinion explaining his views on how the word *another* can mean "the same."[58] In Justice Scalia's only discussion of this issue, he relies not on the original meaning of the Eleventh Amendment to support his bizarre reading, but instead on *Hans v. Louisiana*,[59] a case decided by the Supreme Court in 1890 (ninety-five years after the amendment was ratified), which adopted that strained reading of the Eleventh Amendment with little analysis. Of course, Justice Scalia did not allow stare decisis concerns to block other votes he made to overturn important precedents in such diverse areas as affirmative action, abortion, and commandeering, nor did he ever explain why sometimes he felt bound by precedent and other times he felt free to discard it.

The only justice (Souter) who ever embarked on a detailed analysis of the original meaning of the text of the Eleventh Amendment, and the reasons why *Hans* decided the case in the countertextual way it did, persuasively demonstrated that there is no evidence that the people who ratified the Eleventh Amendment would have interpreted it to block federal question lawsuits against states brought by citizens of those states.[60] Souter argued that the framers would never have associated the doctrine of sovereign immunity with federal question lawsuits against the states because in such cases, the federal government, not the states, is the "sovereign."

Neither Scalia nor Thomas ever responded to Justice Souter's treatise-like discussion of this issue, nor did they put forward persuasive evidence suggesting the Eleventh Amendment was intended only as one form of sovereign immunity (among other nontextual preconstitutional principles) protecting the states from lawsuits. The Eleventh Amendment is an example of the reality of Justice Scalia's decision making as captured by one Court commentator: "in cases where historical evidence might be inconsistent with his cherished political views, Scalia would simply ignore it."[61]

When justices who say they are committed to text and original meaning change the definition of a clear word like another to mean "the same," affecting numerous civil rights statutes and other federal laws making it much more difficult for Congress to hold states accountable in federal court for violations of federal law, the burden of proof surely is on those justices to justify their departure from their own doctrinal philosophy – a burden they have not met. Maybe our country is better off if states cannot be sued by their own citizens for money damages in federal court, just as maybe the anticommandeering rule adopted in *New York* and *Printz* may strike the proper balance between state and federal powers, but the justifications for these limitations on congressional power must be based on policy concerns, not on text or original meaning. For Justices Scalia and Thomas, as is true for all Supreme Court justices, these policy concerns should be fair game when trying to apply the majestic phrases in the Constitution to modern problems. What is not fair, however, is for these justices to sternly lecture us (and other justices), about the importance of adhering to text and original meaning when they, whenever they deem it important enough, also stray from those principles.

E. STANDING

Both Justice Scalia and Justice Thomas have taken an extremely strong view of Article III's requirement that the federal judicial power only extends to a "case" or a "controversy." There is no debate that advisory opinions fall outside the federal judicial power as both a textual and historical matter. In other words, federal courts require two adversarial parties before they will hear a case. Scalia and Thomas, however, have also dogmatically insisted that every plaintiff in every federal case must allege a unique personal injury.[62] This requirement keeps many public interest actions (suits brought by nonprofit organizations to broadly reform allegedly illegal practices) out of federal court.

Justice Scalia has defended the personal injury requirement on a policy basis (it furthers the separation of powers) without ever trying to ascertain Article III's original meaning.[63] If he did, he would discover that "strangers to the court" were allowed at common law, and there is little evidence the framers intended to alter that practice.[64] This conclusion that personal injury is not a constitutional requirement imposed by Article III was embraced by no less an originalist than Raoul Berger in his seminal article, "Standing to Sue in Public Actions: Is It a Constitutional Requirement?"[65] Moreover, Justice Harlan, no liberal, reached the identical conclusion in his dissenting opinion in *Flast v. Cohen*.[66]

Justices Scalia and Thomas never tried to establish that so-called
"public actions" brought to vindicate the public interest are barred by
Article III's original meaning. In such cases, there are usually adverse
parties disagreeing over governmental decisions, which allegedly have
negative effects on real people. Those disputes literally satisfy the case
or controversy requirement. Yet, both Scalia and Thomas have consistently used a nontextual, nonhistorical personal injury requirement
to close the courthouse doors to these lawsuits challenging governmental policies. This standing doctrine may further the separation of
powers and be good judicial policy, but compelling plaintiffs in all
federal cases to establish personal injury is simply not required by text
or original meaning.

Professor Michael Ramsey has argued that in many of Justice
Scalia's opinions, including *Printz* (anticommandeering), *Seminole
Tribe* (sovereign immunity), and *Lujan v. Defenders of Wildlife* (standing), Scalia did shirk textualism, but not originalism. Ramsey, a
thoughtful advocate for originalism, and the host of "The Originalism
Blog" argues that that these and other Scalia opinions show that the
late justice often relied on "non-textualist structural reasoning" based
on his views about original ratification-era understandings.[67] Ramsey
further argues that scholars such as Erwin Chemerinsky, and this
author, have failed to understand this aspect of Scalia's originalist
methodology.[68]

Professor Ramsey thinks that Scalia was true to his originalist
leanings in these cases because Scalia relied on, in Ramsey's own
words, "founding-era assumptions [that] are derived largely from
conjectures based on constitutional structure rather than specific
practices or founding-era commentary."[69] But in *Printz, Seminole
Tribe*, and *Lujan*, Scalia voted to strike down federal laws, where
the text did not require that result, as admitted by Ramsey, and
where there were detailed arguments supporting more specific
originalist-era practices than the personal assumptions Scalia used
to invalidate those laws. As discussed earlier in this chapter, *The
Federalist Papers* clearly reject an anticommandeering rule, Justice
Souter has shown in painstaking detail that the Founding Fathers
did not expect states to be immune from federal lawsuits based on

federal questions, and Raoul Berger argued strenuously that as an original matter personal injury was not necessary to support federal jurisdiction.[70]

Professor Ramsey would likely respond that all that shows is that reasonable people can disagree over how these cases should be decided as an original matter, not that Scalia was not an originalist. The problem with that defense, however, is that to the extent Scalia embraced and applied clearly contestable assumptions about our constitutional structure, based on nontextual and largely contested historical evidence, he is simply doing what any living constitutionalist would do. If Scalia had deferred to legislatures in those cases where the plaintiffs could not demonstrate with clear originalist evidence that the laws should be struck down, then Scalia [and Ramsey] could justifiably label that an originalist methodology. But in fact, Scalia did exactly the opposite by consistently striking down laws even where there was abundant originalist and textualist evidence against that interpretation. Even Ramsey concedes that Scalia showed a "perhaps surprising willingness to go beyond the text and direct evidence of its meaning to employ structural reasoning based on implications from founding-era assumptions."[71] Those "implications" derive as much from Scalia's modern sensibilities, based on values and politics, as originalist sources.

Ramsey also concedes that Scalia often used historical evidence from both well before and well after the relevant ratification eras to support his judicial opinions.[72] It is at best unclear, as Ramsey concedes, whether the use of such evidence suggests an originalist methodology. Moreover, Scalia never sketched out the reasonable boundaries of the use of such evidence or his own personal rules for limiting the discretion that such a timeless historical approach obviously provides a judge. A method of constitutional interpretation that allows a judge to use assumptions "derived largely from conjectures based on constitutional structure rather than specific practices or ... commentary," with a time frame ranging from Edward Coke in 1628,[73] to many years postratification, simply does not privilege ratification-era evidence enough to justify the label originalist.

F. CRIMINAL PROCEDURE

Justices Scalia and Thomas sometimes disagreed with each other in important criminal procedure cases arising under the Fourth, Fifth, and Sixth Amendments. Whereas Justice Thomas consistently votes against criminal defendants with the other conservatives and occasionally Justice Breyer, Justice Scalia at times surprised people by adopting a more defendant-friendly view. Due to the hundreds of cases both justices heard in this area of the law, it is difficult to assess whether either's votes are consistently supported by or contradicted by the text and history of the Fourth, Fifth, and Sixth Amendments. However, there is one opinion written by Justice Scalia that is so reflective of a "living constitutionalism" approach that it must be included in this section.

The issue in *Minnesota v. Dickerson*,[74] was whether the Fourth Amendment allows the seizure of contraband detected by a police officer during a protective search permissible under *Terry v. Ohio*, which allows police to make sure people they stop do not possess hidden weapons.[75] The Court held that the police officer in *Dickerson* violated the Fourth Amendment's ban on "unreasonable searches and seizures" by "'squeezing, sliding and otherwise manipulating the contents of the defendant's pocket' – a pocket which the officer already knew contained no weapon."[76]

Justice Scalia wrote a concurring opinion, the beginning of which adopts hard-core originalism. He began by saying that "I take it to be a fundamental principle of constitutional adjudication that the terms in the Constitution must be given the meaning ascribed to them at the time of their ratification."[77] Therefore, according to Scalia, the right to be free from "unreasonable searches and seizures," must be construed in light of what those words meant when the Constitution was adopted. Scalia then suggested that he was not sure whether the *Terry* rule, allowing a person to be frisked prior to arrest to ensure he has no hidden weapons, properly interpreted the Fourth Amendment. Scalia doubted that "the fiercely proud men who adopted our Fourth Amendment would have allowed themselves to be subjected, on mere suspicion of being armed and dangerous, to such indignity."[78]

Scalia went on, however, to articulate a distinctively living constitutionalism approach to this case. He said that, "even if a 'frisk' prior to arrest would have been considered impermissible in 1791 . . . perhaps it is only since that time that concealed weapons capable of harming the interrogator quickly . . . have become common – which might alter the judgment of what is 'reasonable' under the original standard."[79] In other words, even if the framers had specifically considered the validity of protective frisks prior to arrest, and even if they thought that such frisks were invalid, the identical issue may be decided differently by today's judges because of factual developments that have taken place since the Constitution was adopted. If, according to Scalia, the interpretation of the word *unreasonable* to a given set of facts can change, which he said it could, why can't the meaning of phrases like "cruel and unusual punishments," "equal protection," and "due process," also change?

In his *Dickerson* concurrence, Justice Scalia employed the same method of constitutional interpretation that underlies many of the precedents, such as those relating to abortion and same-sex marriage, that he so harshly criticized. For Scalia, Thomas, and all the justices, as Professor tenBroek observed in 1939 about the justices of his day,[80] historical sources are used when they support the justices' policy preferences, but are dropped when they get in the way of those preferences.

This chapter has identified major swaths of constitutional law where Justices Scalia and Thomas did not vote in an originalist manner. Other scholars have listed numerous other areas such as the justices' takings, free speech, and commerce clause jurisprudence, to name just a few, where the same objections could be made.[81] What Professor Rick Hasen said in his excellent biography of Justice Scalia, is true as to Justice Thomas as well:

> [Scalia] wrote that his ideas could increase the legitimacy of judicial decision-making yet his attacks on his opponents may have undermined it. He offered jurisprudential theories to guide all cases, yet these doctrines were flexible enough to allow him in most of the cases important enough to him to deliver opinions consistent with his ideology. He was an originalist who believed constitutional provisions should be interpreted in line with their public meaning at time of enactment except when he wasn't.[82]

It would be quite difficult to identify many modern cases where originalist analysis played a major role in the court's decisions. There is one case, however, that originalists of all stripes use to argue how far originalism has come among the justices – *District of Columbia v. Heller*.[83] The next chapter explains why this conventional wisdom is incorrect, and why originalism without great deference to more accountable political decision makers simply cannot work.

8 ORIGINALISM WITHOUT STRONG DEFERENCE CANNOT WORK

Originalism has a way of subverting the constitutional principles it purports to uphold.

Scott Lemieux[1]

In *District of Columbia v. Heller*,[2] the Supreme Court ruled for the first time in American history that the Second Amendment provides an individual right to own firearms in the home for self-defense. Justice Scalia's long majority opinion devoted substantial attention to both the original meaning of the Amendment and to the history of gun rights in this country, as did Justice Stevens's long dissent (which came to the opposite conclusions). The general storyline told by originalists about *Heller* is that it is not important whether one sides with the history of the Second Amendment as recounted by Scalia or Stevens. What is important is that both justices devoted their opinions to comprehensive reviews of originalist sources reflecting the ascendency of originalism as a method of constitutional interpretation.[3] Non-originalists, by contrast, have argued that what *Heller* demonstrates is the bankruptcy of an originalist method of constitutional interpretation in the hands of judges, liberal, conservative, or moderate, who are not equipped to conduct serious historical analysis.[4]

The Second Amendment provides the following: "A well-regulated Militia, being necessary to the security of a free state, the right of the people to keep and bear arms shall not be infringed."[5] From the Second Amendment's ratification until the *Heller* decision in 2008, the Supreme Court had never interpreted the Amendment to protect an individual right to own guns, and virtually every federal court to consider the issue assumed the Amendment only applied to official militia service (as its text seems to indicate).[6]

The facts and background of *Heller* were summarized succinctly and accurately by Professor Jamal Greene:

> Heller was a test case engineered by lawyers at the libertarian Cato Institute and the Institute for Justice in the wake of dramatic shifts in elite opinion in favor of an individual rights view of the Second Amendment. Dick Heller is a libertarian activist and a security guard at the Federal Judicial Center, which sits less than a half mile away from the Supreme Court building and serves in part as an annex for the Supreme Court's library. From 1976 until *Heller* was decided, Washington, D.C. had among the strictest gun control laws in the country, essentially prohibiting possession of handguns, requiring that all other guns be either unloaded and disassembled or bound by a trigger lock, and preventing Dick Heller from registering a gun for use in his D.C. home.[7]

In a 5–4 opinion written by Justice Scalia, the Court held that the District's law violated Heller's right to keep a gun in his home for self-defense. Justices Scalia and Stevens both agreed that the central purpose of the Second Amendment was to stop the national government from disarming official state militias.[8] Unlike Stevens, however, Scalia did not believe that protecting state militias was the Amendment's only purpose. Instead, along with the four other conservative justices, Scalia found that the Amendment also protected the right to self-defense and the right to hunt.

Although the majority found for Heller because the law completely banned the possession of an arm commonly in use (handguns), the Court did not decide what other weapons were protected by the Second Amendment, whether something less than a complete ban would be constitutional, or even what level of constitutional review applied to gun restrictions. In addition, in an important paragraph limiting the reach of its holding, the Court stated the following: "[N]othing in our opinion should be taken to cast doubt on longstanding prohibitions on the possession of firearms by felons and the mentally ill, or laws forbidding the carrying of firearms in sensitive places such as schools and government buildings, or laws imposing conditions and qualifications on the commercial sale of arms."[9]

Two years after *Heller*, the Court held, in another 5–4 opinion divided along the same ideological lines, that the Second Amendment, though intended as a limitation on federal power like most of the Bill of Rights, also applies to the states, like most of the Bill of Rights.[10] The *McDonald* case was the last Supreme Court decision interpreting the Second Amendment, and the lower courts have struggled with a wide array of gun control laws ever since.[11]

Both Justice Scalia's and Justice Stevens's opinions in *Heller* purport to be based on their review of history as opposed to balancing the importance of gun ownership against public safety concerns. Perhaps it is just a coincidence that all five conservatives voted to strike down the D.C. law, while all four liberals voted to uphold it (or perhaps not). The important point, however, is that both Justices' review of history has been lambasted by most historians. Thus, the *Heller* decision, rather than supporting originalism as a proper method of constitutional interpretation, reflects how dangerous, incoherent, and misleading the doctrine can be in the hands of Supreme Court justices who are not competent at historical analysis.

Most legal scholars and historians agree with Professor Paul Finkleman's statement that *Heller*'s and *McDonald*'s holdings that "individual self-defense is 'the central component' of the Second Amendment right . . . runs counter to the plain meaning of the text of the Amendment" and is contrary to "virtually all of the serious historical scholarship on the Founding."[12] Similarly, Saul Cornell, the Chair of Fordham University's History Department, has written extensively on the *Heller* and *McDonald* decisions, originalism, and the implications of the holding that the Amendment guarantees an individual right to own guns: "*Heller* and *McDonald* cast aside more than 75 years of established precedent to hold that individual citizens have a right to bear arms for personal use . . . the two decisions [are] incoherent and historically dishonest. And lower courts have now heard more than a thousand cases generated by the confusion *Heller* wrought."[13] Another scholar has written that Scalia's historical analysis is "disingenuous and unprincipled" as well as "objectively untenable."[14] Yet, another probably said it best when he concluded that *Heller* represents "law office history" and "the strained efforts of advocates, and the legions of law clerks and researchers at the Court's disposal, to find every shred of evidence that might support their position (as opposed to an unbiased search for all sources)."[15] The reactions by other historians to *Heller* and *McDonald* are full of such statements while scholars supporting the historical analysis in the opinions, or for that matter supporting the historical analysis in Justice Stevens's dissent in *Heller*, are truly rare.[16]

It is beyond the scope of this book to document all the poor research and historical analysis in both the *Heller* majority opinion and Justice Stevens' dissent. The scholars cited earlier, along with many others, have already done that work. However, two examples supply all the proof needed to demonstrate that, if *Heller* is an example of originalist decision making, then originalist decision making is not something other judges should emulate.

Justice Scalia held that the Second Amendment applies to guns that are "commonly used" for self-defense and hunting. This formulation, however, in the words of Saul Cornell "has no foundation in the text, structure, or history of the Second Amendment. In fact, this view gives gun makers – not legislatures, or even courts – the power to determine public policy on guns. Which is exactly why the Founders would have spurned it."[17] According to Cornell, any market-driven interpretation of the Second Amendment is just historically wrong:

> The Second Amendment was not designed to hobble government regulation. At the time, men arrived for military service already armed with guns the government required them to purchase ... the law did not countenance Americans simply showing up with whatever weapons they owned – that is, what was in common use. Without specific regulations ... most Americans would likely have shown up for active duty with fowling pieces, which were more like shot guns than muskets, because these were better suited for putting food on the table. In other words, the Founders recognized that if left to the free market and people's own preferences, America's militias would be prepared to hunt turkeys, not fight a powerful European standing army ... If the Founders had understood the Second Amendment in the way Scalia ... suggest[s], the United States would likely have lost the American Revolution.[18]

Not only did Scalia misinterpret the Second Amendment's history to concoct the "common use" test, but also a major part of his holding has nothing at all to do with originalism. The law that *Heller* invalidated was a complete ban on handgun possession in the District of Columbia (with a few minor exceptions), and the Court's holding was limited to such bans. However, as noted earlier, the majority opinion also explicitly stated that nothing in the ban precludes laws prohibiting "the possession of firearms by felons and the mentally ill, or laws forbidding the carrying of firearms in sensitive places such as schools and government buildings, or laws imposing conditions and qualifications on the commercial sale of arms."[19]

Justice Scalia made up this list of "presumptively lawful regulatory measures" out of whole cloth without a single citation to any historical source, case, or study.[20] He spent fifty-four pages of historical "analysis" supporting the view that the Militia language of the Amendment could be ignored in favor of a personal right to own guns, but not one word justifying the important list of exceptions he carved out from that so-called personal right. These exceptions demonstrate "more than 'judicial lawmaking.' In fact, it demonstrates that even the purest originalist cannot resist the tug to implement, nay, to transport, the 'original meaning' into the context and experience of our living age."[21] The list of exceptions shows that the majority opinion "draws on commonsense and modern-day experience ... without any originalist analysis whatsoever. ... Indeed, it is *activist living constitutionalism* at its best: The Second Amendment must be interpreted to permit restrictions that America's evolution has demonstrated are sensible and necessary. History must give way to reality. The dead hands of the Framers – whether or not their children took their hunting guns to school with them – cannot govern the living two centuries hence."[22] Nelson Lund, a conservative supporter of Second Amendment rights argued that Scalia's opinion, given the list of exceptions not justified by ratification era-sources, makes a "great show of being committed to the Constitution's original meaning, but fails to carry through on that commitment."[23] Lund concluded that the "Court's reasoning is at critical points so defective – and in some respects so transparently non-originalist – that *Heller* should be seen as an embarrassment for those who joined the majority opinion."[24]

Judge Harvey Wilkinson of the US Court of Appeals for the Fourth Circuit compared the judicial aggression in *Heller* to the method of constitutional interpretation employed by the Court in *Roe v. Wade*:

> The Constitution's text, at least, has as little to say about restrictions on firearm ownership by felons as it does about the trimesters

of pregnancy. The *Heller* majority seems to want to have its cake
and eat it, too – to recognize a right to bear arms without having to
deal with any of the more unpleasant consequences of such a right.
In short, the Court wishes to preempt democracy up to point. But
up to what point and why?[25]

Judge Wilkinson also argued in his fine article that any objective
person reading the historical arguments and counterarguments in the
majority and dissenting opinions in *Heller* would have to conclude "'the
arguments about the Second Amendment's meaning are in reasonably
close balance' and that given this indeterminacy, people's positions on
the Second Amendment's meaning will have more to do with their ideas
about policy than with legal principle."[26] Even if Justice Scalia and
Justice Stevens had conducted sound historical analysis, which most
historians claim they did not do, the result would still be a standoff where
something other than that analysis drives the result. If transparency is a
substantial goal of judicial decision making, *Heller* flunks that test.

Another aspect of *Heller* that shows the many flaws of originalism is
the torrent of non-originalist questions the decision unleashed. Judge
Wilkinson foresaw this problem just after the decision was issued. He
predicted lawsuits about what types of weapons are covered by the
Second Amendment; what kinds of people would be outside the reach
of the Amendment (all felons, just violent felons, people who commit
violent misdemeanors); what places would be legally gun-free zones
(schools, hospitals, sporting arenas, college campuses, post offices);
whether states could limit who could carry a gun in public; and what
restrictions could be placed on the commercial licensing of guns,
among many other issues.[27] All of these questions have been or are
being litigated in the lower courts right now, and few if any of them can
be usefully analyzed through an originalist or historical lens. How
would one even go about trying to determine the original meaning of
the Second Amendment as applied to small, dangerous weapons or
semi-automatic weapons the Founding Fathers and the people living at
the time could never have anticipated? How would the history of the
Amendment possibly be relevant to balancing the supposed right to
own guns with the government's interest in the safety of 100,000
people at a college football game? The list of public policy issues
surrounding gun control measures grows every year, and they will

not and cannot be decided according to the original public meaning of the Second Amendment. As Judge Wilkinson concluded back in 2009:

> So now, predictably and inevitably, the litigation will take off. Courts across the country will face detailed questions about firearms regulations and will provide varied and often inconsistent answers. Circuit splits and open questions will persist for our lifetimes. And for what purpose? What justifies the judiciary asserting its primacy in yet another new arena? Surely not its greater expertise. Surely not, as in apportionment, a dysfunctional political process. As Justice Stevens observed in Heller, 'no one has suggested that the political process is not working exactly as it should,' in firearms regulation. Accordingly, the Court should honor the structure of our constitution, stay out of the thicket, and leave the highly motivated contestants in this field to press their agendas in the political process where the issue properly belongs and where for centuries it has remained.[28]

These problems raised by an originalist approach to the Second Amendment are replicated in virtually every other area of constitutional law. Unless a historical inquiry includes a strong presumption that the challenged law is constitutional, a judge using original meaning as the primary method to resolve modern cases will find little that helps and will eventually apply her own modern sensibilities to the broad principles that underlie most constitutional litigation. This is not to say that the study of ratification-era evidence and history (from the Founding to the present) can't at times inform a judge's application of constitutional values. But contrary to what many originalists contend, the evaluation of history does not trump the justices' personal ideologies nor could it (absent strong deference). The important cases demonstrating this thesis could fill a treatise, but here are a few representative ones.

A First Amendment question that has long bothered the conservatives on the Court, including Justices Scalia and Thomas, is whether states may impose mandatory fees on public-sector workers who are represented by unions. Nonconsenting employees who don't want to join unions argue that these fees fund ideological speech with which they disagree. Therefore, they contend that state laws requiring them to pay union fees against their will violate their right to free speech.

The states' counterargument is public-sector union activities redound to the benefit of all employees, and in any event, nonconsenting employees may engage in as much counterspeech as they want against the union's activities. In *Abood v. Detroit Board of Education,*[29] decided in 1977, the Supreme Court held that imposing mandatory union fees on state employees does not violate their First Amendment rights if the fees are used for collective bargaining purposes related to workplace conditions, not political causes.

Just a few years, ago, the Court limited *Abood's* reach in a case involving quasi-state workers who provide end-of-life-care in the home,[30] and the conservatives on the Court made clear their desire to reverse *Abood* in an appropriate case. These justices seemed to be sympathetic to the argument, rejected in *Abood,* that all public-sector employer–union bargaining raises ideological issues. The Court granted certiorari the next year in a similar case probably to reverse *Abood,*[31] but after Justice Scalia passed away, the Court deadlocked 4–4, which meant the lower court decision, which followed *Abood,* was affirmed.[32] The justices recently decided to hear another case raising this question and placed it on the docket for the 2017–18 term.[33]

Original meaning has not yet been a part of the Court's discussions of this legal issue for an obvious reason: there were no public-sector unions in either 1787 when the Constitution was ratified or in 1868 when the Fourteenth Amendment (applying the First Amendment to the states) was ratified. We can't begin to figure out the original public meaning of free speech as applied to union fees when the notion of collective bargaining for government workers would have been completely foreign to the framers. Moreover, even if we could somehow explain these ideas to the Framers, they would also need to know the history of union/employer relationships in the twentieth and twenty-first centuries, and the growth of government bureaucracies to fully grasp the issues. By the time we pour that new information into a search for the First Amendment's original public meaning, our biases and prejudices would substantially affect the story we tell. In other words, the supposed discovery of original public meaning in this context would simply lead to the application of our modern values to a distinctively contemporary problem, which is exactly what living constitutionalists would do.

These same difficulties arise for most other constitutional law cases. Take, for example, whether women should have a constitutional right to terminate their pregnancies, or whether gays and lesbians have a legal right to marry. A coherent posture for a judge to take in both cases would be to place a high burden of proof on plaintiffs to demonstrate with clear and convincing evidence that either unambiguous text or strong ratification-era evidence supports them (in which case the plaintiffs would likely lose both cases). Another coherent position for a judge to take would be that because society changes dramatically, and neither clear text nor history forbids the plaintiffs from winning those cases, the judge will do what he thinks best considering text, history, precedent, and likely consequences, and then he'd explain his decision as transparently as possible. What is an incoherent position for a judge to take, however, is to canvass originalist sources, try to figure out the best we can what the people living in 1787 or 1868 thought about the problem, or do what a hypothesized originalist "objective meaning" of the text requires.

The people who wrote and/or ratified the Fourteenth Amendment had views about women that are completely taboo in the United States today (I hope). Women didn't have the right vote, were excluded from many professions, and were largely second-class citizens under the law and in practice. The issue of abortion, in 1868 or today, whether one is pro-life or pro-choice, is wrapped up in balancing many aspects of a woman's individual autonomy with the rights, if any, of the fetus. We simply don't know how people living in 1868 would balance those questions if they held our common assumptions about women and equality. Suggesting we have any way of translating those times to ours in the context of abortion is facetious, at best.

The same is true for same-sex marriage. The concept of a homosexual person (as opposed to homosexual conduct) barely existed in 1868, so how much valuable information could people living at that time offer us?[34] Moreover, the institution of marriage was fundamentally different in many important ways. More generally, what does it even mean to try to define the "original meaning" of the word *equal* in the Fourteenth Amendment to a society and a people so radically different from our own? Historical analysis simply can't help unless we place the burden on the plaintiffs to prove that the text or

universally agreed-upon assumptions about the text obviously forbid
the practice at issue. It is the rare modern case, however, that satisfies
that condition.

The problems with arguing that original meaning should play a
primary role in constitutional interpretation are not just evident in
high-profile constitutional cases like those implicating freedom of
speech, abortion, and same-sex marriage. Our current administrative
state, where executive agencies like the Environmental Protection
Agency or the Department of Health and Human Services, and so-
called independent agencies such as the Federal Election Commission
wield so much authority would have been completely unknown to the
Founding Fathers. As late as 1933, prior to the New Deal, there were
less than twenty federal agencies while today there are hundreds.[35]
Virtually all areas of American life are governed not by laws passed by
Congress but by administrative regulation. As Phillip Hamburger,
among others, has written, the rise of these agencies, coupled with
Supreme Court decisions legitimizing them and their broad powers,
has allowed them to occupy "a sort of juridical monad that can interpret, execute, and legislate its statutory norms and facts in clear violation of the principle of the separation of powers."[36] Whether or not we
can justify this fundamental shift in power from Congress and the
states through some method of living constitutionalism, the twin real-
ities are that we are not going to go back to the preadministrative state
(though there may be occasional slides), and more important, new
questions of separation of powers must be analyzed through a realistic
lens of an administrative world that no one living in 1787 could
possibly have anticipated. In Hamburger's words, "although much
administrative state power is economically inefficient, all of it is
unconstitutional."[37]

These problems were highlighted in the 1980s when the Court
decided a series of important separation of powers cases in which
plaintiffs challenged the constitutionality of important new aspects of
our federal regulatory practice, all designed to deal with different
features of our sprawling federal government. In these cases, the Court
devoted little attention to the original meaning of the various constitutional provisions at issue, and for good reason. No one living in
1787 could have possibly expected the Executive Branch to function

like it does today. Any opinions those people could have had on the various issues raised by these cases would be of little or no value.

For example, the question in *I.N.S. v. Chada*[38] was whether Congress could pass a law, signed by the president, which allowed one branch of Congress to veto a decision by the president to suspend the deportation of an alien who stayed past the time allowed by his visa. The original law giving the president that discretion went through the constitutionally required process of bicameralism (both Houses of Congress must approve a bill) and presentment (all bills must be signed by the president or his veto must be overruled by two-thirds of both Houses). The argument made by the Executive Branch was that if Congress wanted to overrule the president's deportation decision, it had to do so through the normal requirements of bicameralism and presentment despite the authority given one House of Congress in the original and validly enacted immigration law. The Congress's primary response to that argument was that, in the new Administrative State, the Executive makes law routinely through delegated authority from Congress. Thus, one House's authority to veto the suspension of a deportation was also constitutional if the president signed the original bill granting that discretion. Although the facts of *Chada* were relatively narrow, Congress had placed legislative vetoes in over two hundred laws as a way of controlling Executive Branch discretion, so the stakes of this case were extremely high.

The Court ruled that the legislative veto was unconstitutional because it violated the separation of powers. Although the majority opinion cited some history to support the broad requirements of bicameralism and presentment, there was no reliance on original meaning for the Court's conclusion that the legislative veto was different in substance than other examples of valid lawmaking that do not have to go through bicameralism and presentment. This absence of originalist authority makes sense because the Executive Branch in 1983 and the Executive Branch in 1787 have so little in common. The purpose of the legislative veto was to fix a problem (Executive Branch lawmaking) that barely existed prior to the 1930s. As Justice White explained in dissent:

The prominence of the legislative veto mechanism in our contemporary political system and its importance to Congress can hardly be overstated. It has become a central means by which Congress secures the accountability of executive and independent agencies. Without the legislative veto, Congress is faced with a Hobson's choice: either to refrain from delegating the necessary authority, leaving itself with a hopeless task of writing laws with the requisite specificity to cover endless special circumstances across the entire policy landscape, or, in the alternative, to abdicate its law-making function to the Executive Branch and independent agencies. . . . Accordingly, over the past five decades, the legislative veto has been placed in nearly 200 statutes. The device is known in every field of governmental concern: reorganization, budgets, foreign affairs, war powers, and regulation of trade, safety, energy, the environment, and the economy.[39]

No amount of historical study, analysis, or investigation into original meaning could have led to a persuasive conclusion about the constitutional validity of the legislative veto, which is probably why the Court didn't go down that path. How can the world of 1787 possibly help us solve a problem that the people at the time did not contemplate? This is not to say that political practices over time and the actions of the three branches of the federal government are not highly relevant to the justices' considerations in separation of powers cases. In both *NLRB v. Noel Canning*[40] and *Zivotofsky v. Kerry*,[41] the Court's majority opinions strongly emphasized how much of a role prior political practices play in giving shape to the vague constitutional provisions that trigger most separation of powers cases.[42] But the job of reviewing more than two hundred years of congressional, executive, and judicial reflections and actions regarding hard separation of powers issues is hardly an originalist task given how inevitable a role subjectivity (and modern considerations and balancing) must play in that enterprise.

The difficulty of applying original meaning to modern separation of powers issues can be seen by examining other contemporary problems. To provide just three examples: may the president constitutionally execute an American citizen who is likely a dangerous terrorist living in a foreign country without giving him any judicial due process; what are the limits of the provision in Article I, Section 8, giving Congress the power to declare war given the repeated use of military forces by numerous presidents without such authorization; and does the writ of habeas corpus apply to alleged terrorists who America holds for long periods of time outside the United States in places where the United States has de facto control?[43] The resolution of these questions, whether by judges, scholars, or politicians simply cannot be substantially aided by canvassing 1787 sources and materials. These and most other constitutional law problems implicate broad and conflicting principles, and as Terrance Sandalow once wrote, "choice among the various [principles] is inescapable, and through that choice contemporary values are given expression."[44] Similarly, Judge Richard Posner said in a slightly different, but related context:

> What would the framers of the [Fourth Amendment] have thought about [n]ational security surveillance of people's emails[?] That is a meaningless question. It is not an interpretive question, it is a creative question. … The [Constitution] cannot resolve it … by thinking about the intentions, the notes of the constitutional convention, [or] other sources from the 18th century. This seems to be the standard problem for judges. … It is not interpretation, it is just trying to find … a solution to a question that has not been solved by the legislature.[45]

Most constitutional questions revolving around the Fourth Amendment's prohibition on "unreasonable searches and seizures" cannot be usefully analyzed through any form of originalist analysis. Professor Matthew Tokson explains how little 1791 evidence can help with modern Fourth Amendment issues:

> The Founders had little reason to specify the scope of the "search" concept, because most Founding-era searches were easy to identify – they involved physical violation of the home or other property. Modern search questions only arose in the radically changed context of the Twentieth Century, when police officers could use listening devices to record private activities or access intimate conversations transmitted through wires over long distances. Neither the telephone, nor the "bug," nor even the professional police officer existed in 1791.[46]

To recap, in most areas of litigated constitutional law, originalism, whether defined as original meaning, original intentions, or some hybrid of the two, cannot be the primary method of constitutional interpretation if that means judges must reconstruct history to come up with the most accurate interpretation of vague constitutional text. The examination of originalist evidence can provide context and background to a hard problem and support judicial decisions reached on other grounds, but it will not decidedly point to one solution or another. The people living in the United States in 1787 or 1868 inhabited a substantially different country than ours today. Most constitutional law cases raise difficult issues of balancing governmental power against the asserted rights of people claiming they have been injured by official action. These issues "will often bear scant resemblance to what the constitutional framers . . . envisioned, and thus the normative questions joined in today's litigation must typically draw on a host of considerations – a configuration of values – that have no real roots" in the original meaning of the Constitution.[47]

The Original Originalists argued that those asserting constitutional rights had a heavy burden of proof to justify those alleged rights through clear text or original intentions. This theory is coherent, but judges do not apply it, and it is most unlikely they will adopt it anytime soon. The New Originalists, while rejecting a heavy burden of proof for constitutional plaintiffs, implicitly recognized the futility of historical emphasis through their theory of constitutional construction, which admits that normative judgments not originalist materials inevitably drive constitutional litigation. Or, in the alternative, some New, New Originalists, dodge the futility of history by claiming that a decision is originalist if the judge first labels the relevant text as "general" not "specific" before applying a living constitutionalism approach to the controversy at hand.[48]

Professor Robert Bennett has explained why in practice originalism is doomed to failure. He cites the following four reasons why "no plausible version of what is called originalism has the resources to stem a substantial flow of evolving values into our constitutional law, even if they are different from the original animating ones."[49]

1) Most litigated constitutional text is general and ambiguous;
2) The text was debated by large numbers of people with different views on practical applications;

3) The problems judges face today bear "scant resemblance" to the problems these words were trying to address; and
4) Court decision making in the United States emphasizes consequences "in the here and now." Judicial responsibility propels judges "towards thinking in terms they can comfortably relate to today."[50]

Originalism with great deference might make sense but fails miserably as a descriptive or, sadly, predictive account. Most other forms of originalism don't take ratification-era evidence seriously as a decision-generating device for the reasons given by Bennett. In fact, as Chapter 9 argues, no prior legal rule or theoretical precommitment, much less originalism, has ever successfully outweighed the role of personal ideology and values as drivers of constitutional adjudication. If people are going to retain faith in our Supreme Court, it must be for reasons separate from the belief that text and original meaning generate Supreme Court decisions.

9 VALUES AND IDEOLOGY, NOT LAW, DRIVE SUPREME COURT CASES

The life of the law, has not been logic; it has been experience.
Oliver Wendell Holmes[1]

Never in American history, thankfully, have a majority of the Justices accepted originalism.
Erwin Chemerinsky[2]

Political scientists who have studied and written about the Supreme Court often argue that legal sources such as text, history, precedent, and prior positive law play less of a role in the justices' decision making than their political and personal values.[3] This description, often called the attitudinal model, is a minority position among law professors and judges, but the dominant view among political scientists. In the succinct words of Professor Michael Gerhardt, "[l]aw professors believe the Constitution and other laws constrain the Court, while most political scientists do not."[4] Because the justices don't have to follow precedent, are usually faced with vague text with contested historical origins, and have the final say on important societal issues, it is fair to ask why legal scholars would expect the justices to do anything other than what they think best, and what the public will tolerate, all things considered.

One answer may be that lawyers, legal scholars, and judges are strongly discouraged by the profession from thinking this way. There seems to be a need among many legal professionals to believe that prior rules, doctrines, and legal formulae guide judicial decision making instead of the justices' values. This need is most apparent in the rhetoric and myths surrounding originalism. There seems to be a consensus among many Originalists that judges engaged in constitutional interpretation must place primary reliance on text and original meaning.

Yet, as discussed in Chapter 7, and more fully in this chapter, the Supreme Court does not decide cases in an originalist fashion (unless we drain that term of any real meaning), and more important, ideology not law plays the dominant role in Supreme Court decision making, just as most political scientists contend.

One way to demonstrate the importance of values, politics, and ideology in Supreme Court decision making is to document the large number of fundamentally important doctrinal reversals the Court has engaged in over the years despite no change in the constitutional text or new discoveries about its history. What accounts for these major changes in doctrine is not changes in prior law, but the reality that justices with different values will inevitably reach different results in important and hard cases.

Another factor contributing to major doctrinal changes in constitutional law is that when times change outside the courts, such as with the New Deal or the social turbulence of the 1960s, the justices' values change as well. In other words, Supreme Court made constitutional law depends little on text and history and more on values and changed cultural, social, economic, and political conditions. This description is not intended to generate cynicism about how the Court operates, just accuracy.

It would take an entire book to provide the relevant case law to support these claims.[5] The representative and important examples that follow, however, should make the case that neither originalism nor any other single interpretative methodology is, in the words of Professors Baude and Sachs, "our law." Rather, when it comes to Supreme Court constitutional doctrine, ideology and values writ large, meaning both legal and nonlegal considerations, is "our law."

A. PAPER MONEY

The US Constitution allows Congress to "coin Money [and] regulate the Value thereof."[6] Nothing in the document explicitly authorizes the federal government to print paper money. During the Civil War, Congress issued "greenbacks" to help defeat the South. After the War ended, debtors wanted to pay back their loans with the new paper currency, but many creditors demanded coin. On February 7, 1870, the Court issued its momentous decision in *Hepburn v. Griswold* siding with a disgruntled creditor and holding that Congress lacked authority to make paper money legal tender.[7]

The decision was 5–3, with four Democrats and one Republican in the majority and three Republicans in dissent. At the time, the Republican Party generally represented the debtor class and the Democrats the creditor class. The majority opinion held that allowing Congress to increase its enumerated powers by making paper money legal tender would give the national government too much power, and that the law legalizing paper money unconstitutionally interfered with the creditor's preexisting contract rights.[8] The dissent strenuously disagreed, arguing that there was a critical need for paper money during the Civil War, and without it, both the government and the Constitution "would have perished."[9] The importance of this case cannot be overstated. One commentator later announced that the issues had been "argued and reargued by numerous and distinguished counsel. It is probable that never in the history of the Court [to that time] has any question been more thoroughly considered before decision."[10]

At the time of the opinion, the Court had eight justices, and one of them, a Democrat, had already announced his retirement. Shortly after the decision, Republican President Ulysses S. Grant nominated two Republican justices, both of whom were expected to vote differently on the legal tender issue. Just over a year later, with these two new justices on the Court giving the Republican Party a clear majority, the Court reversed itself and held that Congress did have the authority to make paper money legal tender.[11] The majority did not point to any new information or facts but simply disagreed on the fundamental issues resolved just the year before. President Grant was accused by Democrat-leaning newspapers of packing the Court. One said that the decision was not based on law and "is generally regarded not as the solemn adjudication of an upright and impartial tribunal, but as a base compliance with Executive instructions by creatures of the President placed upon the Bench to carry out his instructions."[12] The year was 1871.

Like virtually all constitutional law cases, the issues in the Legal Tender Cases were not susceptible to persuasive resolution based on prior positive law materials. Although the justices in both cases discussed traditional legal sources, their politics and values, not text or original meaning, governed the matter. Although the timing (two identical and important cases decided in opposite ways only one year apart) and the grave significance of the Legal Tender Cases might be somewhat unusual, the lessons of the two cases are not. The justices decide hard constitutional law cases based on their values, politics, and examinations of consequences, not legal sources such as text, history, or precedent.

B. PAROCHIAL SCHOOL AID

The first time the Supreme Court interpreted the command in the First Amendment that the government make no law "respecting an establishment of religion" was in 1947. In *Everson v. Board of Education*, the Court rejected an Establishment Clause challenge to state payments to parents for bus transportation to and from religious schools.[13] After a second decision in 1968 allowed state governments to lend secular textbooks to children in religious schools,[14] the issue of public support for private religious schools became hotly contested in the courts, state legislatures, and Congress.

Starting in 1971,[15] the Court dramatically changed constitutional course and adopted a series of seemingly contradictory rules governing what assistance religious schools could receive from both the federal and state governments. By the mid-1970s, the Court had disallowed most publicly funded educational materials including books other than textbooks, as well as chalk, erasers, maps, films, and other school supplies.[16] The Court also didn't allow public-school employees to teach secular subjects in the religious schools, although they could provide diagnostic and psychological testing.[17] Commentators lamented how arbitrary this doctrine had become by observing that, under the justices' interpretation of the Establishment Clause, religious schools were allowed to receive textbooks with maps from state governments but not maps themselves.[18] This led a US Senator to wonder with sarcasm where Atlases fit into the Court's bizarre categories of permissible and impermissible aid.[19] No one could plausibly argue that this line-drawing doctrine was based on the language or original meaning of the First Amendment.

After Justice Thomas replaced Justice Marshall in 1991, and the political balance of the Court changed, the justices dramatically reversed course. The Court now allows state and federal governments to provide virtually all educational and instructional equipment to religious schools provided the same support is available to public schools (which of course it always is) and private nonreligious schools.[20] The Court's decision to stop policing the line between permissible and impermissible aid to religious schools was not caused by a change in constitutional text or new scholarly discoveries about the history of the First Amendment or any new originalist arguments. In fact, applying originalism to the issue of parochial aid would lead nowhere, given that the role of public and private schools when the Constitution was adopted, or even in 1868, was so much different than today.

As one commentator, writing in 2001, observed, "the Supreme Court is hardly immune to cultural and political trends. . . . the political preferences of voters wield considerable influence on the Court. . . . The current wave of religious revivalism is likely to exert similar influence on the Court."[21] Shortly thereafter, the Court radically liberalized the law regarding parochial school aid. Whether the justices' personal perspectives on this issue were shaped by the "cultural and political trends" of the late 1990s, or whether the justices helped shape those trends is hard to say. But what is easy to say is that the Court's decisions about the proper balance between church and state were not determined by constitutional text, history, or precedent, but by the justices' personal perspectives regarding the appropriate relationship between church and state in today's public and private schools.

C. FREE SPEECH

Prior to 1976, numerous Supreme Court cases suggested that pure commercial speech (speech advertising the selling of a product for profit) either received no or limited First Amendment protection.

For example, in 1942, the Court reviewed a New York law that prohibited the distribution of handbills that advertised commercial matters but allowed those handbills concerning "information or a public protest."[22] The plaintiff wanted to encourage people to visit his submarine tied up at the Port of New York. On one side of his handbill he protested certain pier policies, and on the other he advertised his submarine. He was told by New York officials that his handbill was illegal, and the Supreme Court upheld the law, saying that "the Constitution imposes no restraint on government as respects purely commercial advertising. Whether, and to what extent, one may promote or pursue a gainful occupation in the streets, to what extent such activity shall be adjudged a derogation of the public right of user, are matters for legislative judgment. ... If the respondent was attempting to use the streets of New York by distributing commercial advertising, the prohibition of the code provision was lawfully invoked against his conduct."[23]

The Court continued to refuse First Amendment protection for commercial speech throughout the 1960s and into the early 1970s. Around that time, a few academics began advocating for more judicial protection for business interests as did a prominent attorney in Virginia, whose wealthy clients included the US Chamber of Commerce.[24] He wrote a confidential memorandum suggesting that socialism in the United States was on the rise, and the free market system was under attack.[25] Among other suggestions to address these issues, he recommended that the Chamber use the Supreme Court more aggressively to challenge laws governing commercial activities. He argued that under "our constitutional system, especially with an activist-minded Supreme Court, the judiciary may be the most important instrument for social, economic and political change. ... Other organizations and groups, recognizing this, have been far more astute in exploiting judicial action than American business. ... This is a vast area of opportunity for the Chamber."[26] The author of that memorandum was Lewis F. Powell Jr., who shortly afterwards was nominated by President Nixon for a position on the Supreme Court.

Just a few years later, with Powell joining the majority opinion, the Court in *Virginia State Board of Pharmacy v. Virginia Citizens Consumer Council, Inc.,*[27] changed its mind about commercial speech and held that such speech does receive First Amendment protection. *Virginia Pharmacy* involved a state law prohibiting pharmacists from advertising prescription medicine prices. The Court held that if the advertising of a commercial product is honest and does not advocate illegal activity, it is entitled to constitutional protection. This dramatic shift came about without any discussion of the original meaning of the Constitution. What did change was the attitudes and values of the justices who sat on the Court. The decision was 8–1 with Justice Rehnquist writing a bitter dissent lamenting the Court's overruling of prior cases holding that commercial speech received little or no constitutional protection. He argued that "while there is again much to be said for the Court's observation *as a matter of desirable public policy,* there is certainly nothing in the United States Constitution which requires the Virginia Legislature to hew to the teachings of Adam Smith in its legislative decisions regulating the pharmacy profession."[28]

Although it took a while, eventually the Rehnquist and Roberts Courts would not only fully protect commercial speech, but would also adopt an aggressive policy striking down laws limiting such speech.[29] Harvard Law School Professor Fredrick Schauer labeled this trend "First Amendment opportunism" and worried that if "every time government regulation touched on speech [and we treat it] as a First Amendment problem, [it] would jeopardize a considerable amount of ... the post-New Deal regulatory state."[30] Schauer also suggested that "if we use the First Amendment for almost everything, will it be there when we need it the most?"[31]

Whether speech proposing or discussing purely commercial transactions should receive full, little, or no legal protection is admittedly a tough question. The lines between commercial and noncommercial speech may be quite difficult to draw leading to arbitrary decisions where judges have significant discretion to choose which laws they uphold and which they strike down. On the other hand, the robust commercial speech protections adopted by the Roberts Court interfere with state and federal efforts to protect consumers. The one thing that we can be sure of, however, is that the Court's fluctuations concerning commercial speech have little to do with text, original meaning, or case law and everything to do with the justices' perspectives on the relationships between government, consumers, and business interests.

Other hard issues involving free speech such as questions concerning campaign finance reform, obscenity, and defamation, are similarly immune to originalist judicial resolution because there is virtually no helpful history regarding the First Amendment's adoption. As one scholar has noted:

> The legislative history of the Amendment sheds almost no light on its scope or meaning, especially with respect to free speech. There are no records of the Senate deliberations or the relevant ratification debates in the state legislatures. The House debates are not illuminating either. Moreover, the concept of freedom of speech itself "had almost no history as a concept or a practice prior to the [ratification of the] First Amendment or even later."[32]

Taking a slightly different tack, Professor Jud Campbell recently wrote an important article suggesting that the evidence shows that the framers' views on free speech were substantially more limited than much of the Court's modern First Amendment doctrine.[33] In either event, trying to ascertain the original meaning of the First Amendment as applied to virtually any current controversial free speech issue simply will not point the way to helpful answers. There is little or nothing there to help, and inevitably judges will simply mistake their own values for those of people living centuries ago, who never considered most of the hard speech questions judges must face today.

D. COMMERCE AMONG THE STATES

Article 1, Section 8 of the Constitution allows Congress to regulate "commerce among the states." Between 1903 and 1918, the Supreme Court gave Congress significant authority to regulate the movement of commercial goods across state lines without much consideration of whether the legislation substantially affected interstate commerce.[34] During these years, the Court allowed Congress to regulate or prohibit the interstate shipment of lottery tickets, meat that had not been federally inspected, mislabeled eggs, and even women being transported for "prostitution and debauchery."[35] The rationale of these cases harkened back to the Court's first commerce clause case decided in 1824, where the Court held that Congress could regulate all commerce that "concerns more states than one."[36]

In 1918, however, the Court changed course. In a landmark, and many consider tragic, decision, the Court ruled that Congress lacked the power to regulate the shipment across state lines of goods manufactured by child labor.[37] The federal statute made it illegal to transport goods for profit if they had been manufactured by children who worked more than certain specified hours, or at night, or more than six days a week.[38] In light of prior cases, Congress had every reason to believe this law, which impacted the commerce of more states than one, would be upheld by the justices. Unfortunately for thousands of children working long hours in unsafe conditions, the Court struck down this law saying it exceeded Congress's commerce clause authority.

The Justices were concerned that upholding this statute would give Congress too much power to regulate matters they thought should be left to the states. The Court said that over "interstate transportation, or its incidents, the regulatory power of Congress is ample, but the production of articles, intended for interstate commerce, is a matter of local regulation. ... If it were otherwise, all manufacture intended for interstate shipment would be brought under federal control to the practical exclusion of the authority of the states."[39] The Court suggested that such a result would be inconsistent with the initial federalism plan of the Constitution but did not explain why the regulation of goods shipped across state lines was not a literal regulation of "commerce among the states." The Court distinguished the prior cases upholding similar laws because they all involved products that were themselves harmful whereas the goods made by child labor were "of themselves harmless."[40] This distinction is quite elusive, however, given that one of those prior cases involved women and another mislabeled eggs. Nevertheless, the justices in the majority in *Hammer v. Dagenhart* felt so strongly about their decision that they ended the opinion with this dire warning:

> The far-reaching result of upholding the act cannot be more plainly indicated than by pointing out that if Congress can thus regulate matters entrusted to local authority by prohibition of the movement of commodities in interstate commerce, all freedom of commerce

will be at an end, and the power of the States over local matters may be eliminated, and thus our system of government be practically destroyed.[41]

There was a strong dissent by Justice Oliver Wendell Holmes. He observed that the law in question unquestionably fell within the terms of the commerce power: "The statute confines itself to prohibiting the carriage of certain goods in interstate or foreign commerce. Congress is given power to regulate such commerce in unqualified terms ... it is established by the Lottery Case and others that have followed it that a law is not beyond the regulative power of Congress merely because it prohibits certain transportation out and out. ... "[42] He concluded his opinion by emphatically rejecting the argument that our federal structure requires that the indirect regulation of manufacturing, through laws prohibiting the interstate shipment of goods, should be struck down by the Court:

> The act does not meddle with anything belonging to the States. They may regulate their internal affairs and their domestic commerce as they like. But when they seek to send their products across the state line they are no longer within their rights. If there were no Constitution and no Congress their power to cross the line would depend upon their neighbors. Under the Constitution such commerce belongs not to the States but to Congress to regulate. It may carry out its views of public policy whatever indirect effect they may have upon the activities of the States.[43]

The justices' invalidation of the federal child labor law came in the middle of the Court's *Lochner* era when, as discussed in Chapter 3, the Court was generally hostile to economic regulation. Less than two decades later, with several new justices on the bench, the Court changed its mind and essentially stopped reviewing both state and federal legislation governing employers, employees, labor relations, and the economy.[44] In one of those case, *United States v. Darby*,[45] decided in 1940, less than 25 years after the *Hammer* decision, and despite the dire warnings of the *Hammer* majority that a different result would lead to "our system of government be[ing] practically destroyed," the Court explicitly reversed that case. In *Darby*, the Court upheld federal regulation of wages and overtimes in industries affecting interstate commerce even though such rules regulated manufacturing. As to *Hammer*, which had held manufacturing to be exempt from federal interference, the justices simply concluded "that *Hammer v. Dagenhart*, was a departure from the principles which have prevailed in the interpretation of the Commerce Clause both before and since the decision and that such vitality, as a precedent, as it then had has long since been exhausted. It should be and now is overruled."[46]

The Court's back and forth on what powers Congress may employ to regulate "commerce among the states" was not determined by careful review of originalist principles, text, or precedent. Instead, times changed, the Great Depression occurred, and the justices who emerged in the middle of that chaos simply had different perspectives on the appropriate balance between the states and federal government than the justices who held sway during the *Lochner* era. The recognition that constitutional interpretation as practiced by the Supreme Court depends much more on, as Justice Jackson once observed, the "imperatives of events" and "contemporary imponderables,"[47] than on text and original meaning is not a criticism but rather a realistic appraisal of the long running currents of Supreme Court decision making.

The ebb and flow of the justices' views on what "commerce among the states" means remained stable for decades until, once again, justices with quite different attitudes about federalism appeared on the bench.

Between 1936 and 1994, the justices did not strike down a single federal law as being beyond Congress's commerce power despite the proliferation of statutes regulating what could fairly be labeled local activities. The doctrinal tool the Court used to allow this onslaught of federal regulation was the aggregation test, which held that the commerce clause allows Congress to regulate all local activities that, in the aggregate, substantially affect commerce among the states.[48] Pursuant to this authority, the Court allowed Congress to regulate the home-grown production and consumption of wheat, individual instances of loansharking, and the discriminatory practices of local restaurants and hotels among many other statutes governing local economic transactions.[49]

As is true with virtually every litigated area of constitutional law, however, the justices eventually circled back to a different approach, cutting back on federal power over commerce. In 1990, Congress made it a crime to possess a gun in or near a school zone. A Texas student was arrested for violating the law and challenged the statute on the basis that it exceeded Congress's power under the commerce clause. The issue came before the Court in *United States v. Lopez.*[50]

The government defended the law on the basis that (1) guns pose a serious threat to the nation's schools; (2) the national economy is impacted when schools decline in quality; and (3) housing markets and local businesses are negatively impacted when schools are threatened. Although those arguments may seem strained, prior Courts, as mentioned earlier, had allowed Congress to regulate virtually every aspect of labor relations, discrimination by small businesses, local crime with little connection to the national economy, and home-grown wheat.[51]

The *Lopez* Court distinguished those prior cases on the basis that they involved commercial activity, which the justices said was not true about the gun law.[52] Then, despite reaffirming the "substantial effects" test and the "aggregate" approach, which had led to so many cases affirming federal power under the commerce clause, the justices returned to the rationale of the discredited child labor case and pondered whether there would be any limit on Congress's commerce clause power if the justices were to uphold the gun law. In a 5–4 decision decided along ideological lines, they answered the question in the negative and overturned a federal law under the commerce power for the first time in over fifty years.[53]

The Rehnquist Court, and later the Roberts Court, were not done. Twice more after *Lopez*, the Supreme Court ruled laws beyond federal reach under the commerce clause. In *United States v. Morrison,*[54] the justices invalidated an important provision of the Violence against Women Act,[55] which authorized civil remedies for people who were the victims of gender violence. Congress had conducted years of hearings and commissioned numerous reports concluding that gender violence costs the economy billions of dollars in lost work days, medical bills, and increased insurance costs. Nevertheless, by a 5–4 vote divided along the same liberal/conservative lines, the Court said the provision exceeded congressional power because gender-related violence is not commercial activity. The justices were also concerned that granting Congress this power would lead to unlimited federal authority.[56] The justices in dissent observed that the act "would have passed muster at any time between *Wickard* in 1942 and *Lopez* in 1995" and accused the majority of returning to the "federalism of some earlier time," by embracing the "theory of laissez-faire [that] was [un]able to govern the national economy 70 years ago."[57]

The third case where the justices said that Congress exceeded its commerce clause power was *NFIB v. Sebelius.*[58] In an opinion joined again by five conservatives (with four liberals dissenting from this part of the case), the Court held that Congress could not mandate, under the commerce clause, that people buy health insurance (although the Court did uphold the mandate as a valid tax).[59] The justices concocted an antimandate limiting principle that is nowhere in the text of the Constitution even though early Congresses used mandates to enforce parts of the Constitution other than the commerce clause (so much for originalism).[60] There is much to criticize about the Court's commerce clause analysis, but for our purposes, the important aspect of this case is its inconsistency with a decision just a few years earlier.

After the Court's decisions in *Lopez* and *Morrison*, but before it decided *NFIB*, the justices surprised most people by holding that Congress could regulate the private, noncommercial medical use of homegrown marijuana that was legal under state law.[61] The 6–3 decision was joined by both Justices Scalia and Kennedy, who previously voted to invalidate the laws in *Lopez* and *Morrison*. All the justices who upheld the marijuana law relied on the fact that the restrictions were contained in one small section of an omnibus federal statute regulating the buying and selling of numerous drugs. For example, Justice Scalia said that Congress's goal was to eliminate virtually all uses of schedule one substances including marijuana. Therefore, even though the activity in *Raich*, private use of marijuana for permissible medical purposes under state law, was a local, noncommercial activity, Congress could still prohibit it "as a necessary part of a larger regulation."[62]

Of course, the same thing could have been said about the individual mandate in the Affordable Care Act, which was also "a necessary part of a larger regulation." In response to that argument, both Justices Scalia and Roberts argued that allowing Congress to use mandates somehow violated the "proper" element in the "Necessary and Proper

Clause."[63] However, what is constitutionally "proper" is quite obviously much more in the eye of the beholder than dictated by text, history, or precedent.

Between 1995 and 2012, the Court decided four major commerce clause cases. The justices struck down congressional efforts to regulate guns, violence against women, and health insurance, but affirmed federal power to regulate noncommercial marijuana use. All the liberal justices voted to uphold the laws in every case. All the conservatives voted against federal power under the commerce clause in each case, except Scalia and Kennedy jumped ship in the marijuana decision. From all of this, and the past back and forth history of the commerce clause, it is easy to conclude that what drives the justices' views on the appropriate relationship between federal power and the need for state autonomy is not the text or original meaning of the commerce clause, or the justices' prior cases interpreting the provision. Rather, ideology, values, and politics were the major drivers of these decisions.

There are many other areas of constitutional law where the justices have changed their collective minds on important issues. For example, as discussed in Chapter 8, the Court never held that the Second Amendment protected an individual right to own guns until 2008.[64] As discussed in Chapter 7, the Court's anticommandeering decisions under the commerce clause have gone back and forth between deference and aggressive judicial review for eighty years.[65] In 1989, the Court held that Congress could use its commerce clause power to take away a state's sovereign immunity, but just a few years later, after Justice Thomas replaced Justice Marshall, the Court abruptly changed its mind on this fundamental federalism question.[66] And, the fluctuations in the Court's campaign finance reform and voting rights decisions have generated enormous uncertainty and angst among election law experts as well as local and state governments.[67]

The Supreme Court has updated, backtracked, or dramatically changed its views on most of the litigated constitutional law issues of the last one hundred years. Most of these alterations have been sparked by changes in societal and judicial values, modern technologies, and political considerations. Judicial analysis of text and original meaning has not played a major role in these developments other than to support decisions quite likely made on other grounds. In other words, "interpretations [of text and history] do not, in our practice of constitutional law, determine constitutional decisions."[68]

Originalists who claim that text and history are (or should be) the primary drivers of constitutional litigation must wrestle with this torrent of changing case law interpreting a fixed Constitution. Yet, as the next chapter shows, few have taken on that task. Instead, the claims of originalists are made and defended more as an article of faith than a reasoned response to judicial review as actually practiced or likely to be practiced by the US Supreme Court.

10 ORIGINALISM AS FAITH

Defenses and criticisms of originalism have come to seem to me more
like disputes among theologians than like other academic inquiries.

Mark Tushnet[1]

A. ORIGINALIST TESTIMONY

Professor Lawrence Solum, whose work was discussed in prior
chapters, testified about originalism in front of the Senate Judiciary
Committee during the Neil Gorsuch Supreme Court confirmation
hearings.[2] He described how most originalists, old and new, advocate
for originalism as their favored method of constitutional interpretation.
His remarks were public statements by a leading originalism scholar
designed to persuade the American people and the Senate that originalism is the most, perhaps the only, legitimate method of constitutional
interpretation. Solum's rhetoric strongly suggested that he believed the
doctrine of originalism is the only true constitutional faith. Taking a
close look at his testimony, however, reveals substantial questions that
originalists often refuse to wrestle with and demonstrates many of the
myths surrounding originalism as a theory of constitutional interpretation. The first part of this chapter critically reviews Solum's testimony
while the rest suggests that its dogmatism is consistent with how other
originalists try to spread the word and keep the faith.

One likely objection to this section must be addressed at the start.
Solum's remarks are only twelve pages long. Obviously, he could not
and did not intend to present a comprehensive defense of originalism,
as he has attempted elsewhere.[3] Nevertheless, in his testimony he
made bold and dogmatic statements about originalism and criticized

non-originalist accounts of judicial review by nationally prominent constitutional law scholar David Strauss (whose work was also discussed in prior chapters). Moreover, Professor Solum has made similar arguments in much more scholarly settings, yet he has not supported them even in those academic venues with substantial references to litigated cases and written opinions.[4] When he testified, he entered the most public and political of places, the US Congress, at a key moment in American history, the confirmation hearing for Justice Scalia's replacement, and made strong claims about those who do not believe originalism is a viable method of constitutional interpretation. His comments deserve serious consideration.

Solum argued that for "most of American history, originalism has been the predominate view of constitutional interpretation."[5] He said that originalist judges, like Justice Scalia before he passed, believe that constitutional interpretation is concerned with understanding the original public meaning of the constitutional text. What "[o]riginalist judges do not believe [is] that they have the power to impose their own values on the nation by invoking the idea of a 'living constitution.'"[6]

Few Court followers, originalist, non-originalist, or those in between, agree with Solum's descriptive statement that originalism has been the "predominate view" of constitutional interpretation throughout American history. As already discussed, the legal realists of the 1930s, the critical legal scholars of the 1980s, and many political scientists today believe the Court's decisions are best explained by looking at the justices' values and prior cases, not originalist methodologies.[7] Many of today's leading academics who are not legal realists, such as Philip Bobbitt, Steve Griffin, Laurence Tribe, Mitch Berman, Erwin Chemerinsky, and Mike Dorf, argue that the justices use a pluralistic interpretative model taking into account numerous modalities including text, history, structure, case law, consequences, and values, while originalism plays only a minor role.[8] Even modern originalists such as John McGinnis and Michael Rappaport disagree with Solum's descriptive account that originalism has in practice played a primary role in constitutional interpretation.[9]

Moreover, Solum identified Justice Scalia as a justice committed to originalism. Randy Barnett, Solum's originalist colleague at Georgetown University Law School, has stated the opposite, that Justice Scalia was not a true originalist.[10] Furthermore, as Chapter 7 argued, originalists cannot hold up Justice Scalia (or Justice Thomas) as models of judicial reliance on originalism because throughout their careers they consistently voted for non-originalist outcomes.[11] Their free speech, affirmative action, criminal procedure, anticommandeering, sovereign immunity, and standing decisions, among many others, are all inconsistent with originalism. If Scalia is Solum's model of originalist decision making, the late justice's many non-originalist votes, as well as the description of Scalia by a leading originalist that Scalia did not actually implement the doctrine, suggests there is a significant disconnect between Solum's theoretical claims and the reality of originalism on the ground.[12]

There is no fair argument that Supreme Court constitutional law decisions have been largely driven by originalism if by that term we mean that ratification-era sources played a primary role in constitutional interpretation. Professor Barnett has stated that "I am pretty sure the Constitution will mostly be interpreted in accordance with what the words mean *in the modern context*. And it has mostly been interpreted in that way."[13] Perhaps we could describe the Court's cases as originalist if we take most of the "original meaning" out of originalism and use the broad definition of "inclusive originalism" advocated by Professors Baude and Sachs.[14] However, that kind of originalism brings most of the Warren and Burger Court's liberal decisions, as well as the same-sex marriage cases, into the originalism fold.[15] I doubt Solum would accept that most of those cases were based on the original public meaning of the constitutional text, although in fairness he has never addressed those questions. Even if there is a case to be made that text and ratification-era history have in fact played a significant role in Court decisions, Professor Solum has never tried to make it because he "assiduously avoids discussion of specific constitutional problems."[16] Solum is a careful and thoughtful scholar, but when it comes to his descriptive claims about originalism, he has so far not provided enough case law support to justify his theory.

Solum made a distinction between originalist judges and judges who believe that they "have the power to impose their own values on the nation by invoking the idea of a 'living constitution.'" But the Supreme Court's decisions do not support the claim that so-called originalist justices do not draw on their own values to decide cases.

As Professor Cass Sunstein has remarked, "the views of many self-proclaimed originalists line up, not with those of We the People in 1789, but with those of the right wing of the Republican Party in 2017. Whether we're speaking of campaign-finance laws, commercial advertising, gun rights, affirmative action, gay rights, property rights, or abortion, originalism has failed to prevent judges from voting in accordance with their political predilections."[17]

In his prepared remarks to Congress, Solum responded to what he said were several categorical misunderstandings about Originalism. One of these was, in his words, that "Originalists Cannot Apply the Constitution to New Circumstances."[18] He tried to rebut this alleged myth by claiming that the First Amendment can easily be applied by originalists to the internet even though that specific medium did not exist in 1787, and that we all understand that Nebraska is constitutionally entitled to two senators even though Nebraska as a state did not exist in 1787.[19] These examples, however, do not address the commonly made charge that it is extremely difficult for judges to ascertain the original meaning of centuries old text when they are called upon to resolve actual cases.

No one disputes that new mediums of communication such as the internet are covered by the First Amendment, or that states that came into the union after 1787 are entitled to two senators. There is much debate, however, about how judges should ascertain the Constitution's original meaning as applied to internet threats, abortion restrictions, affirmative action policies, presidential drone attacks, partisan redistricting, police searches of cell phones, and same-sex marriage bans, to name just a few examples of controversies that the worlds of 1787 or 1868 could not have anticipated.

There are many questions about our government resolved by clear constitutional text such as the president must be thirty-five, and all impeachments must be tried by the Senate. Few disputes over these issues ever make it to court. In his other writings, Solum has explained why. When the communicative (nonlegal) content of the text is susceptible to only one reasonable interpretation that matches its legal consequences, judges will be quite hesitant to apply a different meaning.[20] Although the Supreme Court has at times veered away from clear text, such as with its holdings on sovereign immunity and anticommandeering, these are exceptions to the rule.[21] As a general proposition, judges do follow clear text, and few living constitutional-ists would disagree. A fair and important question is why Professor Solum employs strawmen examples of precise constitutional provi-sions (like the president must be 35) that do not get litigated instead of real controversies the Supreme Court must resolve. Again, the disconnect between theory and reality is significant.

In his remarks, Solum criticized Professor David Strauss for his view that the Supreme Court uses a common law system of revising and updating its own precedents to build constitutional doctrine, not an analysis of text and original meaning.[22] Solum said that it "is no accident that Professor Strauss wrote a book entitled *The Living Consti-tution*. The truth is that if the constitutional text does not bind the Supreme Court, then the justices are the equivalent of a super legislature ... [a] committee of nine unelected judges [who] has the power to reshape our Constitution as they see fit."[23]

Solum criticized Strauss, but neither in Solum's testimony (under-standable), or anywhere else in his scholarship, does Solum provide evidence to combat Strauss's descriptive account of how little the original meaning of the constitutional text matters to the justices. Both Strauss and this author have published articles in the *Harvard Law Review* arguing, based on voluminous case law, that the Court's doc-trines are based on a common law method of precedent and ideology, not text and original meaning.[24] Solum's claims that living constitu-tionalism leads to judicial tyranny, but originalism somehow constrains judges, rings hollow, if not false, because Supreme Court constitutional doctrine goes back and forth repeatedly based on the ideological makeup of the Court,[25] and most cases implicate vague text that, even according to Solum, must be constructed in ways that originalist inquiries cannot answer.[26]

As to the objection leveled by many non-originalists that determin-ing the original public meaning of such an old document is too difficult to drive constitutional interpretation, Solum responded as follows: "The constitutional text is old, but it is not the Rosetta Stone. Lawyers, judges, and scholars can work together to unearth the evidence of original meaning in the hard cases. And there are many easy cases, in which the original meaning is clear to any fair-minded reader who consults the historical record."[27] Solum pointed to no such litigated cases however, because there are not any, at least of those that reach the Supreme Court. In virtually every case the justices choose to resolve, the original meaning of the constitutional text will be either hotly disputed by the parties or irrelevant. What does it matter what people living in 1787 or 1868 thought about federal independent agencies that exercise power in a way the framers did not anticipate, or affirmative action policies designed by universities to make up for generations of Jim Crow that the people of 1868 couldn't know about? The idea that judges should try to figure out what the words of the Constitution meant at the time of ratification makes no sense when judges must resolve cases that implicate facts, values, technologies, and events the people living at the time of ratification did not and could not contemplate. Solum does not use real cases to address any of those practical problems with originalism in either his testimony or his scholarship, and neither do most originalists.

Professor Solum ended his testimony with the following statement: "The whole idea of the originalist project is to take politics and ideology out of law. Democrats and Republicans, progressives and conservatives, liberals and libertarians – we should all agree that Supreme Court Justices should be selected for their dedication to the rule of law."[28] This idea, that only originalism can make judging and judicial review consistent with the rule of law, and that only originalism can "take politics and ideology" out of the Supreme Court, are constant refrains of many originalists. Lino Graglia has said that originalism is "almost self-evidently correct."[29] Judge Bork said that interpretative theories other than originalism "must end in constitutional nihilism and the imposition of the judge's merely personal values on the rest of us."[30] Writing for the Cato Institute, Roger Pilon said the following about the late Justice Scalia: "Rejecting the modern living Constitution and the wide discretion that approach to constitutional interpretation affords a judge, [Scalia] argued brilliantly, often in scintillating dissents, that to preserve the rule of law – and, presumably, the legitimacy it entails – judges must ground their decisions in the statutory or constitutional text as understood by those who wrote or ratified it."[31] Professor Richard Duncan has written that to Scalia, "the text of the Written Constitution is law, and the duty of the Court is to interpret the constitutional text based upon its original meaning. The so-called Living Constitution is not law but rather clay in the hands of Justices who shape it to mean whatever they believe it 'ought to mean.'"[32]

These statements about originalism, whether made by legal scholars in law reviews and books, or by judges in written opinions, or by law professors testifying in front of Congress, are designed to promote one central idea: that only originalism can take the politics out of judging and ensure the rule of law is not the rule of the justices' personal values. The problem is none of that is true.

B. ORIGINALISM ON THE GROUND

Originalists themselves disagree, often strenuously, over proper outcomes and appropriate methodology in constitutional cases.[33] As Professors Tom Colby and Peter Smith have shown in detail, Original Originalists, New Originalists, and those in between and after adopt substantially different views on how judges should use originalism and what results judges should reach in specific cases.[34]

Original Originalists such as Judge Bork, Lino Graglia and Raoul Berger would be aghast at Randy Barnett's and Ilya Somin's originalist (and quite libertarian) calls to strike down much of the regulatory state, and to use the Ninth Amendment to enforce a strong libertarian form of judicial review.[35] Allowing judges to pick and choose which economic regulations are valid would leave them enormous discretion increasing judicial subjectivity. As a more general matter, an "originalist" judge today could either advocate strong deference to all state and federal laws in the name of the old, classic originalism, or could adopt Barnett's and Somin's theory of construction to strike down laws banning abortion, affirmative action, gun control, and same-sex marriage. If an originalist judge could reach any, some, or all these results, how does originalism lead to less-personal judging than other methods of constitutional interpretation?

Originalist Professors Michael Rappaport and John McGinnis believe that the type of constitutional construction advocated by Keith Wittington, Randy Barnett, and Lawrence Solum is not only inconsistent with originalism,[36] but also that "constructionist originalists lose most of the advantages of originalism."[37] Originalist Steven Calabresi believes that judges should interpret the Fourteenth Amendment at such a high level of generality that it invalidates most forms of gender discrimination and bans on same-sex marriage.[38] Jack Balkin believes that the New Originalism and living constitutionalism are "flip-sides of the same coin," something most originalists might argue with, but not Randy Barnett, who has said, "I am in agreement with nearly everything Balkin says about [New] Originalism."[39]

There is no theory of originalism that leads to agreement among scholars and judges about how the Supreme Court should decide cases. Some originalists think deference is important; others believe that enforcing the broad libertarian nature of the Constitution is crucial; yet others think the key insight is that the justices should use only those interpretative measures that the framers considered and adopted. Some originalists, like Will Baude and Steve Sachs, even think that originalism is already "our law" in the sense that decisions like *Brown v. Board of Education, Lawrence v. Texas,* and *Obergefell v. Hodges* are based on originalism, despite the unarguable fact that in each of those cases the justices explicitly denied that original meaning generated the outcomes. For example, in *Lawrence,* Justice Kennedy said, "times can blind us to certain truths and later generations can see that laws once thought necessary and proper in fact serve only to oppress. *As the Constitution endures, persons in every generation can invoke its principles in their own search for greater freedom.*"[40] If this is originalism, as Baude and Sachs allege,[41] then everything is originalism, and nothing is originalism.

There are as many different versions of originalism and how judges should use text, original meaning, and precedent, as there are theories of "living constitutionalism." Originalism does not take politics or ideology out of constitutional decision making but instead gives judges any number of ways to reach whatever results they choose in virtually any constitutional case. In that specific sense, originalism and living constitutionalism are no different.

Absent a strong deferential approach to all state and federal laws, which has never been how the modern Court practices constitutional law, the justices will inevitably decide cases largely in conformity with their ideologies. In the words of Dean Erwin Chemerinsky, "[c]onstitutional law is now, will be, and always has been ... largely a product of the views of the Justices."[42]

C. WHY PRETEND ORIGINALISM MATTERS?

Why do so many smart and thoughtful legal scholars advocate that originalism is the only interpretative method to keep personal values out of judging, and that the rule of law requires originalism for judicial review to be legitimate, when those claims do not accurately describe judging today or in the past? Why do some Supreme Court justices and lower court judges so often talk about the importance of originalism in their decisions but consistently vote for non-originalist outcomes? The answer may be that for many legal actors, and for the public, it is a matter of faith that only something called "originalism" can constrain judges.

In one relatively recent survey, 70 percent of the people polled thought the Supreme Court is a political body "too mixed up in politics."[43] Thus, on one level, the American people are not naïve when it comes to wrestling with the confluence of law and politics in the Court's decisions. There is nonetheless great resistance among the people to fully embrace that account of the justices as reflected by the fact that, although the Court's popularity has dipped in recent years, it still is far more popular than Congress or the president.[44]

Professor Karl Coplan has explained why there is so much resistance among law professors, lawyers, judges, and the American people to the legal realist description of constitutional law adjudication:

> If judges ... choose law out of an indeterminate range of outcomes supportable by legitimate legal reasoning, basing their choices on idiosyncratic notions of policy and fairness, then are not judges making legislative choices that more properly belong with the legislature? If the justification for judicial review is the inherent judicial function of applying the rule of decision required by a superior legal document (the United States Constitution, with its Supremacy Clause) as against an inferior legal document (congressional legislation), does not this theoretical justification fall apart in those cases where accepted constitutional legal reasoning will

support more than one outcome, and the judicial choice of
outcomes is based on something other than ineluctable legal
reasoning?[45]

To accept the realist critique would, in the eyes of many observers,
sophisticated and lay, undercut the entire rationale for allowing judges
to strike down acts of more accountable governmental officials.
Although many legal realists disagree that their critique fatally undercuts the rationale for judicial review,[46] legal academics and most
originalists need to be able to justify the Court's decision making on
the basis that preexisting text, or other positive law materials, drive the
justices' opinions. As Jamal Greene has so artfully put it, "the selling of
originalism" is to a large degree centered around the idea that only
strong fidelity to text and original meaning can support unelected
judges possessing so much power in our constitutional, representative
democracy.[47] But this idea glosses over major disconnects between
the rhetoric of originalism and real-life constitutional interpretation by
judges deciding actual cases.

Since the 1980s, the label "originalism" has been an effective
political tool employed by some (certainly not all) conservatives and
libertarians to justify the appointment of judges whose politics and
values they prefer. The claim that originalist judges "apply not make
the law," appeals to the general public's wish to believe that the justices
are above normal politics (even if at some level the public knows that
isn't true). As Professor Greene has pointed out, originalism "is not
only instrumental to a particular political agenda but is also responsive
to a set of demands the public makes during moments of constitutional
engagement ... originalism as a constitutional aesthetic."[48] This "aesthetic" is described along the lines as our side (originalists) believe in
text, original meaning and the law whereas your side (those judges and
scholars who favor the living constitution) impose their own values.
Those ideas were expressed by Professor Solum in his congressional
testimony.

Professor Greene summarizes one of the ways originalism has been
effectively sold to the American public. He recounts the story of Mark
Levin (self-proclaimed "The Great One"), who in 2005 (and today)
was a right-wing radio host and a former member of Ed Meese's Justice

Department. He wrote a book called *Men in Black: How the Supreme Court Is Destroying America.*[49] Levin argued that judges are either originalists who follow the law or activists who make the law in their own image. Rush Limbaugh wrote the introduction and Ed Meese the afterword.[50] This book was almost completely ignored by law professors and the Supreme Court media. It was not reviewed in the *New York Times* or the *Washington Post.* Constitutional Law Professor Mark Tushnet of Harvard said that he did not know anyone who read the book.[51] Yet, the book became a national bestseller, and at the time, Levin's radio show garnered the number one slot in New York's evening commute home.[52] This was originalism for the masses. On the other side, there has never been a living constitutionalism for the masses.

Another example of how conservatives have marketed originalism is Justice Scalia's national speaking tours, where he constantly lamented the living Constitution and advocated for what he repeatedly called the "Dead, Dead, Dead" Constitution.[53] According to the justice, "you would have to be an idiot" to think the Constitution is alive.[54] Scalia said that "[m]y Constitution is a very flexible one ... there's nothing in there about abortion. It's up to the citizens. ... The same with the death penalty."[55] To Scalia, "[t]he only good Constitution is a dead Constitution."[56]

Bruce Allen Murphy, who wrote a biography of the late justice, said that what Scalia meant by all of this "dead" and "alive" talk was that social and political change should come through the people and constitutional amendments, not through creative readings of text and history by nine unelected, lawyers.[57] Scalia repeatedly pressed these arguments in his speeches to law students, college students, the media, and the public at large.[58]

There can be no denying Justice Scalia's impact on constitutional law, judicial politics, and how judges perceive and sell themselves. Murphy said it best writing shortly after Scalia's death: "From among the thousands of younger lawyers and conservative Federalist Society members who revere his judicial opinions, many books, and entertaining speeches, we might see his intellectual heirs rise through the judiciary in the years and decades ahead, with perhaps one or more being appointed to the Supreme Court."[59] This prediction, of course, given the Federalist

Society's direct role in choosing judicial nominees for President Trump and Justice Gorsuch's appointment, has more than come true.[60]

The substantial problem with this rhetoric about Justice Scalia is that he did not vote like the Constitution was "Dead, Dead, Dead," and he did not let text or original meaning stop him from imposing his personal values on the parties who appeared before him. Chapter 7 detailed many examples of Scalia's voting patterns in areas as diverse as affirmative action, federalism, criminal procedure, jurisdiction, and free speech. Although he occasionally broke ranks with conservatives on issues involving criminal procedure and First Amendment freedoms, his votes for thirty years reliably reflected those of the Republican Party. He supported, in the legal sense (as does Justice Thomas), gun rights, term limits, abortion restrictions, same-sex marriage bans, sodomy bans, affirmative action bans, class action limitations, consumer-hostile arbitration agreements, campaign finance restrictions, the death penalty for juveniles and the mentally ill, nontextual limitations granting states sovereign immunity from lawsuits, immunity for states from congressional commandeering, nontextual limitations on Congress's commerce clause authority, and the list goes on and on. In many of these areas, Scalia voted to overturn state and federal laws without support in text or original meaning.[61] Scalia regularly updated the Constitution with nontextual principles he supported on purely policy grounds. This lengthy description of Justice Scalia by one commentator hits the mark:

> The adulation by admirers of Justice Antonin Scalia over his alleged role as a conservative constitutional steward who applied neutral, nonpartisan principles, is pure myth. . . . Justice Scalia was, in fact, one of the most unabashedly partisan judges ever to sit on the Supreme Court. *His manipulation of the constitution was brilliant, and maddening, mostly because he and his followers pretend otherwise.* . . . Sometimes he glorified judicial restraint and vilified his colleagues for . . . expanding constitutional rights. Sometimes he was a clear example of judicial activism.[62]

Professor Paul Campos argued that:

> Scalia had no real fidelity to the legal principles he claimed were synonymous with a faithful interpretation of the law. Over and over

during Scalia's three decades on the Supreme Court, if one of his cherished interpretive principles got in the way of his political preferences, that principle got thrown overboard in a New York minute.[63]

Another scholar used Scalia's commerce clause votes to make the same point:

Scalia is neither a faint-hearted or stout-hearted originalist. He is a *convenient* originalist. He's an originalist when it leads to the result he wants and he's not an originalist when it doesn't. ... And he's perfectly happy contradicting himself to reach the result he prefers. Just compare his ruling in *Raich* to his ruling in the challenge to the Affordable Care Act. ... In *Raich* he agreed that the interstate commerce clause gave Congress the power to regulate the growth of marijuana for personal use – an action that is neither interstate nor commerce – despite that being legal under state law. In the ACA case he argued that the interstate commerce clause did not give Congress the power to regulate the health insurance market, which is, by any definition, a matter of interstate commerce. Ironically, Scalia is exactly what he ... for decades accused liberals of being, a results-oriented judge.[64]

Why do so many law professors and Court commentators pretend that Justice Scalia applied originalism? It cannot be enough to justify the originalist label to talk about text and original meaning but routinely distort or ignore those legal sources to implement your own values. Why was Scalia so effective advocating for a theory of constitutional interpretation he did not adopt? The answer may be that originalism is not a theory of constitutional interpretation judges can effectively use to decide cases but a symbol, an article of faith, that links judicial review and the rule of law.

As discussed at length in Chapters 5 and 6, many originalists today virtually concede that judges must employ normative non-originalist judgments to resolve constitutional cases. Professors Randy Barnett, Lawrence Solum, and Keith Whittington all accept that today's judges will not be able to rely on originalist sources when deciding many or most cases.[65] Jack Balkin, speaking about New Originalism theory, has said that when "the Constitution is silent, or when it uses vague language, standards, or principles, *an inquiry into*

original meaning will not be sufficient to decide most contested questions.
Hence there is a second activity of constitutional interpretation, called
constitutional construction. Constitutional construction builds out
the 'Constitution-in-practice,' fleshing out and implementing vague
and abstract language through doctrine."[66] Along the same lines
Balkin also says that, "the basic [originalist] framework does not settle
most disputed questions of constitutional interpretation; most disputed questions require constitutional construction. ... [A]nswering
these disputed questions *must depend on other kinds of authority than
the originalist account.*[67]

Professor Richard Kay, an Original Originalist, has pointed out that
to "engage in construction is definitionally to go beyond the constitutional text," and that one "prominent theme is that construction
should work out the large values that underlie the constitutional
text."[68] Kay correctly argues that the New Originalist theory of constitutional construction is not originalist at all:

> When judicial decisions are founded on constructions, however,
> they are not "textual imperatives." Instead ... judges in matters of
> construction are deemed to have "discretion to resolve ambiguities
> and vague terms based on extra-constitutional considerations."
> Each judge must select what he or she decides is the appropriate
> "normative theory." Admittedly, such a theory will be connected in
> one way or another to the constitutional text. Inevitably, however, it
> will also be determined, in more or less substantial part, by the
> judges' own estimation of the right principles that ought to govern
> society.[69]

Kay concluded that in "the context of constitutional adjudication,
the endorsement of constitutional construction amounts to the "view
that courts are authorized to impose constitutional rules other than
those adopted by the constitutional [enactors]," a position that more or
less defines non-originalism."[70]

Many New Originalists do not rely on original meaning,
ratification-era evidence, or even history as the primary driver of
constitutional outcomes. Historian Jonathan Gienapp has argued
that New Originalists seek to identify the meaning of words written
long ago "without behaving like historians; they insist that historical
methods are only incidental to their chosen historical inquiry. ...

[T]hey ... presume that historical expertise has little bearing on the recovery of public meaning."[71]

What all of this means is that many, if not most, academics who today try to sell originalism to the public through their books, articles, essays, op-eds, public speeches, and even congressional testimony are promoting a brand of constitutional analysis substantially removed from reliance on text and original meaning and based mostly on the personal values and normative judgments of the justices. Originalism today, as opposed to the kind advocated by Judge Bork and Raoul Berger, is simply living constitutionalism by another name, and it is exactly the method of constitutional interpretation applied by Justices Scalia and Thomas.

Yet, originalism as a brand is selling better today than ever before. In the words of Gienapp, "leading originalists can be found on most esteemed law school faculties and in a growing network of influential constitutional law centers and think tanks. The thriving annual 'Originalism Works In-Progress Conference' at the University of San Diego Law School's Center for the Study of Constitutional Originalism ... is one prominent marker of popularity and influence; the well-funded annual 'Originalism Boot Camp,' which hosts aspiring law students each summer at the Georgetown Center for the Constitution is another. A new mountain of originalist scholarship and new lines of influence linking this academic work with the world of political and judicial action, meanwhile, appears every year."[72]

So why are all these scholars and judges using the brand name originalism to describe a method of constitutional interpretation far removed from ratification-era analysis? Why do Professors Will Baude and Steve Sachs argue, against all reason, that *Brown*, *Roe*, and *Obergefell* are examples of "inclusive originalism"? Why did Scalia tour the country ranting that the Constitution is "Dead, Dead, Dead," when his jurisprudence kept it very much alive and in sync with the times?

It is impossible to get in the heads and hearts of other people. To most Americans, however, the term *originalism* likely correlates both to conservative judges and to judges who "interpret but don't make the law." Those ideas were the main arguments in Solum's congressional testimony, Levin's book, and Scalia's roadshows. Maybe the myth that originalism can reduce the role of personal values in the Court's decisions is one that is necessary to allow people to keep faith in the Court. But this faith is misplaced, and as the next section argues, the myth is not needed to adequately justify judicial review.

D. LEGAL REALISM AND STRUCTURAL JUDICIAL REVIEW

Chief Justice John Marshall set forth the original rationale for judicial review in *Marbury v. Madison*, decided in 1803. Marshall explained how judicial enforcement of constitutional rules is an integral part of our country's devotion to the idea of limited government:

> The Constitution is either a superior, paramount law, unchange-able by ordinary means, or it is on a level with ordinary legislative acts, and like other acts, is alterable when the legislature shall please to alter it ... Certainly, all those who have framed written consti-tutions contemplate them as forming the fundamental and para-mount law of the nation, and consequently the theory of every such government must be, that an act of the Legislature, repugnant to the constitution, is void ...
>
> It is emphatically the province and duty of the judicial department to say what the law is. Those who apply the rule to particular cases, must of necessity expound and interpret that rule. If two laws conflict with each other, the Courts must decide on the operation of each. ... This is the very essence of judicial duty.[73]

Marshall explained that the judicial duty is to enforce paramount constitutional law over conflicting statutes. The content of the supreme law may either be precise, such as the president must be thirty-five, or imprecise, such as the government must not violate the "due process of law" or the "equal protection of the laws." The former types of provi-sions generally do not give rise to litigation, while the latter cannot be fleshed out by judges with reference to only text and original meaning. A political system that includes judicial review can only make three rational choices when it comes to imprecise constitutional language. One possibility is a culture where judges do not invalidate state or federal laws absent clear proof that such laws contradict clear text or almost universally accepted understandings of what the language means. That type of system was advocated by some of the Original

Originalists such as Raoul Berger and Lino Graglia. Under that model of judicial review, judges would rarely overturn decisions made by other political officials.

An analogy to this type of judicial review would be our current rules regarding when federal appellate judges may reverse the factual findings of trial court judges. Such findings are binding on higher courts unless they are "clearly erroneous."[74] That standard means that "an appeals court must accept the lower court's findings of fact unless the appellate court is definitely and firmly convinced that a mistake has been made. ... It is not enough that the appellate court may have weighed the evidence and reached a different conclusion; the lower court's decision will only be reversed if it is implausible in light of all the evidence."[75] Although there isn't reliable data on how often trial courts are reversed under this standard, this rule has been in place for a long time and seems to work reasonably well even if there are occasionally cases close to the line.

We could ask judges to apply the same or a similar standard to state and federal laws. As discussed in Chapter 2, it is likely that the Founding Fathers expected judges, except for cases implicating their own authority or judicial procedure, to adopt that kind of clear error rule. There would be many benefits to such a system. Such deference would reduce the influence of unelected, life tenured judges over difficult questions of social policy such as abortion, affirmative action, and gun control; it might lead to elected leaders taking their constitutional responsibilities more seriously; and it would almost certainly lead to much more predictability and consistency in constitutional cases.

Such a system of strong deference would also have negative consequences. It might weaken constitutional protections for minorities who don't have access to state and federal legislators and might also weaken our system of checks and balances. I have previously argued that the advantages of great deference outweigh the disadvantages,[76] but there is no reason to repeat that discussion here because our Supreme Court has not employed such deference in many constitutional areas in well over 150 years, and it is most unlikely it will do so in the future.

There are only two other rational ways to view our system of aggressive, nondeferential judicial review. One is to pretend that text and original meaning are important to constitutional cases because we

need that myth to justify the Court's strong role in enforcing constitutional rules. But a coercive governmental institutional that plays a
major role in our system of government should not be based on myth.
The other possibility is to see judicial review for what it really is and
justify it without regard to text and original meaning being important
factors the Court uses to decide constitutional cases.

A different and more realistic justification for judicial review would
center around what Professor Coplan has called the "structural justification."[77] The main idea is that the framers built a constitutional
system of checks and balances with competing branches and different
responsibilities. The judiciary's main role is to provide closure on
fundamental questions not clearly resolved by constitutional text, but
which implicate core constitutional values.[78] The Supreme Court, with
life-tenured justices beholden to no political group once on the Court,
might be the best governmental institution to at least temporarily
resolve contentious social and legal issues that divide the populace.
We hope the justices will be people of principle and good character
who will take a long view of what is in the best interests of the country.
Instead of resorting to taking up arms or violence, we rely on the Court
to decrease our passions on many fundamental questions. Since the
Civil War, and on most issues other than abortion and segregation, this
system has worked reasonably well.

This rationale does not depend on judges overturning state and
federal laws only where text and original meaning compel them to do
so. Nor does it require that the justices act as the direct agents for the
people who ratified the text so many years ago (something this book
has argued they simply cannot do). The people will abide by and
respect the Court's decisions simply because of the role the justices
play in our system of checks and balances.

Professor Coplan used the public's reaction to *Bush v. Gore*[79] to
support his structural theory. He persuasively described how the conservative justices ended the Florida recount giving the election to
President Bush while voting "against their ideological leanings to vastly
expand equal protection analysis in voting rights cases, apparently
motivated by a purely partisan desire to hand the presidency to the
candidate of their ... political party."[80] Coplan notes the intense
and immediate academic condemnation of the opinion both for its

"out-of-character" and oversized interpretation of the Fourteenth Amendment and its interference in resolving a disputed election process, which the constitutional text seems to delegate to Congress, not the Court.[81] Even Justice Stevens's dissenting opinion predicted that the case would severely damage the Court's prestige and public support.[82]

But the pushback and backlash against the Court never came, at least not directly. Perhaps that is partly because Al Gore did not contest the validity of the Court's decision. But it is also likely that the public acceded to this dramatic judicial interference because it accepted the Court's role in "resolving the election and avoiding a perceived threat of political chaos if the election were dragged out beyond the meeting of the electoral college."[83] Richard Posner defended the Court's decision along the same lines relatively soon after the opinion was issued.[84]

The advantage of this structural rationale for strong judicial review is that it can absorb the realist critique. We can accept the broad and imprecise aspirational goals of our constitutional enterprise, such as freedom of speech, freedom of religion, and commitments to federalism and separation of powers, for example, and trust the justices to act in good faith to apply those indeterminate concepts to new events and circumstances, without pretending that answers to hard constitutional issues flow naturally or logically from those precommitments. The justices' ideologies will play a dominant role in those resolutions, but the political process that produces Supreme Court nominees will likely go a long way to ensuring that the justices do not veer too far from dominant political sentiment. As Barry Freidman has persuasively detailed, the justices rarely stray too far from centrist public opinion.[85] This realistic approach to judicial power appeals to both faith *and* reason because "practice must trump theory in the context of constitutional argument."[86]

Professor Balkin's rich descriptive accounts and normative justifications for strong judicial review are in accord with this non-originalist picture of how the Court has operated and is likely to function in the future. Leaving aside his [mis]labeling the theory as "originalism," his detailed analysis of how constitutional change occurs seems correct. The justices do not just make up constitutional law out of whole cloth.

Instead, the justices' constructions result from a complex interplay of social, political, and legal forces, including, of course, the justices' ideologies. Balkin's descriptive analysis is right on the mark:

> History teaches us that courts normally do not engage in significant changes in constitutional doctrine without lengthy prodding from a sustained campaign by social movements and political parties, using not only litigation, but also political mobilization and cultural and social persuasion. ... [C]ourts usually don't get involved in developing new constitutional doctrines ... until political forces are strong enough to make them sit up and take notice. .... Above all, courts translate constitutional politics into constitutional law. It is not as if they have a choice ... The Justices do this not because they are wiser, or more noble, or more restrained, or more farsighted, or more principled, or more sober than the rest of us. Rather, they translate constitutional politics into constitutional law because of how they get their jobs and because they inhabit professional roles in which they must continually hear claims and articulate their answers in terms of the forms, practices and arguments of elite legal culture.[87]

The American people accept this "elite legal culture" and the momentous decisions made by our Supreme Court not because they really believe that vague constitutional texts lead inexorably or logically to the justices' conclusions. At one level the people may expect the justices to act like judges but at a deeper level they know the Court's real job is to provide a peaceful way to resolve some of our most bitter disputes. The most important judge in America over the last two decades, Justice Anthony Kennedy, rarely engages in long, detailed examinations of text and original meaning. It is clear from his four gay rights decisions, his key concurring opinion outlawing term limits for members of Congress, and numerous other important decisions regarding abortion, federalism, and free speech, that Justice Kennedy acts more like a political statesman than a judge concerned with text and original meaning.[88] Although he has often incurred the wrath of both sides of the political spectrum, depending on his vote, Kennedy will likely go down in history as one of our most important and transparent Supreme Court justices.

Like the Court that he has dominated, Kennedy's views have evolved over the years on such issues as abortion, affirmative action, and federalism. His differing votes were likely triggered by the political–legal–social process Balkin describes. That process has little to do with any meaningful version of originalism.

Legal scholars and the American people do not need to overstate the importance of vague text, contested ratification-era evidence and subsequent history, and the values of people who lived long ago to justify strong judicial review. Because it appears the Court is going to continue to play an important role in our system of checks and balances, acceptance of that system and hopefully the good character of the justices to perform their responsibilities in good faith should be enough. Pretending that the justices' decisions are based on nonpersonal factors or prior legal doctrine is not necessary and leads to a disturbing lack of transparency and intellectual dishonesty.

Yesterday and today, the justices made and make decisions based on their own values, priorities, and politics, as well as the culture they grew up in and reside in. If we can't justify their decisions on those grounds, the system should be changed. Before we can adequately have that conversation, however, we must see the Court clearly and recognize that originalism, at least as most scholars, judges, pundits, and the public use that term today, is only a matter of faith.

CONCLUSION

As Dean Chemerinsky said in his prologue, President Trump's promise to nominate only originalist judges, along with the confirmation of Neil Gorsuch, a self-avowed originalist, to replace Justice Scalia, suggests that the doctrine of originalism will continue to be discussed as a viable method of constitutional interpretation for years to come. This book has shown, however, that the people and legal cultures of the relevant ratification eras cannot provide substantial help to judges trying to solve today's constitutional questions. In both 1787 and 1868, white males dominated American society while women and people of color were regularly persecuted and denied basic legal rights. Moreover, new technological advancements as well as changed domestic and international conditions preclude judges from gleaning much useful information from centuries ago. Today's hard legal issues require today's solutions.

Originalism fails to limit the effects of personal values on judging. The only effective way to restrain judges from overturning state and federal laws based on ideology rather than law is for them to adopt a clear error rule where they would act only when the evidence of constitutional error is overwhelmingly clear. Such a deferential system of judicial review is coherent and plausible, but highly unlikely to be adopted by the Supreme Court, which has exercised strong judicial review for well over a century. Like other government officials, the justices are unlikely to limit their own power.

It is understandable that law students, law professors, lawyers, judges, and the American people wish to have faith that the justices decide cases based on prior law such as text, originalist evidence, and previous cases. But this book has shown that justices, not bound by precedent, who have largely unreviewable authority to decide society-defining issues, will not allow imprecise text and contested historical evidence from generations ago to stand in the way of their preferred policy preferences.

There is no single legal theory called originalism, and there is no such thing as an originalist judge. Some self-described originalists believe in strong judicial deference, while others advocate for exactly the opposite, aggressive judicial review. Some originalists believe the Court needs to dramatically change its interpretative methods, while others think originalism is already "our law." Some originalists believe that many litigated cases require non-originalist constitutional construction while others advocate that text and ratification-era methods and evidence are the only proper sources of constitutional law.

What most originalists do have in common is the faith that some combination of text, originalist-era evidence, and history can constrain Supreme Court decision making. But the words of the Constitution are too unclear, and their history too contested, for that to work. If limiting judicial discretion is the goal, only more lawyer-like tools like strong burdens of proof and presumptions of legislative validity can do the job.

To have true faith in the Supreme Court as a governmental institution requires the American people to understand and accept that prior law only plays a small role in the Court's decisions. But that doesn't mean the Court is illegitimate. The justices play an important role in the American commitments to checks and balances and limited government. The Court is a place where some of our society's most difficult social, legal, and political issues can be resolved peacefully without too much public acrimony. We need to have faith that our Justices will do their best to reach sound decisions and, eventually, if they decide cases in a way overwhelmingly displeasing to a large enough segment of the people, the nomination process will over time result in justices who make different decisions. But when that happens, it will be consequences, politics, and values that turn the tide, not the study of text and history.

Supreme Court justices should either stop striking down state and federal laws unless the evidence of unconstitutionality is compelling, or they should openly admit that it is their values writ large that make the difference in those cases where reasonable people can differ over a law's constitutionality (which is almost the entirety of the Court's constitutional docket). The belief that anything other than those values substantially drives the decisions of these life-tenured, governmental officials is nothing more than an overly optimistic, but wholly unrealistic, and ultimately dangerous, article of faith.

NOTES

Chapter 1

1. http://legaltimes.typepad.com/blt/2010/06/kagan-we-are-all-originalists.html, last accessed February 27, 2018.
2. www.merriam-webster.com/dictionary/faith, last accessed February 27, 2018.
3. One scholar has observed that there is "judicial originalism," "official originalism," and "universal originalism." These terms refer to judges, politicians, and ordinary citizens. Mitchell N. Berman, "Originalism Is Bunk" (2009) 84 *New York University Law Review* 1–96 at 14. Originalism discussions have taken place in "newspaper editorials, on blogs, on talk radio . . . and consistently large numbers of Americans report in surveys that they believe Supreme Court Justices should interpret the Constitution solely based on the original intentions of its authors." Jamal Greene, "On the Origins of Originalism" (2009) 88 *Texas Law Review* 1–89 at 2, 3.
4. Supreme Court of the United States, "Building History" www .supremecourt.gov/about/buildinghistory.aspx, last accessed February 27, 2018 (quoting Chief Justice Charles Evan Hughes's Cornerstone Address at the Supreme Court Building).
5. US Constitution, Amendments I and VIII.
6. US Constitution, Amendment XIV.
7. Jonathan O'Neil, *Originalism in American Law and Politics* (Baltimore, MD: Johns Hopkins University Press, 2005), p. 1.
8. Jamal Greene, "Selling Originalism" (2009) 97 *Georgetown Law Journal* 657–721 at 716.
9. 347 US 483 (1954).
10. 410 US 959 (1973).
11. 576 US ___ (2015).
12. 558 US 310 (2010).
13. 517 US 44 (1996).
14. 579 US 2 (2013).
15. Paul Brest, "The Misconceived Quest for the Original Understanding" (1980) 60 *Boston University Law Review* 204–238 at 234.

16. https://newrepublic.com/article/130408/antonin-scalia-death-originalism, last accessed February 27, 2018.

17. Berman, "Originalism Is Bunk," 92.

18. Michael Steven Green, "Legal Realism as Theory of Law" (2005) 46 *William & Mary Law Review*, 1915–2000 at 1920.

19. Richard Kay, "Adherence to the Original Intentions in Constitutional Adjudication: Three Objectives and Responses" (1988) 82 *Northwestern University Law Review* 226–292 at 227 ("[m]ost observers agree that a substantial portion of constitutional law is only tenuously connected to the constitution of 1787, as amended").

20. Richard Posner, *The Problems of Jurisprudence* (Cambridge, MA: Harvard University Press, 1990), p. 442.

21. Frank Cross, "Originalism – The Forgotten Years" (2012) 28 *Constitutional Commentary* 37–51 at 51.

22. Stephen M. Griffin, "Rebooting Originalism" (2008) 2008 *University of Illinois Law Review* 1185–1223 at 1188.

23. Thomas B. Colby, "The Sacrifice of the New Originalism" (2011) 99 *Georgetown Law Journal* 713–778 at 715. (New originalism "affords massive discretion to judges in resolving contentious constitutional issues.")

24. Randy Barnett, "Interpretation and Construction" (2011) 34 *Harvard Journal of Law & Public Policy* 65–72 at 69–70.

25. Colby, "The Sacrifice of the New Originalism," 733 ("[c]onstitutional construction . . . aims to produce a decision that is consistent with original meaning but not deducible from it." (internal quotations and alterations omitted)).

26. See Jamal Greene, Nathaniel Persily, and Stephen Ansolabehere, "Profiling Originalism" (2011) 111 *Columbia Law Review* 356–418 at 358. ("We might imagine originalism to be associated with a set of political outcomes or, alternatively, with a particular political ideology, and supported by those who wish to promote those outcomes or who affiliate with that ideology.")

27. Richard H. Fallon, "Are Originalist Constitutional Theories Principled, or Are They Rationalizations for Conservatism?" (2011) 34 *Harvard Journal of Law & Public Policy* 5–28 at 22.

28. www.judiciary.senate.gov/imo/media/doc/03-23-17%20Solum%20Testimony .pdf, last accessed February 27, 2018.

29. The Blog of Legal Times, "Kagan: 'We Are All Originalists'" (June 29, 2010) http://legaltimes.typepad.com/blt/2010/06/kagan-we-are-all-originalists.html.

30. Justice Neil Gorsuch, "Senate Confirmation Hearing" (March 21, 2017) https://grabien.com/story.php?id=95249, last accessed February 27, 2018.

31. Thomas B. Colby and Peter J. Smith, "Living Originalism" (2011) 59 *Duke Law Journal* 239–307 at 245.

32. Jonathan R. Macy, "Originalism as an Ism" (1995) 19 *Harvard Journal of Law & Public Policy* 301–309 at 308.

33. Berman, "Originalism Is Bunk," 24–25.
34. Brest, "The Misperceived Quest," 205.
35. Berman, "Originalism Is Bunk," 18–20.
36. Ibid., 24.
37. H. Jefferson Powell, "The Original Understanding of Original Intent" (1985) 98 *Harvard Law Review* 885–948 at 936.
38. Berman, "Originalism Is Bunk," 17.
39. Ibid., 17–18.
40. *NLRB v. Noel Canning*, 573 US (2014).
41. www.virginialawreview.org/volumes/content/politicians-robes-separation-powers-and-problem-judicial-legislation, last accessed February 27, 2018.
42. Colby, "The Sacrifice of the New Originalism," 714.
43. Greene, "Selling Originalism," 680.
44. See Chapter 6.
45. Griffin, "Rebooting Originalism," 1191 note 40.
46. Jamal Greene, "On the Origins of Originalism" (2009) 88 *Texas Law Review* 1–90 at 7.
47. O'Neil, *Originalism in American Law*, p. 31 (quoting Justice Benjamin Cardozo).
48. Berman, "Originalism Is Bunk," 86 (quoting Laurence Tribe).
49. Erwin Chemerinsky, "The Vanishing Constitution" (1989) 103 *Harvard Law Review* 43–104 at 91–102.
50. Ethan J. Leib, "The Perpetual Anxiety of Living Constitutionalism" (2007) 24 *Constitutional Commentary* 353–370 at 354 (quoting Jack Balkin).

Chapter 2

1. 5 U.S. 137 (1803).
2. Alexander Hamilton, "The Federalist No. 78" (1788) *Independent Journal.*
3. Hamilton, "The Federalist No. 78" (emphasis added).
4. Hamilton, "The Federalist No. 78" (emphasis in original).
5. *Marbury v. Madison*, 5 U.S. 137 (1803).
6. *Marbury*, 5 U.S. 137 at 177 (1803).
7. Ibid.
8. Powell, "Original Intent," 902–904.
9. Ibid., 897.
10. Ibid., 931.
11. Ibid., 888.
12. Powell, "Original Intent"; Gordon Wood, *The Creation of the American Republic: 1776–1787* (1969).
13. See Chapter 4.
14. John O. McGinnis and Michael B. Rappaport, *Originalism and the Good Constitution* (Cambridge, MA: Harvard University Press, 2013), pp. 154–156.

15. See Chapter 6.
16. U.S. Constitution. Art. III, § 3.
17. Larry Kramer, *The People Themselves* (Oxford, UK: Oxford University Press, 2004).
18. Sylvia Snowiss, *Judicial Review and the Law of the Constitution* (New Haven, CT: Yale University Press, 1990), p. 60.
19. Gordon S. Wood, "The Origins of Judicial Review Revisited, or How the Marshall Court Made More out of Less" (1999) 56 *Washington & Lee Law Review* 787–809 at 799–800 (1999).
20. James Bradley Thayer, "The Origin and Scope of the American Doctrine of Constitutional Law" (1893) 7 *Harvard Law Review* 129–156.
21. William Michael Treanor, "Judicial Review before Marbury", (2005) 58 *Stanford Law Review* 455–562 at 455.
22. Treanor, "Judicial Review before Marbury," 457–458.
23. Ibid., 458–59.
24. *Marbury*, 5 U.S. 137 at 176 (1803).
25. *Commonwealth v. Caton*, 4 Call 5 (1782).
26. This summary of the case is taken largely from Dean Treanor's article, Treanor, "Judicial Review before Marbury," 489–496.
27. Ibid., 491.
28. Ibid., 491 (quoting Edmund Randolph).
29. Ibid., 491 (quoting St. George Tucker).
30. Ibid., 492 (quoting St. George Tucker).
31. Ibid., 492 (quoting St. George Tucker).
32. Ibid., 494 (quoting Chancellor Edmund Pendleton).
33. John McGinnis, "The Duty of Clarity" (2016) 84 *George Washington University Law Review (2016)* 843–919, *882 (quoting Pendleton).*
34. Treanor, "Judicial Review before Marbury," 495–496.
35. Hamilton, "The Federalist No. 78."
36. Treanor, "Judicial Review before Marbury," 496.
37. Ibid., 497.
38. Ibid., 498.
39. McGinnis, "The Duty of Clarity," *881.*
40. Treanor, "Judicial Review before Marbury," 561.
41. Keith E. Whittington, "Judicial Review of Congress before the Civil War" (2009) 97 *Georgetown Law Journal* 1257–1332.
42. 60 U.S. 393 (1857).
43. Whittington, "Judicial Review of Congress," 1258.
44. Ibid., 1259.
45. "A Nation Divided: The Political Climate of 1850s America," in *The Benjamin Hedrick Ordeal: A Portrait of Antebellum Politics and Debates over Slavery* (Omeka), https://cwnc.omeka.chass.ncsu.edu/exhibits/show/benjamin-hedrick/polticalclimate, last accessed February 27, 2018.

46. Mark Graber, "Desperately Ducking Slavery: Dred Scott and Contemporary Constitutional Theory" (1997) 14 *Constitutional Commentary* 271–318 at 271–72 (quoting Christopher L. Eisgruber and Charles Evans Hughes) (internal quotation omitted).

47. Christopher Eisgruber, "Dred Again: Originalism's Forgotten Past" (1993) 10 *Constitutional Commentary* 37–66 at 40–41.

48. *Dred Scott v. Sandford*, 60 U.S. 393 at 404–405 (1857).

49. Graber, "Desperately Ducking Slavery," 274 ("[n]o prominent theorist admits that *Dred Scott* might have been a legitimate exercise of judicial review").

50. *Dred Scott v. Sandford*, 60 U.S. 393 at 405 (1857).

51. Ibid. at 410 (1857).

52. Ibid. at 426 (1857).

53. S. L. Whitesell, "Originalism and Dred Scott," *Tractatus* (January 15, 2013), http://tractatus.typepad.com/tractatus/2013/01/originalism-and-dred-scott .html, last accessed February 27, 2018.

54. Graber, "Desperately Ducking Slavery," 273.

55. Ibid., 280–315.

56. *See* Chapter 5.

57. *See* Chapter 9.

58. Eric J. Segall, *Supreme Myths: Why the Supreme Court Is Not a Court and Its Justices Are Not Judges* (Santa Barbara, CA: Praeger, 2012).

59. Arthur W. Machen Jr., "The Elasticity of the Constitution" (Parts 1 & 2) (1900) 14 *Harvard Law Review* 200–216, 273–285. Much of this section is taken from my (too optimistically titled) article, Eric J. Segall, "A Century Lost: The End of the Originalism Debate" (1998) 15 *Constitutional Commentary* 411–440.

60. Machen, "Elasticity of the Constitution," 200 (emphasis added).

61. Ibid., 201.

62. Ibid., 203.

63. Ibid., 204.

64. Ibid., 205.

65. Ibid., 204.

66. Ibid., 204–205.

67. Ibid., 205–211.

68. Ibid., 215.

69. Ibid., 216.

70. Ibid., 216.

71. Robert H. Bork, *The Tempting of America: The Political Seduction of the Law* (New York: The Free Press, 1990), p. 143–167; Antonin Scalia, Laurence H. Tribe, and Ronald Dworkin, *A Matter of Interpretation* (Princeton, NJ: Princeton University Press, 1997), p. 24–28.

72. Machen, "Elasticity of the Constitution," 273.

73. Ibid., 273 (emphasis added).
74. Ibid., 274.
75. Ibid., 274–275.
76. *Brass v. Stoeser*, 153 U.S. 391 at 403–404 (1894).
77. Machen, "Elasticity of the Constitution," 276.
78. Ibid., 276.
79. Ibid., 277.
80. Ibid., 277–78.
81. Ibid., 280.
82. Ibid., 283.
83. Ibid., 283.
84. William Baude, "Is Originalism Our Law" (2015) 115 *Columbia Law Review* 2349–2408.
85. Eric J. Segall, "Originalism as Faith" (2016) 102 *Cornell Law Review* 37–52 at 40–41.
86. Scalia et al., *A Matter of Interpretation*, pp. 40, 66, 120–122, 145–147.
87. Eric J. Segall, "A Century Lost: The End of the Originalism Debate" (1998) 15 *Constitutional Commentary* 411–440 (1998).

Chapter 3

1. *Youngstown Sheet & Tube Co. v. Sawyer*, 343 U.S. 579 at 634–635 (Jackson, J., concurring) (1952).
2. *Strauder v. West Virginia*, 100 U.S. 303 at 309–311 (1880).
3. These cases are discussed in Chapter 4.
4. *Lochner v. New York*, 198 U.S. 45 (1905).
5. Ibid. at 46.
6. For a wonderful treatment of *Lochner*, see David E. Bernstein, *Rehabilitating Lochner: Defending Individual Rights against Progressive Reform* (Chicago: University of Chicago Press, 2011).
7. *Lochner*, 198 U.S. at 57; Eric J. Segall, *Supreme Myths: Why the Supreme Court Is Not a Court and Its Justices Are Not Judges* (Santa Barbara, CA: Praeger, 2012), pp. 34–35.
8. *Lochner*, 198 U.S. at 60–61.
9. Ibid. at 61; Segall, *Supreme Myths*, p. 34.
10. *Lochner*, 198 U.S. at 53.
11. Ibid., at 75.
12. Ibid., at 76.
13. *Hammer v. Dagenhart*, 247 U.S. 251 (1918).
14. Jacobus tenBroek, "Use by the United States Supreme Court of Extrinsic Aids in Constitutional Construction" (1939) 27 *California Law Review* 399–421 at 404–408.

15. *South Carolina v. United States*, 199 U.S. 437 at 450 (1908), quoted in tenBroek, "Extrinsic Aids," 401 and Jonathan O'Neil, *Originalism in American Law and Politics* (Baltimore: Johns Hopkins University Press, 2005), p. 37.
16. *West Coast Hotel Co. v. Parrish*, 300 U.S. 379 at 402 (1937) (Sutherland, J., dissenting).
17. *Adkins v. Children's Hospital of the District of Columbia*, 261 U.S. 525 at 568–570 (1923) (Holmes, J., dissenting).
18. Segall, *Supreme Myths*, pp. 38–41.
19. *United States v. Carolene Products Co.*, 304 U.S. 144 (1938).
20. Ibid. at 154.
21. Ibid. at 152 note 4.
22. Jacobus tenBroek, "Admissibility and Use by the United States Supreme Court of Extrinsic Aids in Constitutional Construction" (1938) 26 *California Law Review* 287–308; Jacobus tenBroek, "Use by the United States Supreme Court of Extrinsic Aids in Constitutional Constructions" (1938) 26 *California Law Review* 437–454; Jacobus tenBroek, "Use by the United States Supreme Court of Extrinsic Aids in Constitutional Constructions" (1938) 26 *California Law Review* 664–681; Jacobus tenBroek, "Use by the United States Supreme Court of Extrinsic Aids in Constitutional Constructions" (1939) 27 *California Law Review* 157–181; Jacobus tenBroek, "Use by the United States Supreme Court of Extrinsic Aids in Constitutional Constructions" (1939) 27 *California Law Review* 399–421.
23. O'Neil, *Originalism in American Law*, p. 28 (quoting Justice Holmes).
24. Ibid., p. 29.
25. K. N. Llewellyn, "The Constitution as an Institution" (1934) 34 *Columbia Law Review* 1–40 at 40 (quoted in Thomas B. Colby and Peter J. Smith, "The Return of Lochner" (2015) 100 *Cornell Law Review* 527–602 at 542).
26. Colby and Smith, "The Return of Lochner," 542.
27. Some of this section is taken from my article, "Judicial Originalism as Myth," *Vox* (February 27, 2017), www.vox.com/the-big-idea/2017/2/27/14747562/originalism-gorsuch-scalia-brown-supreme-court, last accessed February 27, 2018.
28. tenBroek, "Extrinsic Aids," 26 *California Law Review* 287–308, 26 *California Law Review* 437–454, 26 *California Law Review* 664–681, and 27 *California Law Review* 157–181.
29. tenBroek, "Extrinsic Aids," 27 *California Law Review* 399–421 at 400.
30. Ibid., 404.
31. Ibid., 404.
32. Ibid., 404.
33. Ibid., 404.
34. Ibid., 405.

35. Ibid., 403–06.

36. Ibid., 406–08.

37. Ibid., 411.

38. Ibid., 411.

39. Ibid., 416 (quoting Justice Sutherland).

40. Ibid., 416.

41. Ibid., 416.

42. Ibid., 421.

43. This section on the *Steel Seizure* case is substantially similar to a section in Segall, "A Non-Originalist Separation of Powers" (2018), forthcoming *University of Richmond Law Review*.

44. Neal Devins and Louis Fisher, "The Steel Seizure Case: One of a Kind?" (2002) 19 *Constitutional Commentary* 63–86 at 64.

45. Ibid., 64.

46. Ibid., 64–65.

47. Executive Order 10340 Directing the Secretary of Commerce to Take Possession of and Operate the Plants and Facilities of Certain Steel Companies, 17 Fed. Reg. 3139 (Apr. 10, 1952).

48. Joshua Korman, "Youngstown Sheet & Tube Co. *v.* Sawyer Reevaluating Presidential Power," www.roberthjackson.org/wp-content/uploads/migrated-files/article-calendar-files/korman_primer.pdf, last accessed February 27, 2018.

49. *Youngstown Sheet & Tube Co. v. Sawyer*, 343 U.S. 579 at 589 (1952).

50. Ibid. at 701 (Vinson, J., dissenting).

51. Ibid. at 637 (Jackson. J., concurring).

52. Devins and Fisher, "The Steel Seizure Case," 71.

53. Stephen I. Vladeck, "Foreign Affairs Originalism in *Youngstown's* Shadow" (2008) 53 *St. Louis University Law Journal* 29–38 at 31.

54. Martin S. Flaherty, "The Future and Past of U.S. Foreign Relations Law" (2004) 67 *Law and Contemporary Problems* 169–193 at 172.

55. *Youngstown*, 343 U.S. at 634–635 (Jackson, J., concurring).

56. Vladeck, "Foreign Affairs Originalism," 35 (quoting *Medellin v. Texas*, 552 U.S. 491 at 524 (2008)).

57. National Park Service, "Jim Crow Laws" (April 14, 2015), www.nps.gov/malu/learn/education/jim_crow_laws.htm, last accessed February 27, 2018.

58. The Civil Rights Act of 1875, 18 Stat. 335–337 (1875).

59. *The Civil Rights Cases*, 109 U.S. 3 (1883).

60. Ibid. at 11.

61. Ibid. at 58–59 (Harlan, J., dissenting).

62. Segall, *Supreme Myths*, p. 27 (quoting Justice Joseph Bradley).

63. *Plessy v. Ferguson*, 163 U.S. 537 (1896).

64. Segall, *Supreme Myths*, p. 28.

65. *Plessy*, 163 U.S. at 551.

66. Ibid. at 551–552.

67. Ibid. at 559 (Harlan, J., dissenting).

68. Ibid. at 559 (Harlan, J., dissenting).

69. Laws, "Plessy v. Ferguson," www.pbs.org/tpt/slavery-by-another-name/ themes/jim-crow/, last accessed February 27, 2018.

70. PBS, "Jim Crow and Plessy v. Ferguson," www.pbs.org/tpt/slavery-by-another-name/themes/jim-crow/.

71. *Brown v. Board of Education of Topeka, Shawnee County, Kansas,* 347 U.S. 483 (1954).

72. United States Courts, "History-Brown v. Board of Education Re-enactment," www.uscourts.gov/educational-resources/educational-activities/history-brown-v-board-education-re-enactment, last accessed February 27, 2018.

73. United States Courts, "History-Brown v. Board of Education Re-enactment," www.uscourts.gov/educational-resources/educational-activities/history-brown-v-board-education-re-enactment, last accessed February 27, 2018.

74. United States Courts, "History-Brown v. Board of Education Re-enactment," www.uscourts.gov/educational-resources/educational-activities/history-brown-v-board-education-re-enactment, last accessed February 27, 2018.

75. Lumen, "The Eisenhower Administration," www.boundless.com/u-s-history/textbooks/boundless-u-s-history-textbook/politics-and-culture-of-abundance-1943-1960-28/the-eisenhower-administration-216/the-warren-court-1460-8616/, last accessed February 27, 2018.

76. *Brown,* 347 U.S. at 489, 492–93.

77. Ibid. at 494–445.

78. Gerald N. Rosenberg, *The Hollow Hope: Can Courts Bring About Social Change?* 2nd ed. (Chicago: University of Chicago Press, 2008), pp. 52–54.

79. Stephen M. Griffin, "Rebooting Originalism" (2008) 2008 *University of Illinois Law Review* 1185–1223 at 1200.

80. O'Neil, *Originalism in American Law,* p. 40.

81. *Engle v. School District of Abington Township, Pennsylvania v. Schempp,* 374 U.S. 203 (1963).

82. *Gideon v. Wainwright,* 372 U.S. 335 (1963).

83. *Reynolds v. Sims,* 377 U.S. 533 (1964).

84. *New York Times Co. v. Sullivan,* 376 U.S. 254 (1964).

85. *Griswold v. Connecticut,* 381 U.S. 479 (1965).

86. *Miranda v. Arizona,* 384 U.S. 436 (1966).

87. *Loving v. Virginia,* 388 U.S. 1 (1967).

88. *Katz v. United States,* 389 U.S. 347 (1967).

89. *Brandenburg v. Ohio,* 395 U.S. 444 (1969).

90. *Roe v. Wade,* 410 U.S. 113 (1973).

91. Andre LeDuc, "Striding Out of Babel: Originalism, Its Critics, and the Promise of Our American Constitution" (2017) 26 *William & Mary Bill of Rights Journal* 1–86 at 45.

92. *Reynolds v. Sims*, 377 U.S. 533 (1964).

93. *Baker v. Carr*, 369 U.S. 186 (1962).

94. Carlo A. Pedrioli, "Instrumentalist and Holmesian Voices in the Rhetoric of Reapportionment: The Opinions of Justices Brennan and Frankfurter in *Baker v. Carr*" (2013) 4 *Alabama Civil Rights & Civil Liberties Law Review* 1–31 at 2 (quoting Earl Warren, *The Memoirs of Chief Justice Earl Warren* (New York: Madison Books, 2001), p. 306).

95. *Reynolds*, 377 U.S. at 562.

96. *Brandenburg v. Ohio*, 395 U.S. 444 (1969).

97. Frank Cross, "Originalism – The Forgotten Years," (2012) 28 *Constitutional Commentary* 37–51.

98. Ibid., 500–501.

99. O'Neil, *Originalism in American Law*, p. 40 (quoting Lucas A. Powe Jr., *The Warren Court and American Politics* [Cambridge, MA: Belknap Press of Harvard University Press, 2000], pp. 214–215).

Chapter 4

1. John Locke, *A Letter Concerning Toleration and Other Writings*, in Mark Goldie (ed.), *John Locke: A Letter Concerning Toleration and Other Writings* (Indianapolis, IN: Liberty Fund, 2010), p. 140.

2. Keith E. Whittington, "The New Originalism" (2004) 599 *Georgetown Journal of Law and Public Policy* 599–614 at 600.

3. Ibid., 600.

4. Ibid., 600.

5. Ibid., 600 (quoting William H. Rehnquist).

6. Matthew J. Franck, "The Original Originalist," *National Review* (January 28, 2013), www.nationalreview.com/nrd/articles/337354/original-originalist, last accessed February 27, 2018 (quoting Robert H. Bork).

7. Robert H. Bork, "Neutral Principles and Some First Amendment Problems" (1971) 47 *Indiana Law Journal* 1–47.

8. Ibid., 1.

9. Ibid., 6.

10. Ibid., 6.

11. Frank, "The Original Originalist."

12. Bork, "Neutral Principles," 8.

13. Ibid., 4 (quoted in Whittington, "New Originalism," 600).

14. *Griswold v. Connecticut*, 381 U.S. 479 (1965).

15. Bork, "Neutral Principles," 10.

16. Ibid., 10–11 (emphasis added).

17. Alexander Hamilton, "The Federalist No. 78" (1788) *Independent Journal* (discussed in note 34 in Chapter 2 and accompanying text).

18. Douglas Martin, "Raoul Berger, 99, an Expert on Constitution in 2nd Career," *The New York Times* (September 28, 2000), www.nytimes.com/2000/09/28/us/raoul-berger-99-an-expert-on-constitution-in-2nd-career.html, last accessed February 27, 2018.

19. *Bridges v. California*, 314 U.S. 252 (1941). Some of this section is similar to Eric Segall, 'Judical Engagement, New Originalism, and the Fortieth Anniversary of Government by the Judiciary,' (2017) 86 Fordham Law Review On Line 16.

20. Ibid. at 295–297.

21. Raoul Berger, "Constructive Contempt: A Post-Mortem" (1942) 9 *University of Chicago Law Review* 602–642 at 604–605 (quoted in Jonathan O'Neil, *Originalism in American Law and Politics* (Baltimore: Johns Hopkins University Press, 2005), p. 113).

22. Berger, "Constructive Contempt," 641–642.

23. Ibid., 642.

24. O'Neil, *Originalism in American Law*, p. 114.

25. Raoul Berger, *Government by Judiciary: The Transformation of the Fourteenth Amendment* (Indianapolis, IN: Liberty Fund, 1977).

26. Ibid., p. 403.

27. Ibid., p. 18.

28. Gerard E. Lynch, "Book Review Government by Judiciary: The Transformation of the Fourteenth Amendment" (1978) 63 *Cornell Law Review* 1091–1100 at 1091.

29. Ibid., 1092.

30. Ibid., 121.

31. Ibid., 1096.

32. Ibid., 1094 (quoting Berger, *Government by Judiciary*, p. 407).

33. Lynch, "Book Review," 1094.

34. See Legal Realism discussion in notes 18–19 in Chapter 1 and accompanying text.

35. See Chapters 7–9.

36. Andre LeDuc, "Striding Out of Babel: Originalism, Its Critics, and the Promise of Our American Constitution" (2017) 26 *William & Mary Bill of Rights Journal* 1–86 at 62.

37. O'Neil, *Originalism in American Law*, pp. 123–124.

38. Ibid., pp. 131–132.

39. Robert Post and Reva Siegel, "Originalism as a Political Practice: The Right's Living Constitution" (2006) 75 *Fordham Law Review* 545–574 at 545.

40. Mary Ziegler, "Grassroots Originalism: Rethinking the Politics of Judicial Philosophy," (2012) 51 *University of Louisville Law Review* 201–238 at 209–210.

41. Ibid., 216.

42. Ibid., 213.

43. The Heritage Foundation, "The Case for Originalism" (June 6, 2005), www.heritage.org/commentary/the-case-originalism, last accessed February 27, 2018.

44. Ziegler, "Grassroots Originalism," 218–219.

45. Ibid., 226–227.

46. Edwin Meese, Speech to American Bar Association on "Jurisprudence of Original Intention" (July 9, 1985), www.justice.gov/sites/default/files/ag/legacy/2011/08/23/07-09-1985.pdf, last accessed February 27, 2018.

47. Ibid.

48. Ibid.

49. Ibid.

50. Steven G. Calabresi, *Originalism: A Quarter-Century of Debate* (Washington DC: Regnery Publishing, 2007), p. 2.

51. Edwin Meese, Speech to Tulane University on "The Law of the Constitution" (October 21, 1986), www.justice.gov/sites/default/files/ag/legacy/2011/08/23/10-21-1986.pdf, last accessed February 27, 2018.

52. Ibid.

53. Ibid.

54. *Cooper v. Aaron*, 358 U.S. 1 (1958).

55. Meese, Speech to Tulane University on "The Law of the Constitution."

56. Amy Bach, "Movin' on Up with the Federalist Society," *The Nation* (September 13, 2001), www.thenation.com/article/movin-federalist-society/, last accessed February 27, 2018.

57. O'Neil, *Originalism in American Law*, p. 148.

58. The Federalist Society, "Our Background," https://fedsoc.org/our-background, last accessed February 27, 2018.

59. For the entire story, see Michael Avery and Danielle McLaughlin, *The Federalist Society: How Conservatives Took the Law Back from Liberals* (Nashville, TN: Vanderbilt University Press 2013).

60. O'Neil, *Originalism in American Law*, p. 148 (quoting Charles Cooper, assistant attorney general for the Office of Legal Counsel).

61. O'Neil, *Originalism in American Law*, p. 148.

62. Jamal Greene, "On the Origins of Originalism" (2009) 88 *Texas Law Review* 1–89 at 81.

63. Paul Brest, "The Misconceived Quest for the Original Understanding" (1980) 60 *Boston University Law Review* 204–238.

64. Lawrence B. Solum, "*District of Columbia v. Heller* and Originalism" (2009) 103 *Northwestern University Law Review* 923–981 at 928.

65. Brest, "The Misconceived Quest," 230. See also notes 27–30 in Chapter 3 and accompanying text (discussing work of Raul Berger).

66. Brest, "The Misconceived Quest," 230.

67. Ibid., 230 (quoting Justice Warren).

68. O'Neil, *Originalism in American Law*, p. 100.

69. Daniel A. Farber, "The Originalism Debate: A Guide for the Perplexed" (1988) 49 *Ohio State Law Journal* 1085–1106 at 1089.

70. Mark Tushnet, "Heller and the New Originalism" (2008) 69 *Ohio State Law Journal* 609–624 at 610.
71. H. Jefferson Powell, "The Original Understanding of Original Intent" (1985) 98 *Harvard Law Review* 885–948.
72. H. Jefferson Powell, "Rules for Originalists" (1987) 73 *Virginia Law Review* 659–700.
73. Numerous articles have been written devoted to confirming or criticizing Powell's belief in his Harvard article that the founding fathers would not have wanted judges to try to ascertain the subjective original intent of a constitutional provision. Robert N. Clinton, "Original Understanding, Legal Realism, and the Interpretation of 'This Constitution'" (1987) 72 *Iowa Law Review* 1177–1280; Charles A. Lofgren, "The Original Understanding of Original Intent?" (1988) 5 *Constitutional Commentary* 77–112.
74. Powell, "Rules for Originalists," 661.
75. Ibid., 661.
76. Ibid., 662.
77. Ibid., 662.
78. Ibid., 665.
79. Ibid., 669–670.
80. Ibid., 670.
81. U.S. Constitution Amendment IX.
82. Powell, 'Rules for Originalists', 670.
83. Ibid., 670. The most recent New New Originalists, discussed in Chapter 6 answer this concern by arguing that originalism allows judges to ignore the past if that is what the framers wanted. I respond fully to this argument in Chapter 6.
84. Powell, 'Rules for Originalists', 691.
85. Many on the left claim that affirmative action programs were prevalent at the time of the Reconstruction Amendments and therefore they must be constitutional. See notes 23–32 in Chapter 7 and accompanying text. But the historical issues are far more complex than that for many reasons, not the least of which is that we were just coming out of slavery.
86. O'Neil, *Originalism in American Law*, p. 197 (quoting Richard S. Kay, "Adherence to the Original Intentions in Constitutional Adjudications: Three Objections and Responses" (1988) 82 *Northwestern University Law Review* 226–292 at 244).
87. Lane V. Sunderland, "Critical Legal Studies and the Constitution" (1994) 23 *The Political Science Reviewer* 204–236 at 209.
88. Ibid., 208 (quoting Mark Tushnet, "Following the Rules Laid Down: A Critique of Interpretivism and Neutral Principles" (1983) 96 *Harvard Law Review* 781–827 at 818).
89. Robert W. Bennett and Lawrence B. Solum, *Constitutional Originalism: A Debate* (Ithaca, NY: Cornell University Press, 2011), pp. 8–9.

90. See discussion above at notes 50–55 and accompanying text.

91. Seth Stern and Stephen Wermiel, "Justice Brennan and Edwin Meese: A Constitutional Throwdown," *American Constitution Society* (September 30, 2010), www.acslaw.org/acsblog/node/17140, last accessed February 27, 2018.

92. Ibid.

93. Justice William J. Brennan, Speech at To the Text and Teaching Symposium Georgetown University, (October 12, 1985), https://fedsoc.org/commentary/publications/the-great-debate-justice-william-j-brennan-jr-october-12-1985, last accessed February 27, 2018.

94. Ibid.

95. Ibid.

96. Ibid.

97. Ibid.

98. Ibid.

99. Ibid. (quoting *Weems v. United States*, 217 U.S. 349, 373 (1910)).

100. Stern and Wermiel, "Justice Brennan and Edwin Meese," https://acslaw.org/acsblog/node/17140, last accessed February 27, 2018.

101. Ibid.

102. Justice John Paul Stevens, Speech to the Federal Bar Association, (October 23, 1985), https://fedsoc.org/commentary/publications/the-great-debate-justice-john-paul-stevens-october-23-1985.

103. Ibid.

104. Ibid.

105. Ibid.

106. Lori A. Ringhand, "'I'm Sorry, I Can't Answer That': Positive Scholarship and the Supreme Court Confirmation Process" (2008) 10 *Journal of Constitutional Law* 331–360 at 351–352.

107. Ibid., 340–341.

108. Judge Antonin Scalia, Testimony to Senate Judiciary Committee (August 5 & 6, 1986) Senate Hearing 99–1064 at 48–49, www.loc.gov/law/find/nominations/scalia/hearing.pdf, last accessed February 27, 2018.

109. Ibid.

110. Paul M. Collins, Jr. and Lori A Ringhand, *Supreme Court Confirmation Hearings and Constitutional Change* (New York: Cambridge University Press, 2013), p. 199.

111. Nina Totenberg, "Robert Bork's Supreme Court Nomination 'Changed Everything, Maybe Forever,'" *NPR* (December 19, 2012), www.npr.org/sections/itsallpolitics/2012/12/19/167645600/robert-borks-supreme-court-nomination-changed-everything-maybe-forever, last accessed February 27, 2018.

112. Collins and Ringhand, Supreme Court Confirmation Hearings, p. 199.

113. Ibid., pp. 205–219.

114. Ibid., p. 221.

115. Randy E. Barnett and Josh Blackman, "Restoring the Lost Confirmation," *National Affairs* (Fall 2016), www.nationalaffairs.com/publications/detail/restoring-the-lost-confirmation, last accessed February 27, 2018.

116. Collins and Ringhand, Supreme Court Confirmation Hearings, pp. 214–215 (quoting Judge Robert Bork).

117. Ibid., p. 211 (quoting Judge Robert Bork).

118. Ibid., p. 204 (quoting Senator Joe Biden).

119. Ibid., p. 200.

Chapter 5

1. Steven D. Smith, "Meetings or Decisions? Getting Originalism Back on Track" (2015) Research Paper No. 15–178, University of San Diego, p. 2.

2. Keith E. Whittington, "The New Originalism" (2004) 2 *Georgetown Journal of Law and Public Policy* 599–614 at 603.

3. Ibid., 603–604.

4. Lawrence B. Solum, "Originalism and Constitutional Construction" (2013) 82 *Fordham Law Review* 453–537 at 462–463. See also Stephen M. Griffin, "Rebooting Originalism" (2008) 2008 *University of Illinois Law Review* 1185–1223 at 1188.

5. Whittington, "The New Originalism," 604.

6. Andrew Coan, "Living Constitutional Theory" (2017) 66 *Duke Law Journal* 99–115 at 106–109 ("conservative lawyers, judges, and legal theorists were beginning to realize their own power and were looking for rhetorical and theoretical justifications for using it proactively to advance conservative interests").

7. Jonathan O'Neil, *Originalism in American Law and Politics* (Baltimore, MD: The Johns Hopkins University Press, 2005), p. 191.

8. Whittington, "The New Originalism," 605–606.

9. Antonin Scalia, "Address by Justice Antonin Scalia Before the Attorney General's Conference on Economic Liberties in Washington, DC (June 14, 1986)," in U.S. Department of Justice Office of Legal Policy (eds.) *Original Meaning Jurisprudence: A Sourcebook* (1987), Appendix C, pp. 101–106.

10. Jamal Greene, "The Case for Original Intent," (2012) 80 *The George Washington Law Review* 1683–1706 at 1684 (quoting Justice Antonin Scalia).

11. Greene, "Case for Original Intent," 1684 (quoting Justice Antonin Scalia).

12. Robert H. Bork, *The Tempting of America* (New York: The Free Press, 1990), p. 144.

13. Solum, "Originalism and Constitutional Construction," 463–464.

14. Robert W. Bennett and Lawrence B. Solum, *Constitutional Originalism: A Debate* (Ithaca, NY: Cornell University Press, 2011), p. 97 (quoting Gary Lawson, "On Reading Recipes ... and Constitutions" (1997) 85 *Georgetown Law Journal* 1823–1836).

15. Bennett and Solum, "Constitutional Originalism," p. 97 (quoting Michael Stokes Paulsen, "Does the Constitution Prescribe Rules for Its Own Interpretation?" (2009) 103 *Northwestern University Law Review* 857–922).

16. Randy E. Barnett, "An Originalism for Nonoriginalists" (1999) 45 *Loyola Law Review* 611–654 at 621.

17. Ibid., 621–622.

18. Ibid., 622 (quoting Ronald Dworkin).

19. Ibid., 623.

20. Randy Barnett, "Welcome to the New Originalism: A Comment on Jack Balkin's *Living Originalism*" (2013) 7 *Jerusalem Review of Legal Studies* 42–48 at 43.

21. Barnett, "Originalism for Nonoriginalists," 624.

22. Ibid., 624 (quoting Paul Brest).

23. Ibid., 625–627.

24. Griffin, "Rebooting Originalism," 1190–1191.

25. Ibid., 1189.

26. Ibid., 1189 (quoting Keith Whittington).

27. Thomas B. Colby and Peter J. Smith, "Living Originalism," (2009) 59 *Duke Law Journal* 239–307 at 251–252.

28. Ibid., 254.

29. Solum, "Originalism and Constitutional Construction," 464.

30. Ibid., 464.

31. Ibid., 464.

32. Mark Tushnet, "Heller and the New Originalism" (2008) 69 *Ohio State Law Journal* 609–624 at 612.

33. Colby and Smith, "Living Originalism," 254.

34. Griffin, "Rebooting Originalism," 1197–1198.

35. Ibid., 1197–1198.

36. Ibid., 1193–1195.

37. Solum, "Originalism and Constitutional Construction," 468.

38. Ibid., 469.

39. Ibid., 469–473.

40. Smith, "Meanings or Decisions," at 5 (emphasis added).

41. Mitchell N. Berman and Kevin Toh, "Distinguishing Old from New Originalism" (2013) 82 *Fordham Law Review* 545–576 at 554 (quoting Whittington, "The New Originalism," 612).

42. Randy E. Barnett, "Interpretation and Construction" (2011) 34 *Harvard Journal of Law & Public Policy* 65–72 at 69–70.

43. Jack M. Balkin, "The New Originalism and Uses of History" (2013) 82 *Fordham Law Review* 641–719 at 645–647.

44. Andre LeDuc, "Striding Out of Babel: Originalism, Its Critics, and the Promise of Our American Constitution" (2017) 26 *William & Mary Bill of Rights Journal* 1–86 at 27.

45. Steven G. Calabresi and Julia T. Rickert, "Originalism and Sex Discrimination," (2011) 90 *Texas Law Review* 1–101 at 2–3; Ilya Somin, "Why Same-Sex Marriage Bans Qualify as Sex Discrimination," *Volokh* (February 7, 2012), http://volokh.com/2012/02/07/same-sex-marriage-bans-and-sex-discrimination/, last accessed February 27, 2018.
46. Somin, "Same-Sex Marriage Bans."
47. Ibid.
48. Calabresi and Rickert, "Originalism and Sex Discrimination," 11–15.
49. Ibid., 7.
50. See Chapter 4.
51. Orin Kerr, "Is There an Originalist Case for a Right to Same-Sex Marriage?" *The Washington Post* (January 28, 2015), www.washingtonpost.com/news/volokh-conspiracy/wp/2015/01/28/is-there-an-originalist-case-for-a-right-to-same-sex-marriage/, last accessed February 27, 2018.
52. Jack M. Balkin, "Abortion and Original Meaning" (2007) 24 *Constitutional Commentary* 291–352 at 292.
53. Ibid., 293 (emphasis added).
54. Ibid., 293.
55. Jack M. Balkin, "Framework Originalism and the Living Constitution" (2009) 103 *Northwestern University Law Review* 549–614 at 551.
56. Jack M. Balkin, *Living Originalism* (London: The Belknap Press of Harvard University Press, 2011).
57. Balkin, "The New Originalism," 652.
58. Balkin, "Abortion and Original Meaning," 319–320.
59. Ibid., 321–326.
60. Ibid., 352.
61. Barry Friedman and Scott B. Smith, "The Sedimentary Constitution" (1998) 147 *University of Pennsylvania Law Review* 1–90 at 80–85.
62. Randy E. Barnett, "Underlying Principles" (2007) 24 *Constitutional Commentary* 405–416 at 411.
63. Steven Smith, "Are We Really All Living Originalists Now?" *Balkanization* (April 9, 2015), https://balkin.blogspot.com/2015/04/are-we-really-all-living-originalists.html, last accessed February 27, 2018.
64. Jamal Greene, "*Heller* High Water? The Future of Originalism" (2009) 3 *Harvard Law & Policy Review* 325–345 at 328.
65. Coan, "Living Constitutional Theory," 108.
66. Solum, "Originalism and Constitutional Construction," 456.
67. Ibid., 456.
68. Ibid., 456.
69. Bennett and Solum, *Constitutional Originalism*, p. 151.
70. Ibid.
71. Ibid.
72. Ibid.

73. Coan, "Living Constitutional Theory," 110.
74. Smith, "Meanings or Decisions," 2.
75. Colby and Smith, "Living Originalism," 274 (quoting and responding to Keith Whittington, *Constitutional Interpretation: Textual Meaning, Original Intent, and Judicial Review* [Lawrence: University of Kansas Press, 1999], p. 56).
76. Evan Bernick, "Lochner Lives! Why Conservative Are Finally Giving One of the Supreme Court's Most Underrated Decisions the Respect It Deserves," *Huffington Post* (April 24, 2015), www.huffingtonpost.com/evan-bernick/loch ner-lives-why-conserv_b_7130820.html, last accessed February 27, 2018.
77. See Colby and Smith, "Living Originalism," 247–262.
78. Saul Cornell, "Meaning and Understanding in the History of Constitutional Ideas: The Intellectual History Alternative to Originalism" (2013) 82 *Fordham Law Review* 721–756; James E. Fleming, "Are We All Originalists Now: I Hope Not" (2013) 91 *Texas Law Review* 1785–1814; Thomas B. Colby, "The Sacrifice of the New Originalism" (2011) 99 *Georgetown Law Journal* 713–778.
79. Ilan Wurman, *A Debt against the Living: An Introduction to Originalism* (New York: Cambridge University Press, 2017). See also Eric Segall "David Strauss Guess What: You are an Originalist After All" Originalism Blog (8/22/2017).
80. Ibid., p. 95.
81. Ibid.
82. Ibid.
83. David A. Strauss, "The Supreme Court: 2014 Term – Foreword: Does the Constitution Mean What It Says?" (2015) 129 *Harvard Law Review* 1–61.
84. Wurman, A Debt against the Living, pp. 39–40.
85. Ibid., pp. 114–115.
86. Ibid., p. 8 (emphasis added).

Chapter 6

1. William Baude, "Is Originalism Our Law?" (2015) 115 *Columbia Law Review* 2349–2408.
2. John O. McGinnis and Michael B. Rappaport, *Originalism and the Good Constitution* (Cambridge, MA: Harvard University Press, 2013).
3. Andrew Coan, "Living Constitutional Theory" (2017) 66 *Duke Law Journal* 99–115 at 111 (quoting Justice Antonin Scalia, "Originalism: The Lesser Evil" (1989) 57 *University of Cincinnati Law Review* 849–866 at 852).
4. See William Baude and Stephen E. Sachs, 2016 Originalism's Bite, 20 Green Bag 2d 103–108.
5. This discussion of Baude and Sachs is taken largely from Eric J. Segall, "Originalism as Faith" (2016) 102 *Cornell Law Review* 37–52.
6. Baude, "Is Originalism Our Law?" 2349.

7. David A. Strauss, "The Supreme Court: 2014 Term – Foreword: Does the Constitution Mean What It Says?" (2015) 129 *Harvard Law Review* 1–61 at 61.

8. Baude, "Is Originalism Our Law?" 2365.

9. Ibid., 2352.

10. Ibid., 2353.

11. Ibid., 2352 note 5.

12. Eric Segall, "Originalism on the Ground," *Dorf on Law* (November 2, 2015), www.dorfonlaw.org/2015/11/originalism-on-ground.html [https://perma.cc/FA5X-PLTN], last accessed February 27, 2018.

13. Baude, "Is Originalism Our Law?" 2352.

14. Ibid., 2352.

15. Ibid., 2352–2353.

16. Ibid., 2355 (emphasis omitted).

17. Ibid., 2356.

18. Ibid., 2356.

19. *See infra* text accompanying note 26.

20. Ibid., 2357.

21. Ibid., 2358.

22. Ibid., 2360.

23. Ibid., 2352.

24. *Brown v. Board of Education of Topeka, Shawnee County, Kansas,* 347 U.S. 483 (1954).

25. *Obergefell v. Hodges,* 135 S. Ct. 2584 (2015).

26. *Home Building & Loan Association v. Blaisdell,* 290 U.S. 398 (1934).

27. U.S. Constitution. Art. 1, § 10; *Home Building & Loan Association,* 290 U.S. 398 at 447–448.

28. *Home Building & Loan Association,* 290 U.S. 398 at 425–426 (quoting *Wilson v. New,* 243 U.S. 332 at 348 [1917]).

29. Ibid. at 426.

30. Ibid. at 426.

31. Baude, "Is Originalism Our Law?" 2378.

32. Ibid., 2378.

33. Ibid., 2378 (quoting Thomas B. Colby, "The Sacrifice of the New Originalism" (2011) 99 *Georgetown Law Journal* 713–778 at 767).

34. Baude, "Is Originalism Our Law?" 2377–2378, 2395–2397.

35. Eric J. Segall, "Constitutional Change and the Supreme Court: The Article V Problem" (2013) 16 *University of Pennsylvania Journal of Constitutional Law* 443–452 at 446–447.

36. Segall, *Constitutional Change,* 446–47.

37. Baude, "Is Originalism Our Law?" 2377–2378.

38. Ibid., 2352–2353.

39. *Obergefell v. Hodges,* 135 S. Ct. 2584 (2015).

40. Baude, "Is Originalism Our Law?" 2382.
41. *Obergefell*, 135 S. Ct. 2584 at 2629 (Scalia, J., dissenting) ("[The majority] discovered in the Fourteenth Amendment a "fundamental right" overlooked by every person alive at the time of ratification, and almost everyone else in the time since.").
42. Baude, "Is Originalism Our Law?," 2382 (quoting *Obergefell*, 135 S. Ct. 2584 at 2598).
43. William Baude, "Originalism and the Positive Turn" (2015) *Public Law and Legal Theory Working Paper No. 510* 15–23 at 16 (emphasis added).
44. Baude, "Is Originalism Our Law?" 2382 (quoting *Obergefell*, 135 S. Ct. 2584 at 2598).
45. Baude, "Is Originalism Our Law?" 2382–2383.
46. Ibid., 2383.
47. *Lawrence v. Texas*, 539 U.S. 558 at 578–579 (2003) (emphasis added).
48. Barry Friedman and Scott B. Smith, "The Sedimentary Constitution" (1998) 147 *University of Pennsylvania Law* Review 1–90 at 15–21 (tracing the Supreme Court's use of the "living Constitution" approach in the nineteenth and twentieth centuries).
49. Baude, "Is Originalism Our Law?" 2380.
50. Ibid., 2380.
51. Ibid., 2380–2381 (quoting *Brown v. Board of Education of Topeka, Shawnee County, Kansas*, 347 U.S. 483 at 489).
52. *Brown v. Board of Education*, 347 U.S. 483 at 494 n.11 (citing multiple social science sources to establish that segregation psychologically harms children).
53. Baude, "Is Originalism Our Law?" 2380–2381.
54. Stephen M. Griffin, "Rebooting Originalism" (2008) 2008 *University of Illinois Law Review* 1186–1224 at 1200.
55. Griffin, "Rebooting Originalism," 1202–1203.
56. Baude, "Is Originalism Our Law?" 2355 (describing strict originalists as those who think "judges should look only to the original meaning of the Constitution" while disallowing any "other sources of law, such as precedent or practice or policy").
57. Griffin, "Rebooting Originalism," 1188–1189 (claiming that the "old originalism" of Bork and others in the 1980s was designed to cure what they perceived to be the judicial activism of the Warren and Burger Courts).
58. Friedman and Smith, "The Sedimentary Constitution," 3–8. Even if we concede that cases like *Heller* represent authentic originalism, these cases make up only a small portion of all cases and thus a small portion of "our law."
59. Friedman and Smith, "The Sedimentary Constitution," 11–33 (describing a number of nineteenth- and twentieth-century "living constitution" cases, which exemplify the type of cases Baude would have to reconcile with his "inclusive originalism" theory).

60. *See* Chapter 1.

61. Lawrence B. Solum, "Originalism and Constitutional Construction" (2013) 82 *Fordham Law Review* 453–537 at 456.

62. Baude, "Is Originalism Our Law?" 2377–2378. Baude approves of the reasoning used by the Court in *Home Building & Loan Association v. Blaisdell*, 290 U.S. 398, despite disagreeing with the outcome.

63. *See*, e.g., *Obergefell v. Hodges*, 135 S. Ct. 2584 at 2589–2590 (relying heavily on prior Court decisions when legalizing same-sex marriage); *Brown v. Board of Education*, 347 U.S. 483 at 492–493 (refusing to give weight to the original meaning of the Fourteenth Amendment).

64. Stephen M. Griffin, *American Constitutionalism: From Theory to Politics* (Princeton, NJ: Princeton University Press, 1996) pp. 144–149 (summarizing the works of these scholars).

65. Saul Cornell, "New Originalism: A Constitutional Scam," *Dissent Magazine* (May 3, 2011), www.dissentmagazine.org/online_articles/new-originalism-a-constitutional-scam [https://perma.cc/SD5A-H3KH], last accessed February 27, 2018.

66. James E. Fleming, "The Inclusiveness of the New Originalism" (2013) 82 *Fordham Law Review* 433–452 at 436.

67. Ronald Dworkin, *Freedom's Law: The Moral Reading of the American Constitution* (Cambridge, MA: Harvard University Press, 1996) p. 2 (introducing his theory of moral reading).

68. Stephen E. Sachs, "Originalism as a Theory of Legal Change" (2015) 38 *Harvard Journal of Law and Public Policy* 817–888 at 820–822.

69. Sachs, "Originalism as a Theory," 838.

70. Ibid., 852 ("Often we explain important developments in our law by describing them as applications of unchanging rules to changing facts.").

71. Ibid., 856 (downplaying the victory of a post-Founding practice that conflicted with original constitutional text by explaining that the court "was willing to treat post-Founding tradition as a source of law because doing so had already been authorized at the Founding"); Baude, "Is Originalism Our Law?," 2382 (acknowledging that the Court in Lawrence rejected history as a dispositive factor but arguing the decision still had "an originalist pedigree" because the Court realized that the Founders intentionally left room for evolution in future application of the Fourteenth Amendment).

72. Kelley Beaucar Vlahos, "Judge Bork: Judicial Activism Is Going Global," *Fox News* (September 11, 2003), www.foxnews.com/story/2003/09/11/judge-bork-judicial-activism-is-going-global.html [https://perma.cc/8WY6-ZHN4], last accessed February 27, 2018.

73. Michael W. McConnell, "The Role of Democratic Politics in Transforming Moral Convictions into Law" (1989) 98 *Yale Law Journal* 1501–1544 at 1525 (reviewing Michael J. Perry, *Morality, Politics, and Law* [New York: Oxford University Press, 1988]) ("The appeal of originalism is that the

moral principles so applied will be the foundational principles of the Ameri-can Republic – principles we can all perceive for ourselves and that have shaped our nation's political character – and not the political-moral prin-ciples of whomever happens to occupy the judicial office.").

74. See Richard A. Posner, *How Judges Think* (Cambridge, MA: Harvard Uni-versity Press, 2008) p. 9 (noting it is "rather frequent" that judges are influenced by "their own political opinions or policy judgments, even their idiosyncrasies").

75. Eric J. Segall, *Supreme Myths: Why the Supreme Court Is Not a Court and Its Justices Are Not Judges* (Santa Barbra, CA: Praeger, 2012) p. 187 (conclud-ing that Supreme Court justices make decisions based on "their subjective value preferences and personal life experiences").

76. John O. McGinnis and Michael B. Rappaport, *Originalism and the Good Constitution* (Cambridge, MA: Harvard University Press, 2013).

77. McGinnis and Rappaport, *The Good Constitution*, p. 1 (emphasis added).

78. Ibid., p. 8.

79. Ibid., p. 8.

80. Ibid., p. 2.

81. Ibid., p. 3.

82. Ibid., p. 11.

83. Ibid., p. 3.

84. Ibid., p. 93.

85. Ibid., p. 93.

86. Ibid., pp. 93–94.

87. Ibid., p. 116.

88. Edward J. Erler, "Originalist Sin" (2014) 14 *Claremont Review of Books* 48–51 at 48–49 (quoting McGinnis and Rappaport, *The Good Constitution*, p. 116).

89. Whitley Kaufman, "Originalism and the Good Constitution" (2014) 24 *Law and Politics Book Review* 52–57 at 54.

90. Kaufman, "Originalism and The Good Constitution," 52; Erler, "Originalist Sin," 48. ("Whatever might be said for or against consequentialism as a way to organize a life or a country, it would appear difficult, at the very least, to establish that the Constitution of the United States is good, and that adhering to its original meaning is particularly good, without relying in some fashion on contestable assertions about what goodness entails." McGinnis and Rap-paport acknowledge but do not solve this problem.).

91. McGinnis and Rappaport, *The Good Constitution*, p. 107.

92. Ibid., p. 109–110.

93. Kurt T. Lash, "Originalism All the Way Down?" (2014) 30 *Constitutional Commentary* 149–166 at 152.

94. www.dorfonlaw.org/2015/10/stare-decisis-and-originalism.html, last accessed February 27, 2018.

95. McGinnis and Rappaport, *The Good Constitution*, pp. 108, 110.
96. See discussion notes 53–62 and accompanying text in Chapter 5.
97. McGinnis and Rappaport, *The Good Constitution*, p. 124.
98. Lash, "All the Way Down?" 158–159.
99. Ibid., 158–166.
100. Ibid., 165–166.

Chapter 7

1. Doug Kendall and Jim Ryan, "Originalist Sins," *Slate* (August 1, 2007), www.slate.com/articles/news_and_politics/jurisprudence/2007/08/original ist_sins.html, last accessed February 27, 2018.
2. Randy E. Barnett, "Scalia's Infidelity: A Critique of 'Faint-Hearted' Originalism" (2006) 75 *University of Cincinnati Law Review* 7–24 at 13.
3. See discussion at notes 27–42 and accompanying text in Chapter 3.
4. Jamal Greene, "*Heller* High Water? The Future of Originalism" (2009) 3 *Harvard Law & Policy Review* 325–345 at 330.
5. Justice Rehnquist began his career advocating for originalism, but he abandoned that emphasis over time in favor of a pragmatic conservatism that favored states' rights and judicial restraint, See Jeffrey Rosen, "Rehnquist the Great?," *The Atlantic* (April 2005), www.theatlantic.com/magazine/archive/2005/04/rehnquist-the-great/303820/, last accessed February 27, 2018.
6. Much of this analysis in this section is taken from Eric Segall, "The Constitution According to Justices Scalia and Thomas: Alive and Kickin'" (2014) 91 *Washington University Law Review* 1663–1674, Eric J. Segall, "Justice Thomas and Affirmative Action: Bad Faith, Confusion, or Both" (2013) 3 *Wake Forest Law Review Online* 11, Eric J. Segall, "Will the Real Justice Scalia Please Stand Up" (2015) *50 Wake Forest Law Review* 101–108.
7. Segall, "Justice Thomas and Affirmative Action" 11 (stating that Justice Thomas "often claims that fidelity to original intent and constitutional text is the most important element of constitutional interpretation," and additionally "claims that the best way for a judge to keep his personal views out of his judicial decisions is through rigid adherence to the text and history of the Constitution"); Mary Wood, "Scalia Defends Originalism as Best Methodology for Judging Law," *University of Virginia School of Law News and Media* (April 20, 2010), www.law.virginia.edu/html/news/2010_spr/scalia.htm, last accessed February 27, 2018 (stating that "[o]riginalism suggests that the Constitution has a static meaning," and that originalism is "to know the original meaning of constitutional provisions").
8. See Erwin Chemerinsky, "The Jurisprudence of Justice Scalia: A Critical Appraisal" (2000) 22 *University of Hawai'i Law Review* 385–402 at 389–390 (quoting Justice Scalia's statement in *Michael H. v. Gerald D.* regarding judicial decision making, stating that "[b]ecause such general traditions provide

such imprecise guidance, they permit judges to dictate rather than discern the society's views. The need, if arbitrary decision-making is to be avoided, to adopt the most specific tradition as the point of reference ... Although assuredly having the virtue (if it be that) of leaving judges free to decide as they think best when the unanticipated occurs, a rule of law that binds neither by text nor by any particular, identifiable tradition is no rule of law at all" (citing *Michael H. v. Gerald D.*, 491 U.S. 110 at 127 note 6 (1989)).

9. Clarence Thomas, "Judging" (1996) 45 *University of Kansas Law Review* 1–8 at 4 (quoted in Segall, "Justice Thomas and Affirmative Action").

10. *Obergefell v. Hodges*, 125 S. Ct. 2584 at 2629 (2015) (Scalia, J., dissenting); *Planned Parenthood of Southeastern Pennsylvania v. Casey*, 505 U.S. 833 at 979 (1992) (Scalia, J., concurring in part and dissenting in part).

11. Remarks by Justice Antonin Scalia at Oral Argument in the Supreme Court of the United States in *McDonald v. Chicago*, 561 U.S. 742 (March 2, 2010) (transcript available at www.buckeyefirearms.org/sites/buckeyefirearms.org/files/publicfiles/pdf/McDonald-v-Chicago-Oral-Arguments.pdf).

12. Ushma Patel, "Scalia Favors 'Enduring,' Not Living, Constitution," *Princeton University News* (December 11, 2012), www.princeton.edu/news/2012/12/11/scalia-favors-enduring-not-living-constitution, last accessed February 27, 2018.

13. Mitch Kokai, "Scalia: Originalism Not a 'Weird Affliction,'" *Carolina Journal* (November 1, 2007), www.carolinajournal.com/news-article/scalia-originalism-not-a-weird-affliction/, last accessed February 27, 2018.

14. *McCutcheon v. Federal Election Commission*, 134 S. Ct. 1434 at 1462 (2014) (Thomas, J., concurring).

15. *McConnell v. Federal Election Commission*, 540 U.S. 93 at 248 (2003) (Scalia, J., concurring); *Federal Election Commission v. Wisconsin Right to Life, Inc.*, 551 U.S. 449 at 483 (2007) (Scalia, J., concurring); *Davis v. Federal Election Commission*, 554 U.S. 724 (2008); *Citizens United v. Federal Election Commission*, 558 U.S. 310 at 385 (2010) (Scalia, J., concurring).

16. *Adarand Constructors, Inc. v. Pena*, 515 U.S. 200 at 239–241 (1995) (Scalia, J., concurring) (Thomas, J., concurring).

17. *Printz v. United States*, 521 U.S. 898 at 923–924 (1997); *Seminole Tribe of Florida. v. Florida*, 517 U.S. 44 at 67–69 (1996).

18. Michael Ramsey, "Eric Segall on Justice Scalia's 'Snake Oil Originalism,'" *Originalism Blog* (June 29, 2016), http://originalismblog.typepad.com/the-originalism-blog/2016/06/, last accessed February 27, 2018.

19. *Obergefell v. Hodges*, 125 S. Ct. 2584 at 2629 (Scalia, J., dissenting).

20. *McCutcheon*, 134 S. Ct. 1434 at 1462 (Thomas, J., concurring); *Citizens United*, 558 U.S. 310 at 385 (Scalia, J., concurring).

21. *Citizens United v. Federal Election Commission*, 558 U.S. 310 at 386 (Scalia, J., concurring).

22. David H. Gans, "Citizens United and the Bankruptcy of Conservative Originalism at the Supreme Court," *American Constitution Society Blog* (January 26, 2010), www.acslaw.org/acsblog/citizens-united-and-the-bank ruptcy-of-conservative-originalism-at-the-supreme-court, last accessed February 27, 2018; Jeffrey Rosen, "If Scalia Had His Way," *The New York Times* (January 8, 2011), www.nytimes.com/2011/01/09/weekinreview/09rosen .html, last accessed February 27, 2018.

23. *Citizens United v. Federal Election Commission*, 558 U.S. 310 at 428 (Stevens, J., concurring in part and dissenting in part).

24. *Citizens United*, 558 U.S. 310 at 387 (Scalia, J., concurring) ("Even if we thought it proper to apply the dissent's approach of excluding from First Amendment coverage what the Founders disliked, and even if we agreed that the Founders disliked founding-era corporations; modern corporations might not qualify for exclusion.").

25. Gans, "Bankruptcy of Conservative Originalism."

26. *McCutcheon*, 134 S. Ct. 1434 (2014).

27. Lawrence Lessig, "Originalists Making It Up Again: McCutcheon and 'Corruption,'" *The Daily Beast* (April 2, 2014), www.thedailybeast.com/articles/ 2014/04/02/originalists-making-it-up-again-mccutcheon-and-corruption.html, last accessed February 27, 2018.

28. *Planned Parenthood of Southeastern Pennsylvania v. Casey*, 505 U.S. 833 at 979 (Scalia, J., concurring in part and dissenting in part); *United States v. Windsor*, 133 S. Ct. 2675 at 2697 (2013) (Scalia, J., dissenting).

29. *Adarand Constructors, Inc. v. Pena*, 515 U.S. 200 at 239–241 (Scalia, J., concurring) (Thomas, J., concurring).

30. Scott Lemieux, "Scalia and Thomas: Originalist Sinners" (June 29, 2017), http://prospect.org/article/scalia-and-thomas-originalist-sinners, last accessed February 27, 2018.

31. Eric J. Segall, *Supreme Myths: Why the Supreme Court Is Not a Court and Its Justices Are Not Judges* (Santa Barbara, CA: Praeger, 2012) p. 97.

32. Stephen A. Siegel, "The Federal Government's Power to Enact Color-Conscious Laws: An Originalist Inquiry" (1998) 92 *Northwestern University Law Review* 477–590 at 550–551 ("Although by 1869 a few citizens had begun to agitate for integrated schools, Congress spurned all such suggestions and allowed school segregation to continue in the District until the Supreme Court held it unconstitutional in 1954.").

33. Eric Schnapper, "Affirmative Action and the Legislative History of the Fourteenth Amendment" (1985) 71 *Virginia Law Review* 753–798 at 754 ("From the closing days of the Civil War until the end of civilian Reconstruction some five years later, Congress adopted a series of social welfare programs whose benefits were expressly limited to blacks.").

34. See discussion at notes 63–70 and accompanying text in Chapter 3.

35. Andrew Douglas Pond Cummings, "*Grutter v. Bollinger*, Clarence Thomas, "Affirmative Action and the Treachery of Originalism: 'The Sun Don't Shine Here in This Part of Town'" (2005) 21 *Harvard Blackletter Law Journal* 1–74 at 46 (citing Schnapper, "Affirmative Action and Legislative History"; Siegel, "The Federal Government's Power," 499; Christopher E. Smith, "Clarence Thomas: A Distinctive Justice" (1997) 28 *Seton Hall Law Review* 1–28 at 11).

36. *Grutter v. Bollinger*, 539 U.S. 306 at 349 (2003) (Thomas, J., concurring in part and dissenting in part).

37. *Grutter*, 539 U.S. 306 at 349 (quoting Frederick Douglass, "What the Black Man Wants: An Address Delivered in Boston, Massachusetts" (January 26, 1865)).

38. Cummings, "Treachery," 47 (quoting Fredrick Douglass).

39. Ronald Turner, "On Parents Involved and the Problematic Praise of Justice Clarence Thomas" (2010) 37 *Hastings Constitutional Law Quarterly* 225–242 at 241 (quoting Frederick Douglass, "Celebrating the Past, Anticipating the Future: An Address Delivered in Philadelphia, Pennsylvania" (April 14, 1875)).

40. Much of the discussion of affirmative action in this section comes from Segall, "Justice Thomas and Affirmative Action."

41. U.S. Constitution Amendment X.

42. U.S. Constitution Art. 6, cl. 2.

43. *United States v. California*, 297 U.S. 175 at 180–181 (1936).

44. Ibid. at 184.

45. *National League of Cities v. Usery*, 426 U.S. 833 (1976).

46. *Garcia v. San Antonio Metropolitan Transit Authority*, 469 U.S. 528 (1985).

47. Ibid. at 549.

48. *New York v. United States*, 505 U.S. 144 at 149 (1992) ("while Congress has substantial power under the Constitution to encourage the States to provide for the disposal of the radioactive waste generated within their borders, the Constitution does not confer upon Congress the ability simply to compel the States to do so."); *Printz v. United States*, 521 U.S. 898 at 935 ("Congress cannot circumvent that [the rule of *New York*] by conscripting the State's officers directly. The Federal Government may neither issue directives requiring the States to address particular problems, nor command the States' officers, or those of their political subdivisions, to administer or enforce a federal regulatory program.").

49. *Printz v. United States*, 521 U.S. 898 at 905.

50. Alexander Hamilton, "The Federalist No. 27," *New York Packet*.

51. *Printz*, 521 U.S. 898 at 899.

52. Ibid. at 947–948 (Stevens, J., dissenting).

53. *United States v. California*, 297 U.S. 175 at 184.

54. U.S. Constitution Amendment XI (emphasis added).

55. *Seminole Tribe of Florida v. Florida*, 517 U.S. 44 at 54–57.

56. *Seminole Tribe*, 517 U.S. 44 at 100–102 (Souter, J., dissenting).

57. Carols Manuel Vázquez, "What Is Eleventh Amendment Immunity?" (1997) 106 *Yale Law Journal* 1683–1806 at 1686 ("[T]he Court went further and interpreted the Amendment to protect states from being sued even by their own citizens, though the Amendment does not so provide. In subsequent cases, the Court has held that the Amendment also protects states from suits brought by foreign states, and Indian tribes, even though neither category of plaintiff is mentioned in the Amendment."); John F. Manning, "The Eleventh Amendment and the Reading of Precise Constitutional Texts" (2004) 113 *Yale Law Journal* 1663–1750.

58. In his only written opinion on the Eleventh Amendment, a dissent, Thomas simply assumed the Court's prior cases were good law. *Central Virginia Community College v. Katz*, 546 U.S. 356 at 379–380 (2006).

59. *Hans v. Louisiana*, 134 U.S. 1 (1890).

60. *Seminole Tribe*, 521 U.S. 44 at 100–102 (Souter, J., dissenting).

61. Scott Lemieux, "Antonin Scalia and the Death of Originalism," *New Republic* (February 24, 2016), https://newrepublic.com/article/130408/antonin-sca lia-death-originalism, last accessed February 27, 2018.

62. *Lujan v. Defenders of Wildlife*, 504 U.S. 555, 560–561 (1992).

63. Antonin Scalia, "The Doctrine of Standing as an Essential Element of the Separation of Powers" (1983) 17 *Suffolk University Law Review* 881–890 (1983).

64. F. Andrew Hessick, "Standing, Injury in Fact, and Private Rights" (2008) 93 *Cornell Law Review* 275–328 at 279–286, 299 n. 141.

65. Raoul Berger, "Standing to Sue in Public Actions: Is It a Constitutional Requirement?" (1969) 78 *Yale Law Journal* 816 at 827.

66. *Flast v. Cohen*, 392 U.S. 83 at 120 (1968) (Harlan J., dissenting).

67. Michael D. Ramsey, "Beyond the Text: Justice Scalia's Originalism in Practice" (2017) 92 *Notre Dame Law Review* 1945–1976 at 1950–1951.

68. Ibid., 1947 note 7.

69. Ibid., 1951.

70. See discussion at notes 50–51, 60–61, and 65–66 and accompanying text in Chapter 7.

71. Ramsey, "Beyond the Text," 1952.

72. Ibid., 1952–1962.

73. Ibid., 1956–1958.

74. *Minnesota*, 508 U.S. 366 (1993). The point of this discussion relating to Scalia's originalism was first made in Lawrence Lessig, "Understanding Changed Readings: Fidelity and Theory" (1995) 47 *Stanford Law Review* 395 at 398–401. I also summarized this case in my article, Eric Segall, "A Century Lost: The End of the Originalism Debate" (1998) 15 *Constitutional Commentary* 411 at 428.

75. *Terry v. Ohio*, 392 U.S. 1 at 26–27 (1968).
76. *Minnesota*, 508 U.S. 366 at 378.
77. Ibid. at 379 (Scalia, J., concurring).
78. Ibid. at 381 (Scalia, J., concurring).
79. Ibid. at 382 (Scalia, J., concurring).
80. See discussion at notes 28–33 and accompanying text in Chapter 3.
81. Julie K. Collins, "Scalia's *Raich* Concurrence: A Significant Departure from Originalist Interpretation" (2007) 90 *Marquette Law Review* 1043–1068 (commerce clause); Michael Lewyn, "When Scalia Wasn't Such an Originalist" (2016) 32 *Touro Law Review* 747–751 (takings clause).
82. Richard L. Hasen, *The Justice of Contradictions: Antonin Scalia and the Politics of Disruption* (New Haven, CT: Yale University Press 2018) at ix.
83. *District of Columbia v. Heller*, 554 U.S. 570 (2008).

Chapter 8

1. Scott Lemieux, "The Limits of Originalism," *The American Prospect* (April 18, 2016), http://prospect.org/article/limits-originalism, last accessed February 27, 2018.
2. *District of Columbia v. Heller*, 554 U.S. 570 (2008).
3. Jamal Greene, "*Heller* High Water? The Future of Originalism" (2009) 3 *Harvard Law & Policy Review* 325–345 at 325 (adding additional sources in note 3). For an alternative view see Rory K. Little, "*Heller* and Constitutional Interpretation: Originalism's Last Grasp" (2009) 60 *Hastings Law Journal* 1415–1430 at 1418 ("Heller in fact is the 'last gasp' of originalism.").
4. William G. Merkel, "*The District of Columbia v. Heller* and Antonin Scalia's Perverse Sense of Originalism" (2009) 13 *Lewis & Clark Law Review* 349–382 at 352.
5. U.S. Constitution Amendment II.
6. Eric J. Segall, *Supreme Myths: Why the Supreme Court Is Not a Court and Its Justices Are Not Judges* (Santa Barbara, CA: Praeger, 2012) p. 79.
7. Greene, "*Heller* High Water?" 334.
8. Ibid., 334–336.
9. *District of Columbia v. Heller*, 554 U.S. 626–627.
10. *McDonald v. City of Chicago*, 561 U.S. 742 at 778 (2010).
11. Saul Cornell, "Guns Have Always Been Regulated," *The Atlantic* (December 17, 2015), www.theatlantic.com/politics/archive/2015/12/guns-have-always-been-regulated/420531/, last accessed February 27, 2018.
12. Paul Finkelman, "The Living Constitution and the Second Amendment: Poor History, False Originalism, and a Very Confused Court" (2015) 37 *Cardozo Law Review* 623–662 at 623–624.
13. Cornell, "Guns Have Always Been Regulated."
14. Merkel, "Scalia's Perverse Sense of Originalism," 351–352.

15. Little, "Originalism's Last Grasp," 1418.

16. Support for *Heller's* literal holding, that the Second Amendment protects an individual right to own guns, as opposed to just a right connected to the militia, is more common but almost invariably on grounds different than those offered by Justice Scalia. Akhil Reed Amar, "*Heller*, HLR, and Holistic Legal Reasoning" (2008) 122 *Harvard Law Review* 145–190; Sandy Levinson, "United States: Assessing *Heller*" (2009) 7 *International Journal of Constitutional Law* 316–328.

17. Cornell, "Guns Have Always Been Regulated."

18. Ibid.

19. *Heller*, 554 U.S. 570, 128 S. Ct. 2783 at 2786.

20. Ibid. at 626–627 n. 26.

21. Little, "Originalism's Last Grasp," 1420.

22. Ibid., 1427.

23. Nelson Lund, "The Second Amendment, Heller, and Originalist Jurisprudence" (2009) 56 *UCLA L. REV.* 1343–1376 at 1345 (2009).

24. Lund, "Heller," 1345.

25. Judge Harvie Wilkinson III, "Of Guns, Abortions, and the Unraveling Rule of Law" (2009) 95 *Virginia Law Review* 253–323, 273.

26. Wilkinson, "Of Guns, Abortion," 271 (quoting Mark V. Tushnet, *Out of Range: Why the Constitution Can't End the Battle over Guns* [New York: Oxford University Press, 2007], p. xvi).

27. Ibid., 281–288.

28. Ibid., 288.

29. *Abood v. Detroit Board of Education*, 431 U.S. 209 (1977).

30. *Harris v. Quinn*, 134 S. Ct. 2618 (2014).

31. "Friedrichs *v.* California Teachers Association," *SCOTUS Blog* (2017), www.scotusblog.com/case-files/cases/friedrichs-v-california-teachers-association/, last accessed February 27, 2018.

32. *Friedrichs v. California Teachers Association*, 578 U.S. ____ (2016).

33. "Janus *v.* American Federation of State, County, and Municipal Employees, Council 31," *SCOTUS Blog* (2017), www.scotusblog.com/case-files/cases/janus-v-american-federation-state-county-municipal-employees-council-31/, last accessed February 27, 2018.

34. *Lawrence v Texas*, 539 U.S. 558 at 568–569 (2003).

35. Gerardo Muñoz, "A Constitutional Absolutism? On Philip Hamburger's *The Administrative Threat*," *Infrapolitical Deconstruction* (June 30, 2017), https://infrapolitica.wordpress.com/2017/06/30/a-constitutional-absolutism-on-philip-hamburgers-the-administrative-threat-by-gerardo-munoz/, last accessed February 27, 2018.

36. Ibid.

37. Ibid. (quoting Philip Hamburger, *The Administrative Threat* [New York: Encounter Books, 2017] p. 2).

38. *I.N.S. v. Chada*, 462 U.S. 919 (1983).

39. Ibid. at 967–68 (White J., dissenting).

40. *National Labor Relations Board v. Noel Canning*, 134 S. Ct. 2550 (2014).

41. *Zivotofsky v. Kerry*, 135 S. Ct. 2076 (2015).

42. *See* Brianne J. Gorod, "Originalism and Historical Practice in Separation-of-Powers Cases" (2016) 66 *Syracuse Law Review* 41–62 at 42.

43. The latter of these issues was addressed in *Boumediene v. Bush*, 553 U.S. 723 (2008).

44. Robert W. Bennett and Lawrence B. Solum, *Constitutional Originalism: A Debate* (Ithaca, NY: Cornell University Press, 2011) pp. 112–113 (quoting Terrance Sandalow, "Constitutional Interpretation" (1981) 79 *Michigan Law Review* 1033–1072 at 1061–1062).

45. Eric J. Segall, "The Constitution Means What the Supreme Court Says It Means" (2016) 129 *Harvard Law Review Forum* 176–188 at 178 (quoting Judge Richard Posner).

46. Mathew Tokson, "Blank Slates" forthcoming, *Boston College Law Review*.

47. Bennett and Solum, *Constitutional Originalism*, p. 125.

48. See Chapter 6.

49. Bennett and Solum, *Constitutional Originalism*, p. 165.

50. Ibid., p. 142.

Chapter 9

1. Edmund Fuller, "Oliver Wendell Holmes, Jr.," *Encyclopedia Britannica* (2017), www.britannica.com/biography/Oliver-Wendell-Holmes-Jr, last accessed February 27, 2018.

2. Erwin Chemerinsky, "Democrats Should Filibuster Gorsuch's Nomination," *Los Angeles Daily News* (February 8, 2017), www.dailynews.com/2017/02/08/democrats-should-filibuster-gorsuchs-nomination-erwin-chemerinsky/, last accessed February 27, 2018.

3. Jeffrey A. Segal and Harold J. Spaeth, *The Supreme Court and The Attitudinal Model* (Cambridge, UK: Cambridge University Press, 1993) pp. 64–65; Harold J. Spaeth and Jeffrey A. Segall, *Majority Rule or Minority Will: Adherence to Precedent on the U.S. Supreme Court* (New York: Cambridge University Press, 1999).

4. Michael J. Gerhardt, "Attitudes about Attitudes," (2003) 101 *Michigan Law Review* 1733–1763 at 1733.

5. I did make such an attempt in my prior book. Eric J. Segall, *Supreme Myths: Why the Supreme Court Is Not a Court and Its Justices Are Not Judges* (Santa Barbara, CA: Praeger, 2012).

6. U.S. Constitution Art. 1, § 8.

7. *Hepburn v. Griswold*, 75 U.S. (8 Wall.) 603 at 618 (1870). I discussed the *Legal Tender Cases* in a similar way in the Introduction to my book *Supreme Myths*.

8. *Hepburn*, 75 U.S. 603 at 624–626.

9. Joseph M. Cormack, "The Legal Tender Cases – A Drama of American Legal and Financial History" (1930) 16 *Virginia Law Review* 132–148 at 141.

10. Ibid., 140 (citing *Legal Tender Cases*, 79 U.S. (12 Wall.) 457 at 634 (1870) (Field, J., dissenting).

11. *Legal Tender Cases*, 79 U.S. 457.

12. Sidney Ratner, "Was the Supreme Court Packed by President Grant?" (1935) 50 *Political Science Quarterly* 343–358 at 347–348 (quoting Charles Warren, *The Supreme Court in United States History* (Boston: Little, Brown, and Company, 1926), vol. II, pp. 525–526).

13. *Everson v. Board of Education of Ewing Tp.*, 330 U.S. 1 at 17 (1947).

14. *Board of Education of Central School District No. 1 v. Allen*, 392 U.S. 236 at 238 (1968).

15. *Lemon v. Kurtzman*, 403 U.S. 602 at 620 (1971).

16. *Meek v. Pittenger*, 421 U.S. 349 at 362–366 (1975).

17. *Wolman v. Walter*, 433 U.S. 229 (1977).

18. Ethan Bronner, "The Nation: Church, State, and School; Squeezing through the Holes in the Wall of Separation," *The New York Times* (June 28, 1998), www.nytimes.com/1998/06/28/weekinreview/nation-church-state-school-squeezing-through-holes-wall-separation.html?mcubz=1, last accessed February 27, 2018.

19. Ibid.

20. *Mitchell v. Helms*, 530 U.S. 793 at 829 (2000).

21. Wendy Kaminer, "Parochial Schools and the Court," *The American Prospect* (November 14, 2001), http://prospect.org/article/parochial-schools-and-court, last accessed February 27, 2018.

22. *Valentine v. Chrestensen*, 316 U.S. 52 at 53 (1942).

23. Ibid. at 54–55.

24. Elliot Zaret, "Commercial Speech and the Evolution of the First Amendment," *DC Bar* (September 2015), www.dcbar.org/bar-resources/publications/washington-lawyer/articles/september-2015-commercial-speech.cfm, last accessed February 27, 2018.

25. Ibid.

26. Ibid.

27. *Virginia State Board of Pharmacy v. Virginia Citizens Consumer Council, Inc.*, 425 U.S. 748 (1976).

28. Ibid. at 784 (Rehnquist, J., dissenting).

29. Zaret, "Commercial Speech."

30. Ibid. (quoting Frederick Schauer).

31. Ibid. (quoting Frederick Schauer).

32. Mathew Tokson, "Blank Slates" forthcoming in 59 *Boston College Law Review* at 28.

33. www.yalelawjournal.org/article/natural-rights-and-the-first-amendment, last accessed February 27, 2018.

34. "CRS Annotated Constitution," *Cornell Law School* (2017), www .law.cornell.edu/anncon/html/art1frag46_user.html, last accessed February 27, 2018.

35. *Hammer v. Dagenhart*, 247 U.S. 251 at 270 (1918).

36. *Gibbons v. Ogden*, 9 Wheat. (22 U.S.) 1 at 74 (1824).

37. *Hammer v. Dagenhart*, 247 U.S. 251 at 280–281 (1918).

38. Ibid. at 269.

39. Ibid. at 272–273.

40. Ibid. at 272.

41. Ibid. at 276.

42. Ibid. at 277–278.

43. Ibid. at 281.

44. *N.L.R.B. v. Jones & Laughlin Steel Corp.*, 301 U.S. 1 (1937); *U.S. v. Darby*, 312 U.S. 100 (1941); *Wickard v. Filburn*, 317 U.S. 111 (1942).

45. *United States. v. Darby*, 312 U.S. 100.

46. *Darby*, 312 U.S. 100 at 116–117.

47. *Youngstown Sheet & Tube Supply Co. v. Sawyer*, 343 U.S. 579 at 637 (1952) (Jackson, J., concurring).

48. *Perez v. United States*, 402 U.S. 146 at 154–156 (1971).

49. *Wickard v. Filburn*, 317 U.S. 111 (homegrown of wheat); *Perez v. United States*, 402 U.S. 146 (loan sharking); *Katzenbach v. McClung*, 379 U.S. 194 (1964) (discrimination at local restaurant).

50. *United States v. Lopez*, 514 U.S. 549 at 551–552 (1995).

51. Segall, *Supreme Myths*, p. 42.

52. *Lopez*, 514 U.S. 549 at 559–563.

53. Ibid. at 567–568.

54. *United States v. Morrison*, 529 U.S. 598 (2000).

55. Violence against Women Act of 1994, 42 USC § 13981.

56. *Morrison*, 529 U.S. 598 at 615–619.

57. Ibid. at 637, 655 (Souter, J., dissenting).

58. *National Federation of Independent Business v. Sebelius*, 567 U.S. 519 (2012).

59. *Sebelius*, 567 U.S. 519 at 552.

60. C. Eugene Emery Jr., "Harvard Law Professor Says Early Congress Mandated Health Insurance for Seamen and Gun Ownership for Most Men," *Politifact* (January 13, 2012), www.politifact.com/rhode-island/statements/2012/jan/13/einer-elhauge/harvard-law-professor-says-early-congress-mandated/, last accessed February 27, 2018.

61. *Gonzales v. Raich*, 545 U.S. 1 at 22 (2005).

62. Ibid. at 40 (Scalia, J., concurring).

63. *Sebelius*, 567 U.S. 519 at 558–561, 651–655 (Scalia, J., dissenting).

64. Dorothy Samuels, "The Second Amendment Was Never Meant to Protect an Individual's Right to a Gun," *The Nation* (September 23, 2015), www.thenation.com/article/how-the-roberts-court-undermined-sensible-gun-control/, last accessed February 27, 2018.
65. See Chapter 7.
66. Compare *Pennsylvania v. Union Gas Company*, 491 U.S. 1 (1989) with *Seminole Tribe of Florida v. Florida*, 517 U.S. 44 (1996).
67. Mike Sacks, "Supreme Court Reverses Anti-Citizens United Ruling from Montana," *Huffington Post* (June 25, 2012), www.huffingtonpost.com/2012/06/25/supreme-court-reversed-citzens-united-montana_n_1605355.html, last accessed February 27, 2018.
68. Andre LeDuc, "Striding Out of Babel: Originalism, Its Critics, and the Promise of our American Constitution" (2017) 26 *William & Mary Bill of Rights. Journal.* 1–86 at 67.

Chapter 10

1. Mark Tushnet, "Heller and the New Originalism" (2008) 69 *Ohio State Law Journal* 609–624 at 623.
2. Testimony of Lawrence B. Solum at the Hearings on Nomination of Neil M. Gorsuch to the Supreme Court of the United States, at 3 (March 23, 2017), www.judiciary.senate.gov/imo/media/doc/03-23-17%20Solum%20Testimony.pdf, last accessed February 27, 2018.
3. Lawrence B. Solum, "Originalism and Constitutional Construction" (2013) 82 *Fordham Law Review* 454–537; Lawrence B. Solum, "Originalist Methodology" (2017) 84 *University of Chicago Law Review* 268–295.
4. Robert W. Bennett and Lawrence B. Solum, *Constitutional Originalism: A Debate* (Ithaca, NY: Cornell University Press, 2011), pp. 143–164.
5. Solum Testimony, 3.
6. Ibid., 2.
7. G. Edward White, "From Realism to Critical Legal Studies: A Truncated Legislative History" (1986) 40 *Southwestern Law Journal* 819–844 at 819–820, 828.
8. Stephen M. Griffin, "Pluralism in Constitutional Interpretation" (1994) 72 *Texas Law Review* 1753–1770 at 1753–1743; Jeffrey A. Segal and Harold J. Spaeth, *The Supreme Court and the Attitudinal Model Revisited* (Cambridge, UK: Cambridge University Press, 2002).
9. John O. McGinnis and Michael B. Rappaport, *Originalism and the Good Constitution* (Cambridge, MA: Harvard University Press, 2013), pp. 125–126.
10. Randy Barnett, "Scalia's Infidelity: A Critique of Faint-Hearted Originalism" (2006) 75 *University of Cincinnati Law Review* 7–24.

11. Barnett, "Scalia's Infidelity," 13–19.

12. Eric J. Segall, "Originalism on the Ground." *Dorf On Law* (November 2, 2015), www.dorfonlaw.org/2015/11/originalism-on-ground.html, last accessed February 27, 2018.

13. Randy Barnett, "'The End of Originalism' Round Two: Ledewitz Doubles Down," *The Washington Post* (July 9, 2017), www.washingtonpost.com/news/volokh-conspiracy/wp/2017/07/09/the-end-of-originalism-round-two-ledewitz-doubles-down/?utm_term=.b23f17634b42, last accessed February 27, 2018.

14. Eric Segall, "Originalism as Faith" (2016) 102 *Cornell Law Review* 37–52 at 39.

15. See discussion at notes 39–57 and accompanying text in Chapter 6.

16. Bennet and Solum, *Constitutional Originalism*, p. 169.

17. Cass R. Sunstein, "Originalism Put Politics over Principle," *Bloomberg* (January 30, 2017), www.bloomberg.com/view/articles/2017-01-30/originalists-put-politics-over-principle-for-supreme-court, last accessed February 27, 2018.

18. Solum Testimony, 2.

19. Ibid., 2–3.

20. Solum, "Originalism and Constitutional Construction," 469.

21. See Chapter 7.

22. David A. Strauss, *The Living Constitution* (New York: Oxford University Press, 2010), pp. 33–35.

23. Solum Testimony, 7.

24. David A. Strauss, "Does the Constitution Mean What It Says?" (2015) 129 *Harvard Law Review* 1–161 (2015); Eric J. Segall, "The Constitution Means What the Supreme Court Says It Means" (2016) 129 *Harvard Law Review Forum* 176–188.

25. See Chapter 8.

26. *See* Chapter 5.

27. Solum Testimony, 10.

28. Ibid., 12.

29. Lino A. Graglia, "'Interpreting' the Constitution: Posner on Bork" (1992) 44 *Stanford Law Review* 1019–1050 at 1020 (quoted in Thomas B. Colby and Peter J. Smith, "Living Originalism" (2009) 59 *Duke Law Journal* 239–307 at 243).

30. Colby and Smith, "Living Originalism," 243 (quoting Robert H. Bork, "Styles in Constitutional Theory" (1985) 26 *South Texas Law Journal* 383–396 at 387).

31. Roger Pilon, "Justice Scalia's Originalism: Original or Post-New Deal?" in Ilya Shapiro (eds.) *Cato Supreme Court Review 2015–2016* (Washington, DC: Cato Institute, 2016), p. vi.

32. Richard F. Duncan, "Justice Scalia and the Rule of Law: Originalism vs. the Living Constitution" (2016) 29 *Regent University Law Review* 9–34 at 11.

33. For example, compare Ed Whelan's treatment of marriage equality's constitutionality to Ilya Somin's approach. Ed Whelan, "Originalism and Marriage," *National Review* (January 29, 2015), www.nationalreview.com/bench-memos/397485/originalism-and-marriage-ed-whelan, last accessed February 27, 2018; Ilya Somin, "Why Same-Sex Marriage Bans Qualify as Sex Discrimination," *Volokh* (February 7, 2012), http://volokh.com/2012/02/07/same-sex-marriage-bans-and-sex-discrimination/, last accessed February 27, 2018. Another example comes from the differences between Justice Scalia's and Justice Thomas's approaches in *McIntyre v. Ohio Elections Commission*, a free speech case. 514 U.S. 334 at 358–371, 371–385 (Thomas, J., concurring) (Scalia, J., dissenting).

34. Colby and Smith, "Living Originalism," 256–262.

35. Ibid., 256–262.

36. McGinnis and Rappaport, *The Good Constitution*, pp. 145–148.

37. Ibid., p. 153.

38. Steven G. Calabresi and Hannah M. Begley, "Originalism and Same-Sex Marriage" (2016) 70 *University of Miami Law Review* 648–707 at 653, 706–707.

39. Randy E. Barnett, "Underlying Principles" (2007) 24 *Constitutional Commentary* 405–416 at 411, 414 (quoting Jack Balkin, "Abortion and Original Meaning" (2007) 24 *Constitutional Commentary* 291–352 at 348).

40. *Lawrence v. Texas*, 539 U.S. 558 at 578–579 (2003) (emphasis added).

41. See Chapter 6.

42. Erwin Chemerinsky, "The Vanishing Constitution" (1989) 103 *Harvard Law Review* 43–104 at 100.

43. Christopher Olver, "Perceptions of Politicization and Public Preferences toward the Supreme Court," *Journalist's Resource* (October 3, 2011), https://journalistsresource.org/studies/politics/elections/supreme-court-politicization, last accessed February 27, 2018.

44. According to a September 2017 Gallup poll, the Supreme Court's approval rating stands at 49 percent, up from a low of 42 percent in 2016, but still well below the pre-2011 levels that were consistently above 50 percent. Regardless, the 49 percent mark still well exceeds the approval ratings of Congress (13 percent) and President Trump (36.9 percent). Justin McCarthy, "GOP Approval of Supreme Court Surges, Democrats' Slides," *Gallup* (September 28, 2017), http://news.gallup.com/poll/219974/gop-approval-supreme-court-surges-democrats-slides.aspx, last accessed February 27, 2018; Justin McCarthy, "Congress Approval Lowest Since July 2016, at 13%," *Gallup* (October 20, 2017), http://news.gallup.com/poll/220718/congress-approval-lowest-july-2016.aspx, last accessed February 27, 2018; Justin McCarthy, "Trump Job Approval Slips to 36.9% in His Third Quarter," *Gallup* (October 20, 2017), http://news.gallup.com/poll/220742/trump-job-approval-slipped-third-quarter.aspx, last accessed February 27, 2018.

45. Karl S. Coplan, "Legal Realism, Innate Morality, and the Structural Role of the Supreme Court in the U.S. Constitutional Democracy" (2011) 86 *Tulane Law Review* 181–218 at 183–184.

46. Ibid., 204–218.

47. Jamal Greene, "Selling Originalism" (2009) 97 *Georgetown Law Journal* 657–721 at 659–660.

48. Ibid., 660.

49. Ibid., 672.

50. Ibid., 672–673.

51. Ibid., 703–704.

52. Ibid., 673.

53. Katie Glueck, "Scalia: The Constitution Is 'Dead,'" *Politico* (January 29, 2013), www.politico.com/story/2013/01/scalia-the-constitution-is-dead-086853, last accessed February 27, 2018 (quoting Justice Antonin Scalia); Nicole Flatow, "Justice Scalia: The Constitution Is 'Dead, Dead, Dead,'" *Think Progress* (January 29, 2013), https://thinkprogress.org/justice-scalia-the-constitution-is-dead-dead-dead-baf9d39b44aa/, last accessed February 27, 2018.

54. Flatow, "Justice Scalia" (quoting Justice Antonin Scalia).

55. Julie Bolcer, "Justice Scalia: Constitution Is 'Dead, Dead, Dead, Dead,'" *Advocate* (December 11, 2012), www.advocate.com/politics/marriage-equality/2012/12/11/justice-scalia-says-constitution-dead-dead-dead-dead, last accessed February 27, 2018 (quoting Justice Antonin Scalia).

56. Bruce Allen Murphy, "Justice Antonin Scalia and the 'Dead' Constitution," *The New York Times* (February 14, 2016), www.nytimes.com/2016/02/15/opinion/justice-antonin-scalia-and-the-dead-constitution.html?_r=0, last accessed February 27, 2018.

57. Murphy, "The 'Dead' Constitution." Bruce Allen Murphy wrote *Scalia: A Court of One*, a biography described by *The New York Times Book Review* as "the most exhaustive treatment of a sitting justice ever written." Murphy, *Scalia: A Court of One* (New York: Simon & Schuster, 2014).

58. This discussion of Justice Scalia is substantially the same as my blog post here: Eric J. Segall, "Justice Scalia and the Myth of the Originalist Judge," *Dorf on Law* (October 4, 2017), www.dorfonlaw.org/2017/10/justice-scalia-and-myth-of-originalist.html, last accessed February 27, 2018.

59. Murphy, "The 'Dead' Constitution."

60. Lawrence Baum and Neal Devins, "Federalist Court: How the Federalist Society Became the De Facto Selector of Republican Supreme Court Justices," *Slate* (January 31, 2017), www.slate.com/articles/news_and_politics/jurisprudence/2017/01/how_the_federalist_society_became_the_de_facto_selector_of_republican_supreme.html, last accessed February 27, 2018; Jeremy Diamond, "Getting Gorsuch: How Trump Picked His Supreme

Court Nominee," *CNN* (February 1, 2017), www.cnn.com/2017/02/01/pol itics/donald-trump-supreme-court-nominee-neil-gorsuch/index.html, last accessed February 27, 2018.

61. See Chapter 7.

62. Bennett L. Gershman, "Justice Scalia's Faux Originalism," *Huffington Post* (February 8, 2016), www.huffingtonpost.com/bennett-l-gershman/justice-scalias-faux-orig_b_9265726.html, last accessed February 27, 2018.

63. Paul Campos, "Scalia Was an Intellectual Phony: Can We Please Stop Calling Him a Brilliant Jurist," *Salon* (February 18, 2016), www.salon.com/2016/02/18/scalia_was_an_intellectual_phony_can_we_please_stop_calling_him_a_brilliant_jurist/, last accessed February 27, 2018.

64. Ed Brayton, "Scalia's Convenient Originalism," *Patheos* (October 9, 2013), www.patheos.com/blogs/dispatches/2013/10/09/scalias-convenient-original ism/, last accessed February 27, 2018.

65. See Chapter 6.

66. Jack M. Balkin, "The New Originalism and the Uses of History" (2013) 82 *Fordham Law Review* 641–719 at 645–646 (emphasis added).

67. Ibid., 649 (emphasis added).

68. Richard S. Kay, "Construction, Originalist Interpretation and the Complete Constitution" (2017) 19 *Journal of Constitutional Law* 1–25 at 7–10.

69. Ibid., 12.

70. Ibid., 13 (quoting Keith E. Whittington, "Originalism: A Critical Introduction" (2013) 82 *Fordham Law Review* 375–409 at 403).

71. Jonathan Gienapp, "Constitutional Originalism and History," *Process* (March 20, 2017), www.processhistory.org/originalism-history/, last accessed February 27, 2018.

72. Ibid.

73. *Marbury v. Madison*, 5 U.S. 137 at 177–178 (1803).

74. Federal Rules of Civil Procedure Rule 52 ("Findings of fact, whether based on oral or other evidence, must not be set aside unless clearly erroneous, and the reviewing court must give due regard to the trial court's opportunity to judge the witnesses' credibility.").

75. "Clearly Erroneous," *Nolo* (2017), www.nolo.com/dictionary/clearly-errone ous-term.html, last accessed February 27, 2018.

76. Eric J. Segall, *Supreme Myths: Why the Supreme Court Is Not a Court and Its Justices Are Not Judges* (Santa Barbara, CA: Praeger, 2012), pp. 175–183.

77. Coplan, "Legal Realism," 206.

78. Ibid., 206–207.

79. *Bush v. Gore*, 531 U.S. 98 (2000).

80. Coplan, "Legal Realism," 209.

81. Ibid., 209.

82. Ibid., 209.

83. Ibid., 210.

84. Richard A. Posner, *Breaking Deadlock: The 2000 Election, the Constitution, and the Courts* (Princeton, NJ: Princeton University Press, 2001), pp. 252–258.

85. Barry Friedman, *The Will of the People: How Public Opinion Has Influenced the Supreme Court and Shaped the Meaning of the Constitution* (New York: Farrar, Straus and Giroux (2009), p. 370; Coplan, "Legal Realism," 214.

86. Andre LeDuc, "Striding Out of Babel: Originalism, Its Critics, and the Promise of Our American Constitution," 2017 26 *William & Mary Bill of Rights Journal* 1–86 at 64.

87. Jack M. Balkin, "Constitutionalism: It's Political, It's Legal – It's Two Mints in One!" *Balkinization* (March 20, 2008), https://balkin.blogspot.com/2008/03/constitutionalism-its-political-its.html, last accessed February 27, 2018.

88. Eric J. Segall, "Justice Kennedy's Constitution and Why We Need It Now More Than Ever," *Dorf on Law* (June 5, 2017), www.dorfonlaw.org/2017/06/justice-kennedys-constitution-and-why.html, last accessed February 27, 2018.

INDEX